Vulnerability and the Corporate Immune System

Alessandro Capocchi

Vulnerability and the Corporate Immune System

An Integrated and Systemic Approach to Risk Management

palgrave
macmillan

Alessandro Capocchi
University of Milano-Bicocca
Milan, Italy

ISBN 978-3-031-30253-4 ISBN 978-3-031-30254-1 (eBook)
https://doi.org/10.1007/978-3-031-30254-1

This Palgrave Macmillan imprint is published by the registered company Springer Nature Switzerland AG
The registered company address is: Gewerbestrasse 11, 6330 Cham, Switzerland

I wish to dedicate this book to all who have been a part of my education and my teachers and mentors throughout my lifetime.
Teachers and mentors don't always know the true extent of the impact they can have, and they don't often get to hear how much they are appreciated. Often, we don't immediately understand the enormous gift they have bestowed upon us. Often it is only over time and with growing maturity that we can comprehend and appreciate how important they have been in guiding us along the way.
I was fortunate with the teachers and mentors I encountered, and I remain deeply grateful to them.

A special dedication to my wife Sara and to my son Edoardo and Giorgio, and to my daughter Vittoria Luisa.

Preface

We are used to approaching risk management quantitatively using mathematical tools and models that try to measure the probability that an adverse event may occur and/or the effects that the adverse event may cause to the detriment of the company or a socioeconomic system.

The traditional approach that has evolved over the years has always been oriented toward reducing, on the one hand, the probability that the adverse event may occur and, on the other hand, the effects that the adverse event causes. For these reasons, risk management has permanently been anchored to activities aimed at **mitigating** the two dimensions or at trying to reduce them.

Indeed, more needs to be done over the years to attract the attention of scholars and practitioners to the topic of prevention: risk prevention, not risk management.

Risk prevention, like what happens concerning human beings, does not consist of increasing monitoring systems or early diagnosis techniques or methodologies, as they say in the medical field.

Prevention is something much deeper that must take place within companies and complex socioeconomic systems with continuous policies over the years. Prevention, like what happens to humans, is based on education, knowledge, awareness, and the ability to change one's behavior to reduce exposure to risk factors. Factors cannot be eliminated but can be significantly rendered inactive if suitably addressed in time with serious policies projected into the long term.

Prevention does not start with risk: risk is an external variable to the company and the socioeconomic system. Risk is a dynamic variable, and as the experience of COVID-19 teaches us, it is not always visible or predictable.

Prevention originates from the company's and the socioeconomic system's vulnerability level. The vulnerability pertains to the internal and not the external dimension. The vulnerability of a company or a socioeconomic system relates to the health and well-being of which they are the bearers.

Being an internal condition, vulnerability can be adequately managed by those with roles of responsibility and decision-making tasks within the company or the socioeconomic system. To be adequately managed, the vulnerability requires a medium-long-term time perspective as it cannot be limited to the short term. Taking up the dialogue reported in the backstory, the diagnosis ends in the short term, in the exact instant it is conducted. Vulnerability management requires foresight and the ability to plan the company's and socioeconomic system's future.

Passing from an approach linked to risk to one linked to the dimension of greater or lesser vulnerability means substantially changing management models: management must increasingly be projected into the future and adopt a temporal perspective in its decisions that cannot end in a short period. Vulnerability management requires accurate planning skills and, above all, requires constant knowledge, awareness, and education at all levels of the complex organization.

A further difference between the risk and vulnerability approaches is how risks are addressed. Almost all risk management manuals find a long list of corporate risks. By nature, each risk corresponds to recipes and tools to mitigate its probability and/or effects.

Vulnerability management attributes centrality to the company's "health conditions" and the company's "immune system." Vulnerability management aims to strengthen the immune system regardless of the specific nature of the risks to which the company is exposed.

Vulnerability management does not replace risk management. The management of the vulnerability dimension integrates risk management upstream by strengthening the necessary cohesion between the different managerial systems within contemporary complex organizations. This is a part of the COVID-19 lesson.

In this framework, this book is the result of intensive research carried out over the last seven years and aimed at analyzing and observing the complex business phenomenon in Italy and the international context.

The last three years have seen a profound change in the economic dynamics, and business complexity has increased significantly. Over the past three years, we've found that threats are sometimes unpredictable. We have discovered that danger can spread very quickly on a global scale. And we have learned how a microscopic virus manages quickly to undermine the stability of entire complex systems: social, economic, financial, and cultural all over the World. This is modern complexity. And with this contemporary complexity, companies as socioeconomic systems must interact to ensure their survival.

In the contemporary complexity, it is essential to recapture some fundamental elements of the business phenomenon. These include continuity over time and the need to achieve and maintain conditions of lasting economic conditions. Only by keeping conditions of lasting economic equilibrium can the company create social value and contribute to satisfying human needs.

The issue of economic equilibrium assumes a central role also today in the analysis of various business phenomena. This primary role is strictly connected to the theme of the immune system: the immune system is the set of conditions that allow the company to survive over time through turbulence, uncertainty, and adverse events. The immune system is the only answer to contemporary complexity.

This book aims to support the new generations to understand the essence of complexity; understand how the continuity of the business phenomenon is closely linked to the ability to create and maintain long-lasting equilibrium conditions to support the corporate immune system; make it clear how the creation and maintenance of the conditions of lasting equilibrium are linked to the corporate immune system; to facilitate the understanding of the role of managers and managerial systems; finally, make it clear the necessary change of approach from risk to vulnerability management.

This book was written with the awareness that economic and business dynamics run very fast and that by the time this book is available, many of the facts described and analyzed will have already been overcome.

With this awareness, I confirm the commitment to continue the clinical analysis of complex business phenomenology and to guide and drive the new generations toward discovering new entrepreneurship. Entrepreneurship that knows how to deal with complexity and rediscover what those who preceded us have been able to leave us in terms of teachings.

Acknowledgments

Before writing this book, I spent several years of work and relationships with people, managers, and companies I was lucky enough to meet and get to know and from whom I had the good fortune and the ability to learn. In a word, **experience**.

I am trying to remember everyone by name, but I want to underline the many phases in my academic and professional life. Each phase was accompanied by new experiences that left me with several teachings. The experience gained over many years of work is the knowledge I have acquired over time. I hope not to stop being curious and investigate the phenomena surrounding me.

At the same time, I hope to pass on my curiosity and rigor with which I conduct the analyzes to my students, collaborators, my son Edoardo and Giorgio, and my daughter Vittoria Luisa.

Learning is a demanding activity, time-consuming at the base of which there must be curiosity, listening, observation, and passion. We always learn everywhere. I hope the new generations are more and more curious and are not content to find the answers to their questions just within the smartphone screen.

The Backstory

To understand the path that led me to write this book, I want to recount a dialogue I had a few weeks ago, in November 2022, with a very active physician in the fight against smoking—Dr. Biagio Tinghino. The conversation I will describe took place fortuitously at the end of the writing of my book. However, it faithfully expresses the reasons that prompted me to examine this still little-debated topic in Italian and international literature.

For some years now, I have been directing at my university—University of Milano Bicocca—an advanced training course accredited by the Lombardy Region through the Academy of PoliS Lombardia for the physicians that conduct complex structures: i.e., for all the doctors who become directors and as such acquire a managerial role within the structures in which they operate. These are excellent professionals with very high technical skills who, however, do not always possess managerial skills both from a subjective point of view—i.e., related to the awareness of one's role—and from an objective point of view—i.e., linked to the knowledge and use of the managerial tools.

We discussed this doctor's activity in the Italian anti-smoking association at lunch. He offered this observation: technology has dramatically improved diagnostic processes and pathways. Today, thanks to new technologies, we can diagnose lung cancer even at an embryonic stage, as imaging diagnostics can identify infinitely small nodules. The Italian public system, like other European public systems, is moving in the direction of making mass screening increasingly accessible, investing enormous financial resources both in the purchase of new technologies that are used by public structures in which to carry out diagnoses and in the production and provision of diagnostic services on the population at risk. Are we sure that this type of investment should be considered prevention? Wouldn't it be preferable not to talk about prevention but simply the early diagnosis? These are the two questions he asked me, which I have tried to address. In managing a risk represented by lung cancer, for which many studies identify smoking as one of the possible risk-increasing factors, population screening activity cannot be considered prevention. This activity is instead to be regarded as an early diagnosis.

For my doctor at lunch, prevention consists in tackling the causes and, therefore, the factors of risk exposure: in this case, in his opinion, in reducing smoking. For this doctor, prevention means changing the population's habits and not simply increasing the screening activity, which, in any case, even in the face of a negative diagnosis, does not exclude the possibility that the disease may appear later.

The content of this book seeks to analyze this aspect, i.e., the distinction between early diagnosis and prevention. Of course, we are not dealing with human beings in the book, let alone reducing lung cancer. However, there are numerous similarities between the approach that has characterized risk management in recent decades and the approach that we would like to implement in companies with this book: strengthening the corporate immune system.

These similarities appeared evident when the COVID-19 pandemic broke out in Italy, especially in Lombardy in February 2020, with the well-known zero cases of Codogno in the Lodi area. COVID-19 has not only affected human beings with often tragic consequences but also affected our socioeconomic systems with just as many tragic consequences. The consequences of COVID-19 on complex socioeconomic systems are not exhausted today, and the pandemic seems to have loosened its grip. These are consequences whose effects will last for many years and perhaps decades. These effects have severely affected the behavior of individuals and corporate organizations throughout the entire economic system. These consequences cannot fail to raise questions about the stability of our socioeconomic systems. As we have seen, the estate has been tested for COVID-19.

From COVID-19 to the dialogue with the physician in November 2022, the path of study, analysis, and research that guided the drafting of this book begins and ends.

Contents

About the Author

Alessandro Capocchi is a Full Professor of Business Economics at the University of Milano Bicocca (Milan) (https://www.unimib.it/alessandro-capocchi). He currently lectures Business Economics for the first year of the bachelor's degree in economics and business Administration; Risk Management for the master's degree in business economics science. He is the Co-Founder and Chairman of the Board of MIndLab SRL—a Spinoff of the University of Milano Bicocca. With Mr. Giuseppe Caprotti in 2016, he created the Observatory on new entrepreneurship (www.onilab.unimib.it). He is a member of AIDEA (Italian Association of Business Economics) and SIDREA (Italian Society of Accounting and Business Economics), SISR (Italian Society of Accounting History), and in the US, he is a member of ANAHEI Association of North America Higher Education International (https://anahei.org).

List of Figures

List of Tables

PART I

Risk Management and Vulnerability

CHAPTER 1

From Risk to Vulnerability

This chapter focuses on how companies must change their management approach to evolve from the traditional risk centrality model to the new one. This has been necessitated because of the vulnerability that businesses have been exposed to due to the socioeconomic events that have occurred over the last three years at a global level—first, the COVID-19 pandemic and then the conflict in Ukraine. Vulnerability for a company is an internal condition that correct, virtuous, and farsighted behaviors can mitigate.

From the Risk Dimension to the Dimension of Vulnerability

The practice of company risk management began in the seventies, when companies, in response to specific events, began to recognize the importance of risk management and the need to develop models to enhance their risk management capabilities. The evolution of risk management follows the occurrence of significant global events. Initially, it takes the form of an approach oriented to the need to deal with the different types of risk in a differentiated manner, then becomes a unitary system capable of involving the company at the organizational level rather than only addressing a specific source of risk. The transition to an integrated approach to risk management has been enabled by the implementation of enterprise risk management (ERM).

A. Capocchi, *Vulnerability and the Corporate Immune System*,
https://doi.org/10.1007/978-3-031-30254-1_1

In the decades preceding the 1970s, the perception of risk was almost nonexistent because there was a firm conviction, even among economic agents and based on the prevalence of neoclassical economic thought, that markets were perfect and complete. This belief left the burden of absorbing risk to each specific company, allowing companies to neglect the management of this dimension. Soon, events led companies to understand how this belief was incorrect and unrealistic, exposing them to substantial risks resulting from the growing complexity of economic dynamics and hence the need not only to assess risk and to mitigate its impact but also to search for benefits.

Globalization (Stiglitz, 2002), on the one hand, and the race for technological development, on the other, have also played a significant role in this trend. In recent decades, companies have increasingly felt the need to analyze and learn in advance the dynamics of the markets in which they operate to understand how to design their strategies such that they exploit threats and transform them, to the extent possible, into opportunities. The result is a significant reduction in the time dedicated to the management and decision-making processes and the implementation of short-term planning tools.

In the following decades, risk management became an essential business component. Today it assumes an important role, even if it often appears static compared to the highly dynamic market context. When observing risk management models, the sensation plays a "defensive" game in which the company and its management are compelled to reduce the consequences of adverse events. The risk dimension, in fact, mainly concerns the size of the company and the level of its exposure to adverse events.

In this context, the vulnerability dimension is not a substitute for but instead reflects how the risk dimension has evolved following the events that characterized the 2020–2022 period.

The term "vulnerability" can be defined as "the exposure of an economy to exogenous shocks arising out of economic openness" (Briguglio et al., 2008: 1). This term is now present within corporate systems.

The experience of COVID-19 and the subsequent war in Ukraine has made it clear how, in a short time and on a global level, a stable scenario can change with profound repercussions for companies on the strategic and managerial levels. What is striking about these two experiences is not the surprise concerning their unforeseen and unpredictable manifestation but rather the speed with which they have spread globally.

The rapid spread of adverse events is depicted in Fig. 1.1, which underlines how a single event today, precisely because of globalization and technological progress, can, in a short time, affect numerous unrelated or unconnected areas and sectors with significant repercussions.

The speed with which the vulnerability of current socioeconomic systems, even complex ones, has manifested itself is undoubtedly linked to globalization and the profound interconnections and interdependencies between its systems. However, clarifying the relationship between risk and vulnerability is necessary before dealing with this aspect. As discussed previously, the risk mainly concerns the external dimension of the company being linked to the specific and/or potential exposure that

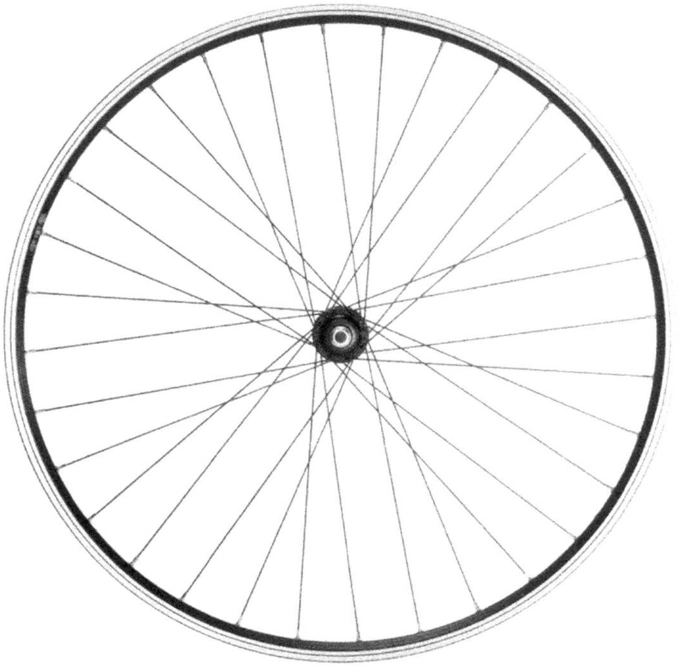

Fig. 1.1 The sunburst effect in the propagation of adverse events on a global scale

the company itself has to hostile events. Vulnerability otherwise affects the internal dimension of the company (i.e., the degree to which it is predisposed to suffer a potentially damaging effect related to a hostile event).

Since risk is external to the company system, it places the burden of building static tools on the company itself. It mitigates the probability that an event will occur and its consequences. The internal vulnerability to the company system leads the company to formulate active and dynamic policies to strengthen its "immune system" and reduce the potential effects of a hostile event. The relationship between vulnerability and risk is controversial in the various strands of scientific literature, and this relationship is not universally accepted. What is certain is that the relationship between risk and vulnerability exists since a close relationship between the two dimensions has been determined in many scientific fields.

In this regard, we can state that risk is determined or determinable as a function between a specific source of danger α, exposure β, and system vulnerability ν and understood as an intrinsic characteristic of the system itself suffering the effects of such events:

$$\text{Risk} = f(\alpha, \beta\ \nu)$$

The above function suggests that vulnerability is a determinant of risk. Therefore, the greater the corporate vulnerability and the greater the company's exposure to risk, the lower its vulnerability and risk exposure. There is, therefore, a direct relationship between vulnerability and risk; thus, reducing vulnerability reduces risk throughout the company. This is why it is necessary to approach risk management innovatively by acting internally to equip the system to face the unpredictable effects of adverse events.

From Economic Vulnerability to Corporate Vulnerability

Numerous studies have been conducted on the vulnerability of economic systems, while more needs to be written concerning corporate systems. This led to the erroneous belief that risk vulnerabilities were external to company systems, and management considered it unnecessary to act scientifically to enhance its risk management function (Chatjuthamard et al., 2022a).

The dimension of vulnerability was first introduced within the scientific disciplines in studying natural disasters in the 1970s. Peter Timmerman proposed it in 1981 and then used it in multiple disciplines such as ecology, economics, sociology, and geography (Bohle et al., 1994; Cutter, 2003; Kienberger & Hagenlocher, 2014; Simelton et al., 2012).

> *Vulnerability, therefore, will refer to the threat to which a community is exposed, taking into account not only the properties of the chemical agents involved but also the ecological situation of the community and the general state of emergency preparedness at any given point in time.* (Gabor and Griffith, 1979)

> *Vulnerability is defined as the ability to resist irreversible damage (which is defined as damage that requires a recovery time more significant than a human life span). Presumably, it is measured by the size of the disturbance necessary to cause irreversible damage.* (Kay, 1979)

The dimension of vulnerability has two faces: “One is vulnerable to attack from, thereby exposing one’s vulnerabilities to—the hazards out there is somehow part of one’s internal weaknesses” (Timmerman, 1981: 19).

Over the years, increased interest in environmental issues has attracted the attention of other scientific sectors to the study of vulnerability, particularly in the social sciences, in which the theme has been mainly studied in the context of sustainability (Vommaro et al., 2020).

The dimension of vulnerability was initially associated with the possibility of damaging even complex systems due to adverse events such as natural disasters. Its definition has evolved over the years into a set of concepts that today include “sensitivity,” “adaptability,” and “resilience” (Li et al., 2022). Scientific studies have transitioned into evaluation methods and embraced the research perspectives typical of the social and economic sciences. The introduction of the evaluation perspective has helped to make explicit the importance of economic vulnerability as the dimension of vulnerability applied to other scientific fields: think, for example, of the field of health and the stability of the health system in the presence of a severe pandemic, to local development and the need for peace of territorial systems, etc. It is, in fact, evidence that the measurement of the economic impact allows us to measure that produced by a hostile event as well as the level of defense that a system must have to reduce its risk exposure. In this context, Briguglio proposed the economic vulnerability index in 1992 and applied it to financial analysis for the first time (Briguglio, 1992).

Since the United Nations Development Program (UNDP) formally introduced the concept of "economic vulnerability" in 1999, researchers have begun to conduct studies on economic vulnerability following multidisciplinary research perspectives. Among the numerous studies, it is worth mentioning those of: Ria et al., who established a system of economic vulnerability assessment indicators based on panel data from 23 countries and proposed countermeasures to reduce economic vulnerability in the context of emerging market economies (Rocha & Moreira, 2010); Araca et al., who collected 118 economic variables and constructed a new economic vulnerability index using least squares factor scores, and then analyzed and assessed the economic vulnerability of urban areas prone to torrential floods using the global assessment method (Estefanía et al., 2018; Li et al., 2022); Gnangnon, who explored the economic vulnerability of 112 developing countries in the context of multilateral trade policy liberalization (Gnangnon, 2018); Ren et al., who comprehensively assessed provincial economic vulnerability and analyzed spatial differences during economic growth using entropy, multilevel extensive assessment, and spatial differences analyses in the theoretical framework of vulnerability (Ren et al., 2018); and Tang, who established a research framework on the economic vulnerability of export-oriented cities and analyzed the economic vulnerability of Foshan city as the spatial and temporal evolution characteristic of a "sensitivity-response" model, set pair analysis, analysis spatial GIS, and other methods (Tang & Lin, 2019).

The effects of hostile events on economic systems have piqued scholarly interest in the impact that the same events can have on corporate systems (Chatjuthamard et al., 2022b; Wongsinhirun et al., 2022). After all, as Italian economics and business science teach, companies are open and dynamic systems and a subunit of the economic system, which in the organic vision has its own life and perspective on temporal continuity (Amaduzzi, 1948; Bertini, 1990; Giannessi, 1970; Zappa, 1927). Hence, the interest is also from institutions that supervise the correct functioning of the markets at national and international levels to prevent damage to corporate systems and systemic crises. For this reason, the vulnerability issue in its current state cannot be limited to economic systems. Still, it must be included within corporate systems and become increasingly integral to management and enterprise organization dimensions.

The Four Types of Vulnerability

There have been many paradigm shifts in risk and vulnerability in recent decades. Among them, the following deserve to be mentioned (Van Westen et al., 2016):

- Technocratic (or behavioral) paradigm: the first approaches to risk were those that likened it to danger relating to the natural sciences (e.g., geologists, engineers, meteorologists).
- Structural paradigm: the concept of vulnerability has been incorporated into risk management. Hence, risk protection focuses on physical protection systems and people's behavior. Including people's behavior among the factors that play a role in vulnerability has encouraged the design and use of early warning systems and educational programs on risks and how to avoid them. The structural paradigm lasted a couple of decades. It was used during the Yokohama Strategy and Action Plan to build a safer world (1994). All efforts were aimed at increasing scientific knowledge on the causes and consequences of natural hazards to reduce the vulnerability of disaster-prone communities.
- Complexity paradigm: A new understanding of the complex interaction between nature and society has emerged, and as such, a challenging new approach to understanding risk needs to be undertaken. The vulnerability affects groups or individuals and is embedded in complex social relationships and processes.

The scientific literature has multiple definitions and conceptual frameworks concerning vulnerability. Among them, we consider that which views vulnerability as the sum of three elements (Van Westen et al., 2016):

$$\text{Vulnerability} = (\text{Exposure}) + (\text{Resistance}) + (\text{Resilience})$$

where:
Exposure: at-risk property and population.
Resistance: measures taken to prevent, avoid or reduce loss.
Resilience: the ability to recover the initial state or achieve a desired post-disaster state.

Following this approach, the dimension of vulnerability is (Van Westen et al., 2016): (i) multidimensional (i.e., physical, social, economic, environmental, institutional, and human factors define vulnerability); (ii) dynamic (i.e., vulnerability changes over time); (iii) scale-dependent (i.e., vulnerability can be expressed at different scales, from human to household to community to country); and (iv) site-specific (i.e., each location may need its approach). Resilience is related to different phases before and after a disruptive event, including the preparation before disasters, the impact of and recovery after disasters, and the long-term impact of disasters. Here, it is possible to identify four types of vulnerabilities:

1. Human-social
2. Physical
3. Economical
4. Environmental.

Each typology can produce direct and indirect effects. Depending on the different types of direct and indirect impacts, vulnerability can be defined as:

1. Physical vulnerability
2. Economic vulnerability
3. Social vulnerability
4. Environmental vulnerability.

Physical vulnerability indicates the potential material impact on the environment, which can be expressed as an "element at risk" (EaR). The degree of damage for a given EaR or set of EaRs resulting from a natural phenomenon of a given magnitude can be expressed using a scale of 0 to 1 (0: no damage; 1: total damage). Economic vulnerability identifies the potential impacts on economic assets and processes (e.g., business disruption, secondary effects such as increased poverty, and job losses), hence the involvement of economic and business systems. The social vulnerability concerns the potential impacts of events on subjects such as the poor, single-parent families, pregnant or breastfeeding women, disabled people, children, and the elderly. Environmental vulnerability identifies the potential impacts of environmental events (e.g., flora, fauna, ecosystems, biodiversity).

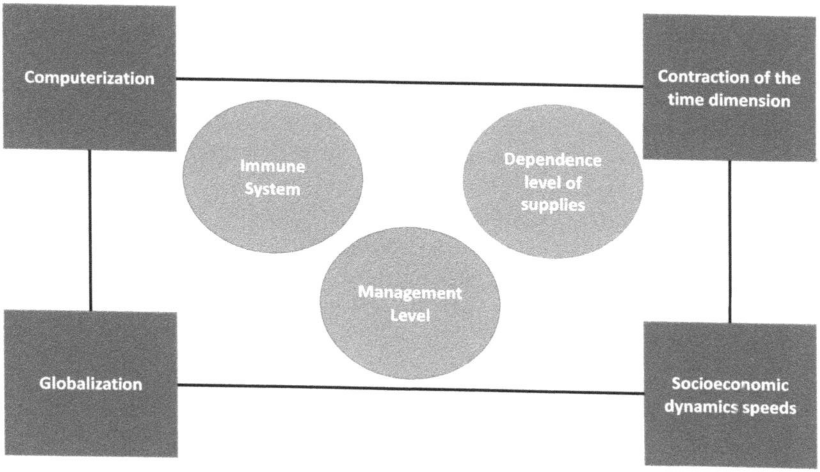

Fig. 1.2 Factors increasing corporate vulnerability

The Growing Vulnerability of Companies in Contemporary Economic Systems

The growing vulnerability of companies is linked to the profound changes in the economic dynamics of markets and the often more remarkable slowness of companies themselves in adapting to the changes taking place. As open and dynamic systems, companies must constantly adapt to changes in the environment in which they operate. The adaptive capacity of the company is linked to its characteristics and the level of structural rigidity that characterizes the organizational dimension. The most significant corporate vulnerability is attributable to elements external to the corporate system and internal to the environmental system and corporate strategy, as shown in Fig. 1.2.

The main factors external to the company system, which are included on the perimeter of Fig. 1.2, that increase vulnerability can be described as follows:

- Globalization is a deep interconnectedness whereby one company's value chain is closely linked to the value chain of other companies. The links between value chains are comparable to the bond that unites a team of climbers on a mountain excursion. If a climber falls, the others act as a net to support the falling climber. If the safety net fails, all climbers will suffer equally.

- Computerization connects the management systems of individual companies using cloud-type data archiving systems, thereby increasing the need to implement IT security systems for the company's information assets.
- The speed of socioeconomic changes in response to economic cycles has rapidly accelerated in recent years.
- The contraction of time dimension has been compressed from 10–15 years to 3–5 years, significantly affecting the planning, production, management, and decision-making processes.

The main internal factors that increase vulnerability are attributable to the following:

- The corporate immune system is shaped by the consistency of the risk to which the company is exposed and its operating status.
- Both the objective and subjective managerial dimensions.
- The dependence on supplies from foreign countries and economies, particularly those in Asia or countries characterized by unstable and/or undemocratic political regimes.

It can be seen in Fig. 1.2 that COVID-19 and the conflict in Ukraine represent real-world stress tests.

In fact, from a socioeconomic point of view, COVID-19 represents a shock on a global level whose real effects—as well as the opportunities it created—can only be described in the coming years. This particular shock involved an event that no one could foresee and which, in a short time, has, on the one hand, stressed the health systems of individual countries and had substantial repercussions at the supranational level and, on the other hand, damaged social and economic systems with significant and detrimental implications for citizens and businesses.

The social effects of COVID-19 are mainly attributable to the lockdowns in individual countries, the interruption of mobility, and numerous activities, including cultural ones. The economic effects produced by COVID-19 are primarily attributable to the supply-side shock it caused, which had significant consequences on entire production chains. The demand-side shock was triggered by multiple factors, such as the restrictive measures on individual mobility, the drop in consumption (in, for example, tourism, retail trade, transport, and mass entertainment), and the more significant uncertainty about the economy's future. In response, many workers have preferred—to the extent possible—to create savings by reducing their consumption but, as restrictions have eased, to limit their non-essential expenditures (Tisdell, 2021).

The supply and demand shocks have produced effects on consumption but also on workers' income. Still, they have also resulted in a wealth effect attributable to the loss in value of financial assets due to the poor performance of financial markets.

It was unclear how long its adverse effects would last during the pandemic, even if efforts were made to ensure it was temporary. Although the pandemic has not been resolved, its effects have progressively decreased. The socioeconomic environment has slowly returned to normal thanks to global vaccination policies. However, we see the connection between the supply- and demand-side shocks today. Specifically, the contraction in demand amplifies the supply shock, thereby generating a wide range of economic repercussions. Some sectors (e.g., think of pharmaceuticals, telecommunications, or high tech) have not suffered any repercussions and, in some cases, have even benefited from the effects of the pandemic. In contrast, other sectors have certainly had to bear significant repercussions.

Further amplification of the effects of the crisis has passed through the financial system: the pandemic has affected the performance of the financial markets, causing a loss in value of the securities held by savers, effectively reducing the financial wealth of households and, consequently, their propensity to consume. In addition, financial intermediaries' ability to obtain financing has suffered due to a decrease in the risk appetite of investors/savers. A further effect that individual countries have tried to counter with supranational policies is attributable to the contraction of credit made available by the banking system for businesses. This will have exposed the production systems to very high risk. However, due to the support policies adopted by individual governments, extreme risks have been avoided for the benefit of both companies and families.

What has been written concerning COVID-19 remains relevant due to the ongoing conflict in Ukraine. On February 24, 2022, Russia invaded Ukraine's territory, raising global geopolitical tensions and significantly affecting the markets, especially energy-related ones. On February 23,

2022, the price of gas in Europe was €88.07 per MWh, and the cost of natural gas in the United States was $4.667. On August 19, 2022, the gas price in Europe reached €262.78 per MWh. This increase in energy costs affects families and businesses, particularly as it relates to consumption. For these reasons, governments immediately tried to implement solutions to mitigate this impact and reduce their energy dependence.

At the European level, the leaders of the 27 EU member states agreed in the Versailles declaration in March 2022 to free the EU from its dependence on Russian fossil fuels as quickly as possible. The March European Council discussed measures to mitigate the impact of high energy prices and secure energy supplies. On May 30–31, 2022, the European Council agreed to ban almost 90% of all Russian oil imports by the end of 2022, with a temporary exception for crude oil supplied by pipeline. Considering different energy mixes and the various circumstances of member states, EU leaders called to diversify energy supply sources and routes further, accelerate the deployment of renewable energies, improve energy efficiency, and improve the interconnections between the gas and electricity networks. On July 26, 2022, EU energy ministers reached a political agreement for a voluntary reduction in natural gas demand by 15% this coming winter. Ministers exchanged views on the energy situation in Europe in the context of Russia's war against Ukraine. They also discussed national contingency plans, measures, and further short-term actions to enhance the EU's energy security. On August 5, 2022, the Council adopted a regulation to reduce gas demand by 15%, following written procedures.

The conflict has affected the energy sector and the food industry, particularly regarding food security and the affordability of food products worldwide.

Thanks to the Common Agricultural Policy (CAP), the availability of food, feed, and fertilizers is relatively low in the EU. Reducing imports of maize, wheat, rapeseed, sunflower oil, and meal from Ukraine impacts feed prices and the EU's food industry. The EU's primary concern remains affordability due to high market prices and inflationary trends.

At the European Council meeting on June 23–24, 2022, EU leaders stressed that Russia is solely responsible for the global food crisis. They urged it to stop targeting agricultural facilities and allow the export of Ukrainian grains.

These are just some more immediate effects of the ongoing geopolitical tension. The results will be assessed only as "a posteriori" based on the duration of the conflict.

To complicate the international economic scenario are added the tensions between China and Taiwan that have returned after the visit of US Congressional spokesperson Nancy Pelosi to Taiwan.

What has been described so far allows us to understand how all the markets are closely connected and how difficult it is to isolate the economy from natural, political, social, and health events. Everything today has an economic impact, and everything is strongly interrelated—hence the pressing need to pay close attention to the dimension of vulnerability even within corporate systems.

Objective and Subjective Management

To understand the impact of vulnerability on decision-making and strategic processes, it is first necessary to clarify the meaning of the term "management." In everyday use, it refers to managing, coordinating, and administering tasks to achieve a specific objective. These activities include defining the strategy, organization, and coordination of efforts to achieve goals given a regime of available but limited resources.

Hence, there is a need to identify the essence of being a manager. Managers are those who, within even complex organizations, must make decisions to guide the organization's activities. Managers are evaluated according to two measurable parameters: compensation and accountability.

The higher the complexity of the manager's decisions, the greater their responsibility will be. Their commitment must be compensated by adequate remuneration. The lower the complexity of their decisions, the lower the degree of responsibility and, thus, the lower the income should be.

In summary, the manager is the one who, within a complex organization, is paid to make decisions for which he is also responsible.

Focusing the term management on the decision-making process allows us to identify two connected areas within the field of management: the first area pertains to so-called subjective management (i.e., to human capital or the individual men and women who comprise company systems); the second area pertains to so-called objective management (i.e., the set of tools that subjective management uses to make its own decisions).

Subjective management within company systems represents the only real non-replicable asset and a real strategic asset. Other assets, such as technology, procurement markets, outlet markets, and financial market relations ship are replicable. Theoretically, one can imagine building two identical companies in a laboratory—Company A and Company B—with the same production process, output, suppliers, outlet markets, and technologies. The only natural non-replicable resource is human capital. If Company A attracts highly qualified talent (i.e., the best managers), Company A will be more competitive than Company B and will develop accordingly.

To carry out its decision-making responsibility, subjective management requires support tools capable of directing and guiding decision-making processes. Objective management is defined as the tools with which managers support their decision-making processes. Over the years, there has been an evolutionary process in the means of supporting management decision-making processes (Fig. 1.3).

Initially, the managerial tools to support the decision-making process were mainly of an accounting nature and based on the integration between the general accounting system—mandatory and aimed at producing financial statements as output—and the optional ability to analyze management's economic and financial dynamics in detail. Over the years, the complexity of economic dynamics has made it necessary

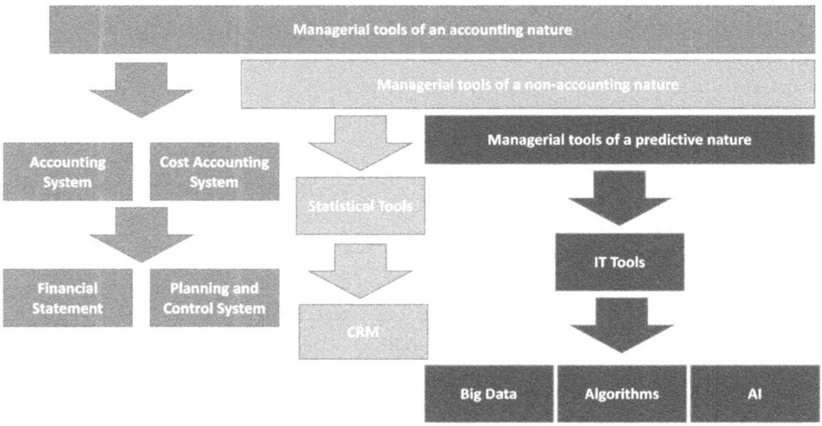

Fig. 1.3 The evolutionary dynamics of managerial tools

to integrate accounting data with non-accounting data. Thus, statistical tools that form the basis of modern CRM systems have entered corporate practice. The implementation of statistical tools on which modern CRM systems are based is consistent with the need for companies to create value through constant customer research, as competitive dynamics are increasingly based on "customer ownership."

The ceaseless quest to acquire "ownership of the customer" has progressively pushed companies to adopt more sophisticated tools capable of analyzing large quantities of data, even those of a heterogeneous nature, and predicting and potentially manipulating consumer behavior. In the current era, companies equip themselves with IT tools capable of managing complex systems based on algorithms, big data, and artificial intelligence.

In the ongoing evolution of managerial tools, the challenges for the future concern the relationship between subjective management and objective management (i.e., the relationship between the objectivity of the data and the subjectivity of the decision-making process or between rationality and irrationality). In the future, it will be essential to understand the instrument's role versus the individual's role. This relationship, which today takes the form of "arm wrestling," will also depend on the training that future managers receive as well as their ability and willingness to not surrender to objectivity and rationality. The writer believes that increasingly sophisticated tools that can process large quantities of heterogeneous data are welcome in a time of high complexity. Still, humans must always make the final decision, not the machine. A human must assume responsibility for their own decisions as it is impossible to delegate the burden of taking responsibility for a decision to the device.

Box 1.1: The story of Mrs. Santos (Time Insider, Investigating Amazon, the Employer. A recent Times project that examined how the tech giant manages its workers took months of reporting and hundreds of interviews. By Maria Cramer, July, the 4th, 2021)

"Dayana Santos, 32, who started at JFK8 in June 2019, appreciated the metrics. "How can I do my job efficiently if the next person isn't doing theirs?" asked Ms. Santos, who sometimes raced with colleagues for fun. "Why does everything have to be a competition with you, Santos?" her boss would tease.

After months of praise from her managers, Ms. Santos had one horrible day. She had been working in robotics but was sent to pick her up because her bus was late. She was offered a different assignment after lunch, but it never came through, and her selection station was occupied. She traversed the warehouse looking for another one, racking up more time off task. That afternoon, she was stunned to discover that she was being fired.
(...)
After repeated inquiries from The Times about the time off task policy and Dayana Santos, the JFK8 worker who challenged her termination, Amazon announced an immediate change: No longer could someone be fired for one bad day. All those who had been are now eligible for rehiring. The company said it had been reconsidering the policy for months."
(https://www.nytimes.com/interactive/2021/06/15/us/amazon-workers.html).

The Impact of Vulnerability on Corporate Decision-Making and Strategic Processes

The increase in complexity and the transition from the risk dimension to that of vulnerability have profound repercussions on complex corporate systems. Risk management, in fact, mainly pertains to the identification of adverse events that can damage a specific subject. Hence the attention paid to the tools that make it possible to mitigate, on the one hand, the probability that the adverse event may occur and, on the other hand, the effects that the adverse may cause. Vulnerability management pertains to a specific condition within the corporate entity exposed to a particular risk. Hence, the focus is not on tools aimed at mitigating the event's probability and/or effects but on tools aimed at strengthening the individual by reducing exposure to risk factors. In summary, the risk is in suffering damage from foreseeable circumstances. In contrast, vulnerability relates to exposure to material and economic damage and depends on the intensity of a given phenomenon.

In this context, decision-making processes must become much faster and more flexible. Speed and flexibility often contrast with the rigidity of organizational structures and the division of roles in corporate hierarchies.

Historical data assume the growing importance of decision-making processes. Using prospective data whose reliability is inversely proportional to the length of the reference time horizon is not plausible.

Hence a growing need within subjective management to support decisions using objective data whose reliability depends on the data selection, processing, and visualization processes. Building integrated systems that can link accounting evidence with non-accounting and statistical evidence is essential while projecting it into the future.

Integrating different managerial tools generates a tug-of-war between objectivity and subjectivity and rationality and irrationality, for which the most effective solution is active management.

In decision-making processes, therefore, it will be less and less essential to have managers with data processing and data collection skills since these activities are increasingly entrusted to managerial tools: managers will instead have to develop strong critical, analytical, and synthesis skills to arrive at clear and coherent decisions.

Within the decision-making process, it will also be essential to implement differential analysis methodologies aimed at measuring not only the effect of a decision in the short term but also its effects in the medium and long term.

References

Amaduzzi, A. (1948). Ragioneria Generale. Casa Editrice Dott. Luigi Macrì.

Bertini, U. (1990). *Il sistema d'azienda*. Giappichelli.

Bohle, H. G., Downing, T. E., & Watts, M. J. (1994). Climate change and social vulnerability: Toward a sociology and geography of food insecurity. *Glob. Environ. Change., 4*(1), 37–48.

Briguglio, L. (1992). Preliminary study on the construction of an index for ranking countries according to their economic vulnerability. *Unctad/ldc/misc, 4*(23), 4.

Briguglio, L., Cordina, G., Farrugia, N., & Vella, S. (2008). *Economic vulnerability and resilience: Concepts and measurements* (Research Paper 2008/055). UNU-WIDER.

Chatjuthamard, P., Ongsakul, V., & Jiraporn, P. (2022a). Corporate complexity, managerial myopia, and hostile takeover exposure: Evidence from textual analysis. *Journal of Behavioral and Experimental Finance, 33*, 100601. https://doi.org/10.1016/j.jbef.2021.100601

Chatjuthamard, P., Chintrakarn, P., & Jiraporn, P. (2022b). *The effect of hostile takeover threats on capital structure: Evidence from half a century* (Vol. 20). Available at: https://refpress.org/ref-vol20-a59/
Cutter, S. L. (2003). The vulnerability of science and the science of vulnerability. *Annals of the Association of American Geographers, 93*(1), 1–12.
Estefanía, A., Bodoque, J. M., García, J., & Andrés, D. (2018). A quantitative methodology for the assessment of the regional economic vulnerability to flash floods. *Journal of Hydrology, 565*, 386–399.
Gabor, T., & Griffith, T. K. (1979). The assessment of community vulnerability to acute hazardous materials incidents. Unpublished paper for Emergency Planning Research Conference, Arnprior, Ontario, June 29–31.
Giannessi, E. (1970). Appunti di economia aziendale. G. Pellegrini.
Gnangnon, S. K. (2018). Effect of multilateral trade liberalization on foreign direct investment outflows amid structural economic vulnerability in developing countries. *Research in International Business and Finance, 45*, 15–29.
Kay, J. J. (1979). *Ecosystem health: A systems approach* (Unpublished Paper).
Kienberger, S., & Hagenlocher, M. (2014). Spatial-explicit modeling of social vulnerability to malaria in East Africa. *International Journal of Health Geographics, 13*(1), 29.
Li, Z., Wu, J., Cui, X., Mi, Z., & Peng, L. (2022). Assessment and influencing factors analysis of economic system vulnerability of the Belt and Road Initiative countries. *PLoS ONE, 17*(1), e0262611. https://doi.org/10.1371/journal.pone.0262611
Ren, C. Q., Zhai, G. F., Zhou, S. T., Chen, W., & Li, S. S. (2018). A comprehensive assessment and spatial difference of China's provincial economic vulnerability. *Sustainability, 10*(4), 1261.
Rocha, K., & Moreira, A. (2010). The role of domestic fundamentals on the economic vulnerability of emerging markets. *Emerging Markets Review, 11*(2), 173–182.
Simelton, E., Fraser, E., Termansen, M., Benton, T. G., Gosling, S. N., South, A., et al. (2012). The socioeconomics of food crop production and climate change vulnerability: A global scale quantitative analysis of how grain crops are sensitive to drought. *Food Security, 4*(2), 163–179.
Stiglitz, J. (2002). *Globalization and its discontents*. Allen Lane The Penguin Press.
Tang, B., & Lin, L. (2019). Economic vulnerability assessment of economic system based on external oriented city: A case study of Foshan city. *Ecological Economy, 03*, 100–106. (in Chinese).
Timmerman, P. (1981). *Vulnerability, resilience and the collapse of society: A review of models and possible climatic applications*. University of Toronto.

Tisdell, C. J. (2021). Determinants of the economic vulnerability of businesses to pandemics and similar events. *Journal of Risk Management, 14*(11), 532. https://doi.org/10.3390/jrfm14110532

Van Westen, Jetten, A., Trigg, H., Brussel, S., Feringa, C.-G., Hossain, A., daSilva, H.-H., & Sijmons, C.-R. (2016). *Caribbean handbook on risk information management*. http://charim.net. Caribbean Disaster Emergency Management Agency (CDEMA) Caribbean Risk Information System (CRIS) website (https://www.cdema.org/cris/) under the Virtual Library (https://www.cdema.org/virtuallibrary/).

Vommaro, F., Menezes, J. A., Barata, M. (2020). Contributions of municipal vulnerability map of the population of the state of Maranhao (Brazil) to the sustainable development goals. *Science of the Total Environment, 706*, 134629.

Wongsinhirun, N., Chatjuthamard, P., Jiraporn, P., & Phiromswad, P. (2022). Do takeover threats influence corporate social responsibility? Evidence from hostile takeover vulnerability. *Corporate Social Responsibility and Environmental Management, 29*(5), 1203–1213. https://doi.org/10.1002/csr.2264

Zappa, G. (1927). Tendenze Nuove negli studi di ragioneria. Discorso inaugurale dell'anno accademico 1926–1927 tenuto nel R. Istituto Superiore di Scienze Economiche e Commerciali di Venezia, Istituto Editoriale Scientifico. http://phaidra.cab.unipd.it/o:51442

CHAPTER 2

The Ant and the Grasshopper—A Business Story

Based on the well-known fairy tale *The Ant and the Grasshopper*, this section highlights the importance of planning, understood as management's ability to prepare for the future. In socioeconomic systems, complexity and dynamism motivate companies and management systems to project their behavior and decision toward the end. Given this, defining the time horizon that drives business strategies in such a complex, turbulent, and dynamic system is essential. In this section, we use the tale of the ant and the grasshopper as a lens through which to explore the possible attitudes that companies can adopt in dealing with risk.

The Story

One warm, sunny day, a grasshopper was bounding through the fields. It was happy and sang a song as it jumped.

As it got tired, it decided to lie on a warm rock in the sunshine and watch the clouds.

The ant passed by, working very hard to carry an ear of corn to his nest. The grasshopper was so enjoying the day that it called out to the ant: "Hey! Why are you working so hard? It's a beautiful day! Come enjoy the sunshine with me!."

The ant called back: "We need to store food for the winter. In not so many days, it will be cold, and we will be hungry."

A. Capocchi, *Vulnerability and the Corporate Immune System*, https://doi.org/10.1007/978-3-031-30254-1_2

The grasshopper thought that was silly. “Why, there’s plenty of food!” it cried. It went back to lazing in the sunshine.

The ant shook its head and went back to work.

The next day, it was again sunny, and the grasshopper decided to visit the riverside. It bounded from leaf to leaf over the crisp, cool water, not a care in the world.

Once again, it saw the ant pass by. This time, the ant was carrying a large leaf. The grasshopper called out again: “Hello, friend! Why are you working so hard again today? Come sit in the shade and enjoy the sound of the river!.”

Once again, the ant refused. “These pretty days are not so many, grasshopper. Soon, the cold will come. We must be ready.”

The ant returned to its work.

On the third day, when the grasshopper awoke, the sun was not shining. It was not warm. Winter had come overnight, and the ground was frozen and covered with snow.

The grasshopper shivered. And when it looked for food to eat, it found nothing.

It walked for hours through the snow, searching for food and shelter. As it walked, it passed the ant’s nest. Inside, it saw ants warm and happy and sharing a delicious-looking meal. Then, it understood that the ant was right all along—not all days are sunny days.

The ant turned then and saw the grasshopper freezing and hungry. It felt pity for the poor grasshopper. “Come, friend,” it called. “There is room here, and there is food. I’ve saved enough for many seasons. Come in and eat.”

And so, the grasshopper was welcomed into the ant’s home, and the ant’s preparations kept the ant, its family, and the grasshopper warm and fed the whole winter long.

(Adapted from Aesop’s Fables, numbered 373 in the Perry Index. Ben Edwin Perry [1965]. *Babrius and Phaedrus*. Loeb Classical Library. Cambridge, MA: Harvard University Press: 487, n. 373. ISBN 0-674-99480-9).

Not All Days Are Sunny

The story of the ant and the grasshopper lends itself well to understanding the importance of the different behaviors that companies can adopt for their business and the risks that may arise—even during moments of stability.

The ant's behavior is profoundly different from the behavior of the grasshopper. The ant has a natural orientation toward planning. For this reason, during a moment of calm—the summer—it works to create the reserves that will allow it and its community to get through the harsh winter. On the other hand, the grasshopper lives daily, is pleased with what it has, and does not plan for itself, never considering the imminent harsh winter that necessitates stockpiling. The grasshopper does not seem to care that not all days are sunny.

The two behaviors symbolize how companies and management must face risks today. Companies and management systems that behave like ants try to prevent adverse events and work to an "immune system" that will help them through a harsh winter. Those that behave like grasshoppers benefit from their position in the market and try to take maximum advantage without considering the future and without adopting any preventive strategies to mitigate the risks that the future may hold.

Theoretically, the ant's behavior appears more suited to protecting the company's interests. In practice, however, one behavior can't automatically be considered better, as there are positive and negative aspects. Figure 2.1 represents the advantages and disadvantages of both behaviors.

It is evident how both behaviors can be considered correct in certain aspects and less correct in others. The effect of the behaviors (negative and positive) depends on the specific moment and the duration. The grasshopper spends the whole summer singing and enjoying the beautiful days.

However, there is no doubt that in the growing complexity of socioeconomic systems, the ant's behavior is preferable to that of the grasshopper, also in line with the economic-business studies that distinguish Italian literature (Giannessi, 1970). Italian literature in which the corporate phenomenon has always been considered long-lasting:

> *an elementary unit of the economic-general order endowed with its own and reflected life, constituted by a system of operations, emanating from the combination of particular factors and the composition of internal and external*

	• He understood the importance of saving (saving is the basis of wealth); • Anticipate problems; • They sacrifice themselves today for the hope of a better future; • Spends money sparingly; • He can cope with winters.	• He lives badly and makes those around him live badly; • It makes it difficult to enjoy life; • It has a short arm; • Has difficulty letting go.
	• She lives happy and carefree; • He is a more pleasant person, he is a companion; • He enjoys himself; • Live in the present and enjoy every moment, • She is cheerful, enthusiastic, and playful.	• He lives in idleness and laziness; • He doesn't care about his future; • He procrastinates the things he should do; • He does not save or does not know how to save; • His hands are pierced and he exaggeratedly spends money; • It doesn't take much to bring everything down, just one winter.

Fig. 2.1 Advantages and disadvantages of both behaviors

> *forces, in which the phenomena of production, distribution, and consumption are prepared for the achievement of a specific economic equilibrium valid over time, capable of offering an adequate remuneration to the factors used and a remuneration, proportional to the results achieved, to the economic subject on whose behalf the activity is carried out.*[1] (Giannessi, 1970: 11)

A company is an open and dynamic system with its own life and designed to last over time regardless of the life of its founder. The company's projection over time aligns with the "going concerned" principle introduced in international accounting and auditing standards. The primary purpose of the company is to ensure its survival. Hence, the need to adopt a management strategy that reflects the behavior of the ant—future-focused and is designed to protect the company's existence as a product combination part of the economic system.

If we analyze the behavior of companies and corporations, we find many things that could be more consistent in management. Inconsistencies whose understanding increasingly passes from the need for companies and management systems to align their behaviors and decisions with the

[1] Translated from Italian: "*unità elementare dell'ordine economico-generale dotata di vita propria e riflessa, costituita da un sistema di operazioni, promanante dalla combinazione di particolari fattori e dalla composizione di forze interne ed esterne, nel quale i fenomeni della produzione, della distribuzione e del consumo vengono predisposti per il conseguimento di un determinato equilibrio economico a valere nel tempo, suscettibile di offrire una rimunerazione adeguata ai fattori utilizzati e un compenso, proporzionale ai risultati raggiunti, al soggetto economico per conto del quale l'attività si svolge.*".

correct time horizon. The time horizon must increasingly guide corporate processes, whether organizational, managerial, or strategic (Woods, 2022).

Enjoy the Sunshine With Me!

Nothing is wrong with enjoying a moment of well-deserved lightheartedness by benefiting from what has been done up to that point. This is how we can read the grasshopper's invitation to the ant. However, we must also pay close attention to whether this moment conflicts or could conflict with the general interest of the company or the community (as in the case of the ant). This depends (the potential conflict) not so much on the present's dimension as the future's size. The future is often partly predictable, even if uncertain.

The ant responds to the grasshopper's invitation by continuing to work and warning it that they should safeguard their community for the imminent arrival of winter. The grasshopper does not immediately understand the ant's response, emphasizing that there is enough food. He will understand its meaning in the middle of the harsh winter when it can find neither food nor shelter from the cold. Then, it will be forced to ask for help precisely from those ants that it had invited to stop work and enjoy the sun and summer.

This passage from the fable draws attention to the need to manage the present while always looking to the future. The behavior of the grasshopper would be entirely acceptable if it did not have to face a harsh winter later. It is the imminence of winter that causes the ants' concern. They prefer to work rather than enjoy the beautiful summer days to prevent a bad situation later. For this reason, the behavior of the ants can be considered correct when looking toward a near future marked by the change of season. At the same time, the behavior of the grasshopper is incautious because in enjoying the present, it doesn't care about what may happen tomorrow.

These Pretty Days Are Not So Many, Grasshopper. Soon, the Cold Will Come. We Must Be Ready

The ant's attitude is based on the awareness that the beautiful days won't last and that the season will soon change, posing new challenges and problems, such as finding food and protecting oneself from the cold.

The context in which the story takes place is pertinent and close to today's economic situation. Our days are characterized by the short-term change of season, with the end of summer and the beginning of autumn and winter. As in the fable, heat (linked to using energy resources) and food (for at least some essential nutrition) are the two aspects that worry us. These two issues are aggravated by issues around the protection of manufacturing activities, with uncontrolled increases in energy and raw material prices in recent months.

The conflict in Ukraine and the COVID-19 pandemic have made everyone understand how economic models, which have worked until now, may now appear inefficient and no longer able to guarantee the satisfaction of the community's needs. This is true even though some would say the system was already broken, and new factors led to the collapse.

In Europe, for example, on August 25, 2022, the gas price on the Amsterdam stock exchange reached €320, causing much concern in the financial markets and for companies whose supplies were significantly affected. A month later, TTF futures finished trading 10% higher at a new all-time high of €321.4 per megawatt-hour as the three-day scheduled shutdown of Nord Stream neared to companies other than those they had supplied before as they waited for a clearer picture of the trend in gas prices (Banca Centrale Europea, 2022).

The concrete result of this scenario was that more and more companies need help finding suppliers. In these weeks, the contracts for the next thermal year are generally renegotiated, starting on October 1st and continuing until September 30th the following year.

In many production sectors, the increase in energy costs ultimately erodes margins to the point of making it more cost-effective for companies to interrupt production and activity. Today, many sectors are strongly affected by the high energy price.

The cost of electricity and gas quadrupled over the summer of 2022 compared to last year's period. Bills are estimated in the millions for the most energy-intensive sectors, whose businesses depend on gas. Even if the problem only affects some countries equally, the manufacturing sector suffers. Some countries may even have an advantage in the current situation.

The energy cost issue is much more complex than the upcoming winter for ants and grasshoppers. Who could have imagined that the situation would quickly change a year ago? Who knew that a possible conflict involving Russia could determine the need to change the gas supply system in Europe radically? Who could have imagined such a rapid change in the balance of power in international markets?

The answer is probably no one. However, this again confirms that the ant's behavior is the most appropriate way of managing the present while looking to the future, with the awareness that external events can disrupt a calm period. It also emphasizes the importance of flexible systems that can adapt to changes, including the ability to look for new solutions in some circumstances, abandoning models and systems that proved valid in the past. This is happening globally concerning the green transition of our economic systems, for example.

"Come, Friend," It Called. "There Is Room Here, and There Is Food. I've Saved Enough for Many Seasons. Come in and Eat"

Every fairytale has its happy ending. At the end of the story, the grasshopper finds refuge with the ants who host it in their home and give it the food they have accumulated over the summer, sufficient to satisfy the needs of many seasons. The tale also has a moral—we must always think about the future, not taking for granted that what we have today can last. Above all, we must always reach out to those in need, even if they don't share our behaviors or decisions.

Of course, the scenario is always more complex in the real world than in a fairytale. Companies compete and are embedded in systems such as individual state laws, regulations, and policies that directly or indirectly affect them. Added to this are the value chains connecting companies from different continents, creating strong interrelationships that affect the destinies of the companies that make up these supply or value chains.

In the real world, it is simplistic to automatically adapt the ant's behavior of working hard during the summer period and facing future challenges. The ability to survive also depends on many other variables over which companies often do not have direct control, such as political stability, financial markets, geopolitical balances, natural events, health events, etc.

In this context, the summer of 2022 was difficult due to increased energy costs, inflationary pressures, and international tensions. Summer 2022 will also be remembered for the extreme climate, water shortages, the drought that affected many countries, and the speed at which the glaciers are melting increased.

The effects of the drought will also be felt from an economic point of view in the coming years. Agricultural production, for example, is essential for many countries, including Italy. Other effects will be detected in the medium to long term. A recent analysis by Bloomberg (https://www.bnnbloomberg.ca/the-world-s-rivers-canals-and-reservoirs-are-turning-to-dust-1.1810753) highlighted the correlations between climate change and the economy in the context of the main waterways. For centuries, the Rhine has been a mainstay of the German, Dutch, and Swiss economies and is set to become impassable, hampering diesel and coal cargoes. The Danube is also clogged, putting the grain trade at risk. France's energy crisis has also worsened because the Rhône and Garonne are too hot to cool nuclear reactors effectively, and the Po in Italy is too low to irrigate rice paddies.

The rivers and canals of the continent carry more than a ton of goods per year for every EU resident and contribute about $80 billion to the region's economy solely as a transport route (Sullivan, 2022). The alarm is widespread. In the Po Valley, home to about 30% of Italian agricultural production, the scorching heat and arid conditions have damaged corn and sunflower crops. When the Po fell to its lowest level in 70 years, rice farmers were forced to cut down crops (Ali et al., 2023).

Even more worrying is that waterways are crucial to the EU's efforts to fight climate change. In its green transition plans, the European Commission aims for a 25% increase in inland waterways and short-sea shipping by 2030 (Silvestri, 2022).

The situation suggests that the solution was designed without considering the complexity of the overall system. Another analysis might be that the solution should have been sought earlier and, due to the urgency, other risk elements must be considered. Whatever the rationale, it is a reminder of the complexity involved (Spanò & Zagaria, 2022).

The Teachings of the Fable

The tale also allows us to draw some important lessons from an economic, business, and managerial point of view:

1. The present can only be managed with an adequate projection into the future. Each behavior, each decision, and in fact, each non-behavior or non-decision affects the future.
2. The primary risk prevention tool is planning. Management must be able to plan its business both in the short and medium to long term.
3. It is essential to understand the period that management should be considering. It seems clear that in reality—unlike in fairy tales—each company has its seasonality with different effects depending on the period. The fairy tale winter may not be as harsh for all companies.
4. Planning makes it possible to mitigate the effects of hostile events and, in some cases, makes it possible to avoid such events. To that end, planning must be based on analyzing previous periods' data and integrating that with future expectations. An effective planning process must be based on something other than the past, and it can be biased toward the end, as the future is uncertain.
5. Finally, solidarity within the system is crucial in a global socioeconomic system. A system is robust if the actors that compose it are strong. A system is weak when some actors dominate the system to the detriment of others.

Solidarity within the system is part of the lesson of the fable. The ants could have left the grasshopper outside, uninterested in its survival. The following summer, they would have also found more food and would have been able to continue their work. However, they welcomed the grasshopper by making their resources available to it. Why did they do this? Because they knew that the grasshopper was needed in the system, and they knew that their strength was not linked to the disappearance of the grasshopper but rather to the ability to safeguard the entire system.

Solidarity must, therefore, be considered as the protection of the entire system within which all the actors—ants and grasshoppers—belong.

References

Aesop's Fables, numbered 373 in the Perry Index. Ben Edwin Perry (1965). Babrius and Phaedrus. Loeb Classical Library. Harward University Press: 487, n. 373. ISBN 0-674-99480-9.s

Ali, I., Golgeci, I., & Arslan, A. (2023). Achieving resilience through knowledge management practices and risk management culture in agri-food supply chains. *Supply Chain Management: An International Journal, 28*(2), 284–299.

Banca Centrale Europea (BCE). (2022). *Bollettino economico, 3.*

Giannessi, E. (1970). *Appunti di economia aziendale*. G. Pellegrini.

OECD. (2021, October 5 and 6). Trust in Global Cooperation. The vision for the OECD for the next decade.

Silvestri, V. (2022). La siccità sta sconvolgendo l'economia in Europa. *Money.it*.

Spanò, R., & Zagaria, C. (2022). Enterprise risk management systems: Emerging issues and future trends. In: Integrating performance management and enterprise risk management systems.

Sullivan, B. K. (2022). *The world's rivers, canals and reservoirs are turning to dust*. Bloomberg Europe edition.

Woods, M. (2022). *Risk management in organisations: An integrated case study approach.* Routledge.

CHAPTER 3

Everything Is Economics

Everything is economics, and everything is measurable. Any behavior, decision, non-behavior, or non-decision has an economic value and is quantitatively measurable. Economic value is not unique, nor is it objective. It depends on the methodology used and the temporal depth to which it is analyzed. Therefore, the principal analysis methodologies are vital for supporting management in decision-making and strategic processes. This chapter describes the principal analysis and measurement techniques to support decision-making: opportunity cost, economic marginalism, differential analysis, and break-even analysis.

The economic value of every behavior, decision, non-behavior, and non-decision has, over the years, changed the composition of organizational systems in the relationship between subjective management (i.e., human capital) and objective management (i.e., managerial tools). Managerial tools are becoming increasingly important in decision-making processes, representing a real threat to subjective management (i.e., management that takes no responsibility and tends to delegate the decision to objective evidence produced by its various analysis techniques).

Technology, big data, algorithms, and artificial intelligence are essential in this context. Companies' almost obsessive pursuit of numbers is the basis of surveillance capitalism. This tug-of-war between subjective and objective management in the digital age must make us reflect

A. Capocchi, *Vulnerability and the Corporate Immune System*, https://doi.org/10.1007/978-3-031-30254-1_3

on two essential issues in companies' decision-making and management processes: the relationship between humans and technology and the relationship between rationality and irrationality.

It Depends—On the Correct Answer to Economic and Business-Economic Questions

Understanding how everything surrounding us takes on economic value requires immediately understanding the effect produced by every action and every non-action. More generally, any behavior, decision, non-behavior, and/or non-decision produces a measurable economic effect. Economic impact measurement is closely linked to the reference time horizon, which means that, according to the projection time horizon (also known as the reference time horizon), the same behavior or decision produces different effects from an economic point of view.

The reference to the reference time horizon in the determination/measurement of the economic effect is linked to all events that occur in the time interval considered and not to the mere passage of time: these are events that directly or indirectly impact behavior and/or decisions.

I often ask my student's economic-business questions with binary answers (on or off, yes or no, negative or positive, black or white, good or bad). They search for the correct answer by focusing on the binary choice. After formulating the question, I point out that, in many cases, questions in the economic and economic-business fields can never be binary: the correct answer is "it depends." Why does it depend? Depends on what?

The correct answer is "it depends" because the implications or effects must be understood to answer an economic or economic-business question. In addition, the effects are never specific but somewhat relative. And the relativity of the impact depends precisely on the temporal depth of the evaluation and projection. It is one thing to evaluate a decision in the short term; another in the medium and/or long term. What is inevitable in all cases is the measurement of the effects in the short, medium, and/or long term.

For example, consider a company that must decide whether to insure a customer against the risk of insolvency. The company turns to an insurance company that, based on an in-depth analysis, determines the premium to insure the selected customer's credit—usually not beyond a specific amount. The higher the tip, the greater the risk of insolvency detected by the insurance company. Sometimes, the same company could also decide not to insure the selected customer.

Suppose the insurance company accepts the risk and decides to insure the customer. In that case, the company must determine if it is convenient today, without knowing what will happen in the future, to assume a specific and immediate cost represented by the premium that it must pay to the insurance company against the security embodied by the collection of the credit that it has extended its insured customer or whether it accepts a risk of future insolvency of the customer without a direct specific cost.

What is the economic effect of the decision that the company must make? The economic impact depends on what happens in the future, namely, the customer's behavior. If the customer remains solvent, the cost to be borne by the company relating to the insurance premium is unavoidable and only has the security of the commercial relationship as a counterpart. Otherwise, if the customer becomes unreliable and insolvent, the cost incurred for the insurance has as a counterpart the collection of the credit even in conditions of insolvency of the customer. This makes the specific cost of the insurance premium negligible compared with the cost that the company would have incurred in the case of default without insurance coverage: the cost represented by the credit loss.

This example clarifies how the "correctness" of a decision and/or behavior can only be evaluated in retrospect according to what happens. At the time of the decision and/or behavior—in our example, the signing of the insurance contract—the company does not have all the elements to ensure that it takes the correct actions, therefore assuming a risk. In the case of insuring the customer, the risk is that the customer remains solvent, in which case there would be no need to activate any insurance coverage for which the specific and immediate cost of the premium was incurred. In the case of not taking out the insurance policy, the risk consists of the customer's insolvency, the cost of which is represented by the loss of the entire credit. The cost in the latter case is far greater than the cost of the insurance premium.

This demonstrates that the decision always involves a choice and that the option—whatever it may be—is always an assumption of risk. The cost of the different scenarios must be evaluated differentially, and the scenario considered the best in the given time and place must be chosen.

Note that the cost does not always appear simultaneously in the decision and the choice. In our example, taking out the insurance policy determines a cost at the subscription time. The decision not to take out the insurance policy determines the potential and future costs incurred if the customer becomes insolvent upon the credit's expiration. This is important because, when making the decision, the company must evaluate different costs both in terms of amount and when they are incurred and, consequently, evaluate which risk to assume: whether the risk of incurring a cost for the insurance premium today or risk incurring a cost in the future (upon expiry of the credit).

This example also clarifies how the decision-making process is based on a non-perfect and non-symmetrical information system: the information available at the time of the decision is not the same as the information that will be available during the event—in our example, the credit expiration. This forms an information asymmetry between the two moments: the moment of the decision and the moment of the event.

Another example familiar to many Italian and non-Italian companies is evaluating opportunities for stipulating contracts to cover the risks associated with increased interest rates. During the covid pandemic, many companies had access to medium- and long-term financing guaranteed by the state at low rates. Before the war in Ukraine, the post-pandemic economic recovery increased the price of raw materials throughout Europe and created an inflationary push that had not been seen for many years. The inflationary push created concerns about the medium- and long-term effects, primarily on consumption. It induced the central authorities to raise interest rates with a consequent increase in the cost of loans taken out by companies. The central authorities decided to use interest rates to curb the inflationary push.

Not knowing a priori the duration of the inflationary push and therefore not knowing by how much interest rates will rise, many companies evaluated financial risk hedging instruments: instruments that, although they protect the future, do so at specific and immediate costs. Even in the face of these assessments, it is impossible to establish in an absolute manner which is the right decision. Once again, by deciding on one scenario or another, the company assumes a risk against which it bears a corresponding current or future cost (Alabdullah, 2022; King et al., 2022; Le Brreton-Miller & Miller, 2022). The current cost is specific: in this example, it is the payment for the hedging instrument. The future cost is potential and consists of the interest the company must pay if interest rates increase. The decision on the correctness of the activation of financial hedging instruments against the risk of an increase in interest rates must

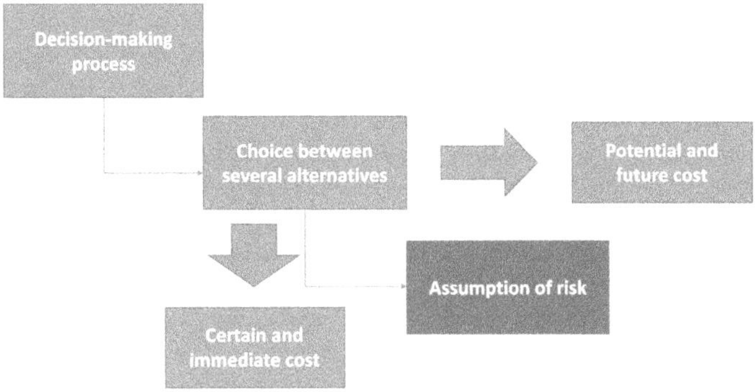

Fig. 3.1 The decision-making process

be based on the answer "it depends:" it depends on the financial structure of the single company, it depends on the company's propensity for risk, and it depends on many other variables internal and external to the company. Only the subsequent verification of the scenarios allows us to establish which behavior was "correct." What has been described to this point appears in Fig. 3.1 and illustrates how the decision-making process consists of choosing between different alternatives and how the different alternatives determine a different assumption of risk and a specific and immediate cost in one case versus a potential and future cost in the other.

Opportunity Cost

What surprises my students is when I point out that, in business economics, not only do behaviors and/or decisions involve costs, but non-behaviors and non-decisions also involve costs. The cost of the non-decision or non-behavior, like the cost of the decision or behavior, is the so-called "opportunity cost." The opportunity cost is the cost of the alternative. Namely, the cost assumed when adopting a particular behavior and/or a specific decision and which necessarily precludes a different option or alternative.

> *The concept of opportunity cost (or alternative cost) expresses the basic relationship between scarcity and choice. If no object or activity valued by anyone is scarce, all demands for all persons and in all periods can be satisfied. There is no need to choose among separately valued options; there is no need for*

social coordination processes that will effectively determine which demands have priority. In this fantasized setting without scarcity, there are no opportunities or alternatives that are missed, foregone, or sacrificed. Once scarcity is introduced, all demands cannot be met. Unless there are 'natural' constraints that predetermine the allocation of end-objects possessing value (for example, sunshine in Scotland in February), scarcity introduces the necessity of choice, either directly among alternative end-objects or indirectly among institutions or procedural arrangements for social interaction that will, in turn, generate a selection of ultimate end-objects. Choice implies rejected as well as selected alternatives. Opportunity cost is the evaluation placed on the most highly valued of the rejected alternatives or opportunities. It is that value that is given up or sacrificed in order to secure the higher value that selection of the chosen object embodies. (…). (Buchanan, 1991: 520)

An opportunity cost is *"the evaluation placed on the most highly valued of the rejected alternatives or opportunities"* (Buchanan, 2008) or *"the loss of other alternatives when one alternative is chosen"* (Oxford English Dictionary, 2010).

Every behavior and every decision has an opportunity cost (Spiller, 2011). The knowledge and determination of the opportunity cost are the basis of the differential analysis methodology within which a decision must be rationally adopted.

The opportunity cost can be determined by applying various calculation methods according to the context. In general, explicit and implicit costs can be considered in determining opportunity costs. Explicit costs are directly linked to a specific activity, behavior, and/or decision. Implicit or economic costs are closely related to the loss of value sustained due to foreclosing on an alternative. The explicit costs are easy to measure, whereas the measurement of the implicit cost is more complex (although not difficult).

Imagine a company that produces mineral water and soft drinks to understand the difference. The production uses the same machinery in the same production facility. If the company produces mineral water in that interval, it cannot produce soft drinks and vice versa. Imagine the company is making several bottles of mineral water in a certain period. The explicit cost is the production cost of water produced in the time interval considered. The company's accounting system quickly measures this cost. The lower value represents the company's implicit cost due to not producing soft drinks in that same time interval. The implicit cost is given by the fact that a liter of water has a lower value on the market than a liter of any other drink, which makes for a lower margin in favor of the company. The margin difference between a liter of water and any soft drink represents an implicit cost for the company linked to the mineral water production. This cost can be measured as the difference between the margin of a liter of any drink other than water and the margin of a liter of mineral water:

$$\text{Implicit Cost} = \text{Margin 1 L Drink} - \text{Margin 1 L of Mineral Water},$$

where

$$\text{Margin 1 L Drink} > \text{Margin 1 L of Mineral Water}.$$

Opportunity cost can only sometimes be fully quantified when a decision is made. Instead, the person deciding can only roughly estimate the results of various alternatives. This means imperfect knowledge can lead to an opportunity cost that will only appear later.

Ultimately, opportunity cost should not be confused with sunk cost, already incurred. As such, it is configured as a retrospective cost differently from the opportunity cost and is configured as a future cost.

Marginal Benefit and Cost

In economic analysis, "marginalism" is essential. It is understood as the method of evaluation based on the marginalistic principle, which guides economic actors in their choices by comparing benefit and marginal cost, where benefit and marginal cost refer to the last unit produced or consumed. The reference to the moments of production and consumption concerns the two main economic actors: the company, whose purpose is to maximize its utility through the production process and thereby maximize profit. The consumer's objective is maximizing utility by allocating his income to support consumption to satisfy his needs.

In marginalist theory, the firm wants to maximize its profit and, if an additional unit of output generates more benefit than the cost of production, does so by producing. When the benefit of use falls below the cost of production, producing is no longer profitable. The consumer wants to maximize the satisfaction of his needs by optimally allocating his limited wealth. Thus the attention to the consumption process. In marginalist theory, the scarcity or limitation of resources (i.e., the constraints that differentiate between the behavior of companies and consumers) plays an essential role.

The marginalistic principle states that an economic subject only takes a given action if the initial satisfaction exceeds the initial sacrifice. The same economic issue continues in step until the increment of sacrifice exceeds the increment of benefit or satisfaction.

The marginalistic principle in economic analysis is possible if sacrifice and satisfaction can be divided into equal and infinitely small doses: the increases in satisfaction decrease. In contrast, the sacrifice can increase or decrease slower than the decrease in satisfaction. When the marginal benefit is less than the marginal cost, the activity, whatever it is, stops. Therefore, the equilibrium that maximizes the advantage for all actors requires the equality of the marginal values of the economic quantities related to the prices.

The marginalist approach was harshly criticized for the excessive individualism it attributed to the behavior of economic actors: business and consumer. This limit was overcome thanks to the contributions of Keynes and other economists who favored a macroeconomic approach increasingly aimed at studying the system's functioning, going beyond the microeconomic analysis to investigate the behavior of individual economic actors. The New Keynesians developed the microeconomic foundations of this theory without escaping criticism from scholars who believed that the prices of goods are not determined by demand but rather by the technical conditions of production.

After the Keynesian and post-Keynesian parentheses, from the 1950s onwards, marginalist thought dominated all other theoretical formulations and is now universally accepted by economists, albeit with nuances and characterizations. The diffusion of the marginalist approach finds confirmation in business and managerial studies in the diffusion of mathematical and statistical tools, whose role has dramatically increased over the years, including within management. Subjective management is increasingly looking for objective support deriving from the available tools. This trend, still ongoing today, has favored the development of mathematical economics, experimental economics, behavioral economics, and game theory over time.

Today it can be affirmed, as better explained below by Zuboff, that marginalism is an integral part of modern management systems, focusing attention on the increasingly detailed study of individual behavior aimed at achieving maximum utility (albeit with a broader definition) in the context of strategic interaction and characterized by uncertainty and complexity. After all, in the digital economy, as an essential American scholar argued, we are in the era of surveillance capitalism where companies strive to "own" the consumer (Zuboff, 2019a, 2019b).

> *Surveillance capitalism's products and services are not the objects of value exchange. They do not establish constructive producer-consumer reciprocities. Instead, they are the "hooks" that lure users into their extractive operations in which our personal experiences are scraped and packaged as the means to others' ends. We are not surveillance capitalism's "customers." Although the saying tells us "If it's free, then you are the product," that is also incorrect. We are the sources of surveillance capitalism's crucial surplus: the objects of a technologically advanced and increasingly inescapable raw-material-extraction operation. Surveillance capitalism's actual customers are the enterprises that trade in its markets for future behavior.* (Zuboff, 2019a, 2019b: 17)

The conquest of consumer ownership is the battleground on which companies compete globally today. This battle assumes different characteristics depending on the sector to which it belongs.

> *Surveillance capitalism can no longer be identified with individual companies or even with the behemoth information sector. This mutation quickly spread from Silicon Valley to every economic sector. Its success birthed a burgeoning surveillance-based economic order that now extends across a vast and varied range of products and services.* (Zuboff, 2019a, 2019b: 11)

Cost–Benefit Analysis

The marginalist model introduces the cost–benefit analysis (CBA) as an analysis tool. The marginal quantity is the increase in the amount for an increase of one unit.

Usually, the concept of marginality is applied to economic quantities to measure marginal costs and revenues. Marginal cost is the cost incurred upon increasing production by one unit. Marginal revenue is the increase in value upon increasing production by one more unit. The use of benefits and marginal costs is the basis of the CBA, intended as "*a methodology for assessing the economic efficiency with which resources are used to support human wellbeing. Its theoretical origins lie in the foundations of welfare economics established by economists such as Hicks (1939), Kaldor (1939), Scitovsky (1941), and Little (1957)*" (James & Predo, 2015: 11).

CBA serves to evaluate the economic efficiency of different alternatives which may be able to achieve some predetermined objectives. CBA is also used in contexts where the public interest is involved. CBA is a social benefit–cost analysis in these cases, focusing on the community's well-being. Well-being is "*the utility experienced in the consumption of goods and services produced by the economic system or that are otherwise made available, such as those provided by natural systems and the environment*" (James & Predo, 2015: 12).

A CBA recalls the setting of the Pareto optimum by which efficient use of resources can be obtained when it is impossible to make specific individuals feel better without making others feel worse. In other words, following Pareto's approach, an economically efficient result is achieved when the net benefits (given by total benefits minus total costs) are maximized.

> *A material image of the company can be had by imagining a container where multiple streams concur, representing the elements of production, and from which a river flows which represents the product.* (Pareto, 1919: 274)[1]

In the CBA model, the benefit is an increase in value and a lower cost, just as a lower benefit can represent a cost. Thus the reference to the willingness to pay is understood as the propensity of the individual or the community to bear a cost at a specific moment and in a particular place (also understood as a minor benefit) to increase one's utility.

The CBA within the decision-making processes is connected to the risk propensity of the subject, who must adopt the decision to choose between alternatives. This methodology is widely used in the economic and engineering fields to conduct project evaluations based on measuring and comparing all costs and benefits directly and/or indirectly connected to them.

> *The basic rationale of cost-benefit analysis lies in the idea that things are worth doing if the benefits resulting from doing them outweigh their costs. This is not, of course, by any means, noncontroversial, but before getting into the controversies, (...).* (Sen, 2000: 934)

[1] Translated from Italian: "Un 'immagine materiale dell'impresa si può avere figurandosi un recipiente ove concorrono molteplici rigagnoli, che rappresentano gli elementi della produzione e dal quale esce un fiume che rappresenta il prodotto" (Pareto, 1919: 274).

The analysis is typically conducted by converting each unit of input into units of elementary costs and each unit of output into units of elemental benefits. An attempt is then made to give the most objective value possible to each of these units, thus making it measurable and comparable. Comparability drives the subsequent decision-making process. The total cost, therefore, is the sum of the values of the single units of elementary costs. In contrast, the full benefit is the sum of the values of the single units of elemental benefits. This system makes it possible to evaluate direct and indirect benefits and costs. To obtain reliable results, one must circumscribe the units of elementary benefits and costs as realistically as possible and evaluate these units using values that are as objective as possible.

For this reason, from an accounting point of view, assessments should be based on direct costs rather than total costs. The entire cost presupposes using indirect costs whose allocation takes place using allocation criteria whose choice always appears subjective. It is, therefore, evident that the evaluation of direct costs, even if not complete, occurs in conditions of greater objectivity than the same evaluation based on full costing.

Differential Analysis

What has been described to this point allows us to introduce differential analysis as an evaluation tool that founded numerous decision-making processes. Differential analysis is an easy-to-implement method that allows one to evaluate and compare alternatives based on economical quantities such as costs, revenues, and margins (the latter obtained from the difference between revenues and costs).

The differential analysis makes it possible to measure specific economic quantities concerning the moment of the evaluation and perspectives, whose synthesis allows a comparison of the different scenarios based on the other available alternatives. Differential analysis is widely used in economics and business science to support decision-making processes and often uses opportunity cost and/or a CBA.

The alternatives are only sometimes immediately comparable. A differential analysis must, therefore, not only measure and compare the different options but must first make them homogeneous and similar. Homogeneity concerns the temporal dimension of the quantities used and their nature.

To understand temporal homogeneity, imagine having to compare the result for the first quarter to monitor the production trend vis à vis the objective the company has included in its annual budget. The comparison must occur through the deviation measurement. The difference between the partial result for the first quarter and the target at the end of the year gives the variance:

$$\text{Deviation} = \begin{array}{l} |\ \text{Partial result in the first quarter} \\ -\text{Target budget at the end of the year}\ | \end{array}$$

We take the absolute value of the deviation measurement because the deviation should not be affected by any interpretation relating to plus or minus signs. An interpretation is applied later by removing the absolute value and checking the sign of the deviation itself. To calculate the deviation, however, the two quantities must be homogeneous in time because, at the end of the first quarter, the partial result for the first quarter must be projected to the end of the year or used to update the final objective on an annual basis. These two alternatives are equivalent and require the determination of a coefficient: in the first case of a projection coefficient and in the second case of a discount coefficient. The coefficient must be determined based on statistical criteria that give the coefficient the maximum possible objectivity.

In our example, the comparison concerned a quantity measured at the end of the first quarter and measured at the end of the year. Given that a year has four quarters, the coefficient for projection and actualization can be given the value of four.

A coefficient of four is correct but assumes a hypothesis that needs to be made explicit. A coefficient of four is based on the hypothesis that the quantity evolves linearly over the year. In our example, the quantity is represented by the volume of activity: the choice of a coefficient of four assumes that the company's production is constant over the year (i.e., it is devoid of seasonality). If this were not the case, the production would be subject to seasonality—think of the production of ice cream or mineral water in the summer months—the coefficient could not be four in such a case. In the case of seasonality, the coefficient must be determined on a statistical basis through the use of historical series. In practice, the company has verified for the last *n* years how production at the end of the first quarter affected the total output at the end of the year and, based on the normalized average of the data, calculates the coefficient which should be greater than four (assuming the production of ice cream or mineral water in which production peaks in the summer months).

To better understand the homogeneity of the quantities, suppose a person wants to invest in Milan by purchasing a hotel. The investor selects two alternatives represented by two already existing and functioning hotels with the same number of rooms, the same classification of several stars, and located in the same area of the city. The investor asks to analyze the accounts of the two hotels. After reviewing them, he realizes that the first hotel does not own the land on which it sits and pays a rent indexed on inflation. In contrast, the second hotel recorded the property in its financial statements at the historical purchase cost and is subject to the standard depreciation procedure.

The two economic structures must be made homogeneous to compare the economic structures represented by the two hotels and analyze which has greater profitability that impacts the return on investment. In this case, homogeneity is obtained by introducing a rental fee into the economic structure of the second hotel even though it owns the property. The inclusion in the economic structure of the second hotel of the rent incurs a notional cost, which is a cost that the company does not bear but must be considered for the analysis and evaluation of the two economic structures. In our example, the rental cost to be included in the economic structure of the second hotel is notional because it is not an actual cost for the company.

Using figurative economic quantities can also concern revenues and not just costs. A figurative revenue is a revenue that a company does not support but must be considered for the analysis.

Break-Even Analysis

One of the applications of differential analysis is the break-even analysis, a simplified analysis model that, within a reference framework of five hypotheses, allows one to evaluate the behavior of various economic functions: total revenue, variable costs, fixed costs, and total costs. The evaluation of the behavior of the economic functions also makes it possible to determine the break-even point (i.e., the point at which total revenues equal total costs).

Break-even analysis is an essential managerial tool to support corporate governance and decision-making processes based on a cost-volume-results analysis model. In turn, is based on the distinction of cost behavior by a single parameter represented by the volume of activity. It is a simplified managerial tool compared with what happens but is very useful for the logic and dynamics that characterize it. In detail, the break-even analysis makes it possible to relate costs to activity volumes and revenues, determining the break-even point between costs and revenues or establishing conditions for certain profit levels.

The model can be developed both from a mathematical point of view and a graphical point of view. Before highlighting the two developments, it appears crucial to report the simplifying assumptions based on the model. There are five simplifying assumptions:

1. The company offers a single product.
2. The company sells (S) everything it produces (P), implying no inventory or variation between the closing inventories and the initial inventories.
3. The price is constant.
4. The unit variable cost is constant.
5. There is no limit to production capacity (i.e., the company can produce and sell infinite output).

Given these simplifying assumptions, we now develop the model mathematically. Let.

$$\text{TC} = \text{Total Cost},$$

$$\text{TR} = \text{Total Revenue}.$$

We start with

$$\text{TR} = \text{TC}.$$

This equation expresses the equality between revenues and total costs. The point at which total costs equal total revenues is the break-even point. The equality between total costs and total revenues makes it possible to determine the quantity of production P or sales S in correspondence with which the same equality occurs.

If total costs TC are represented by the sum of total fixed costs TFC and total variable costs TVC, the above equation becomes

$$\text{TR} = \text{TC},$$

$$TR = TFC + TVC.$$

If the total variable costs TVC are proportional to the only parameter or cost driver represented by the volume q of activity, and the total fixed costs TFC are constant (K) concerning the same cost driver, we have

$$TR = K + (vc \times q),$$

where vc is the variable cost per unit, q is the quantity that expresses the volume of activity, $(vc \times q)$ is the total variable costs TVC, K is the total fixed costs TFC, and TR is the total revenue. If sales revenues are proportional to the quantity q of output produced /sold (i.e., that the production is sold at a constant price p), we have

$$(p \times q) = K + (cv \times q).$$

To determine the break-even point as the volume q of activity and output at which total costs equal total revenues, we have

$$(p \times q) = K + (vc \times q)$$

$$(p \times q) - (vc \times q) = K$$

$$q(p - vc) = K$$

$$q = K/(p - vc).$$

We can thus determine, starting from the equality between total costs and total revenues, the break-even point (i.e., the quantity produced or sold at which the company covers all its costs with its revenues). At the break-even point, the company's profitability is zero. In the equation above, the denominator $(p - cv)$ represents the unit contribution margin, which, if multiplied by q, expresses both at a unit level and an overall level the capacity of the unit price or the revenue (if a general level) to cover fixed costs.

In other words, the contribution margin at the unit level is represented by the difference between the unit price p and the unit variable cost vc. It expresses what remains after the unit price has covered the unit variable cost. Therefore, the contribution margin is the contribution that the unit price makes to cover fixed costs. The contribution margin measures the contribution made by the price or revenues to pay the fixed costs.

A positive contribution margin does not guarantee coverage of fixed costs because this also depends on the extent of the fixed costs. What is certain is that, in the presence of a negative contribution margin, the company cannot create wealth—it cannot even cover its variable costs.

In the equation above, *q* represents the level of output that the firm must produce and sell to cover all costs. The product of *q* and the unit price *p* expresses the company's turnover at the break-even point to cover all fixed and variable costs.

To determine the break-even point as the equilibrium turnover F, we introduce the incidence Y of the unit variable cost *vc* on the unit price *p*, which gives

$$\mathrm{Y} = vc/p$$

$$\mathrm{CVT} = (vc/p) \times q \times p,$$

so the total variable cost is

$$\mathrm{TVC} = \mathrm{Y} \times \mathrm{TR}.$$

Inserting the new formula relating to total variable costs TVC into the initial equation gives

$$\mathrm{Y} \times \mathrm{TR} + \mathrm{K} = \mathrm{TR},$$

from which

$$\mathrm{K} = \mathrm{TR} - \mathrm{Y} \times \mathrm{TR},$$

and

$$\mathrm{K} = \mathrm{TR} \times (1 - \mathrm{Y}),$$

from which we get

$$\mathrm{TR} = \mathrm{K}/(1 - \mathrm{Y}).$$

In the above equation, (1 − Y) represents the effect of the contribution margin on the price because

$$1 - (vc/p) = (p - vc)/p.$$

In addition, TR represents the level of turnover at which the company reaches the break-even point between total costs and revenues.

The break-even analysis model can also be developed graphically using a Cartesian plane. Representation on a Cartesian plane is made possible because the model is two-dimensional. Furthermore, within the Cartesian plane, the representation of the various functions following the simplifying hypotheses on which the model is based allows the reporting of straight lines, not curves. The lines are a direct consequence of the proportionality of the sales or production volumes, with the revenues and the variable costs being the price p and the unit variable cost *vc*, which are assumed to be constant.

From a graphical viewpoint, the Cartesian plane's break-even point is where the total cost line intersects the total revenue line, as shown in Fig. 3.2.

The graphical representation shown in Fig. 3.2 is based on the following characteristics of the functions involved:

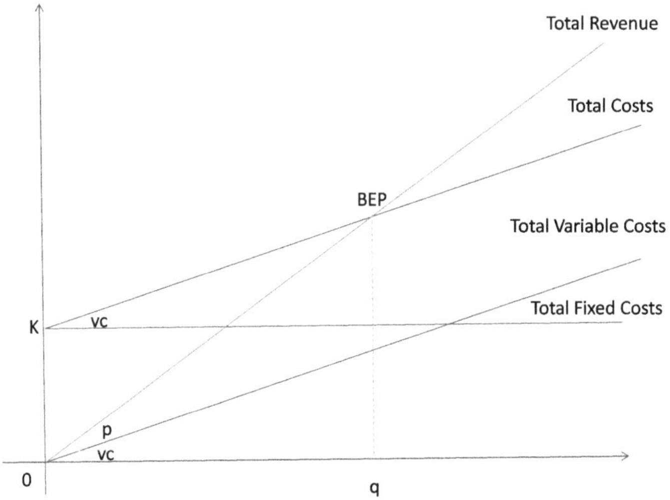

Fig. 3.2 Break-even analysis

- Lines represent all functions.
- The total revenue function (TR) is represented by the straight-line TR having the unit price (p) as the angular coefficient and the origin as an intercept with the *y-axis*. The total revenue line passes through the origin because when the activity level equals zero, total revenue (TR) also equals zero.
- The total fixed cost function (TFC) is represented by a straight-line TFC parallel to the abscissa with an intercept K on the ordinate axis. In the observed relevance range, total fixed costs are constant as the activity level.
- The total variable cost function (TVC) is represented by a TVC line having unit variable cost vc as angular coefficient and the origin as intercept with the *y-axis*. Total variable costs equal zero when the activity level equals zero.
- The total cost function (CT) is given by the sum of total fixed costs (TFC) and total variable costs (TVC). This function is represented by a straight line with the same angular coefficient as the total variable costs (TVC) and an intercept with the ordinate axis, K. In correspondence with an activity level equal to zero, the total costs (TC) assume the value of K; that is, it assumes the total fixed costs (TCF), and the total variable costs are set to zero.

The intersection between the total cost line (TC) and the total revenue line (TR) identifies on the abscissa the break-even activity q and on the ordinate axis the equality between total revenue (TR) and total costs (TC). It then follows that if

$$q' = \text{break} - \text{even point}$$

and

$$q < q',$$

we get

$$\text{CT} > \text{RT}.$$

In addition, if

$$q > q',$$

we get

$$CT < RT.$$

The total costs (TC) exceed the total revenues (TR) for activity levels below the break-even point. The difference also graphically identifies the loss the company suffered economically. The total costs (TC) are less than total revenues (TR) for activity levels above the break-even point. The difference also graphically identifies the economic profit that the company achieves.

In the graphical representation, the contribution margin ($p - vc$) is the difference between the angular coefficient of the total revenue line and the angular coefficient of the total variable cost line.

The graphical representation also enables the so-called sensitivity analysis, which verifies the behavior of the functions at the change of the variables indicated above. Consider, for example, a company that wants to increase the unit sales price p of the output, verifying the consequences in advance through the graphical representation. Suppose the price p increases from p_0 to p_1, where $p_1 > p_0$. In this case, the total revenue line (TR) slope increases, with a consequent upwards translation of the same, the price p, and the angular coefficient.

Other conditions being equal, this determines, as shown in Fig. 3.3, a reduction of the optimal activity level at which the company reaches the balance between total revenues (TR) and total costs (TC).

As shown in Fig. 3.3, with an increase in selling price, the company first reaches the break-even point regarding the volume of activity. However, in the event of a reduction in selling price, a lower slope of the total revenue line is determined by moving forward the break-even point in terms of volume of activity. The sensitivity analysis can also be done by assuming the variation of the other variables or the simultaneous variation of several variables.

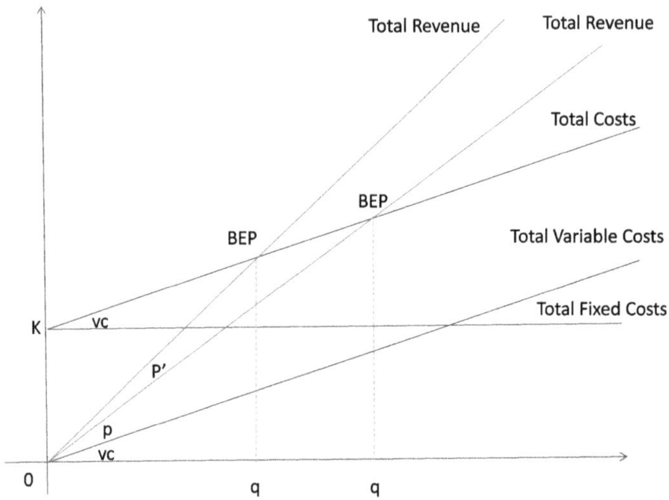

Fig. 3.3 Break-even analysis and sensitivity analysis

Rationality Versus Irrationality

Concerning the objective component (i.e., the tools that support decision-making processes), managerial systems have progressively shifted toward the search for a greater degree of rationality. The greater rationality that forms the basis of decision-making processes has favored the transition from accounting managerial tools to non-accounting managerial tools. Managerial accounting tools refer to general accounting and cost accounting: the balance sheet system, the planning and control system, and the analysis of variance and reporting systems.

Non-accounting managerial tools refer to statistics and customer relationship management systems: these are complex modern systems that help companies strengthen their position within surveillance capitalism by using consumer behavior data to create needs and to direct and "manipulate" the demand. In modern management systems, the accounting component integrates increasingly with the non-accounting component, increasing its role in the complex system. The greater importance of the non-accounting component is also facilitated by technological progress, which favors the collection, selection, and processing of information.

Consider using big data, algorithms, and artificial intelligence in this regard.

In modern managerial systems, the objective component is increasingly replacing the subjective component due to the greater objectivity made possible by modern tools. Objectivity benefits rationality.

A tug-of-war exists between the objective and subjective components in modern accounting systems. Such arm wrestling directly increases management's need for more responsibility in decision-making processes. The de-responsibilization of management favors rationality and the objective part of managerial systems to the detriment of the subjective component.

A management team afraid to assume responsibility and make decisions seeks certainty in managerial tools on to base its choices. In so doing, however, it does not serve the interests of management. Instead, it introduces the idea—wrong in your author's opinion—that, to some extent, technology can replace humans. Algorithms and artificial intelligence have replaced humans in the command post instead of supporting them.

This scenario is not about the future: it is already happening. Are we sure we want to encourage the birth of complex systems where technology decides based on mathematical models? Or do we prefer systems where technology supports processes, but humans always have the last word? I hope humans can maintain their dominant position in processes and modern complex systems by being supported by technological resources. If we leave room for technology, it is easy to imagine that algorithms can influence each other and lead economic actors to homogenize their behavior. This scenario is similar to what happens in the financial markets when algorithms guide mutual funds toward selling positions: the behavior is recorded on the market. It drives the other economic players to do the same, triggering genuine chains.

In a highly dynamic and complex system in which the duration of economic cycles is shortened, the ability to look beyond and make decisions even with an irrational component is fundamental: adopting anti-cyclical behavior in a fast-moving economy is fundamentally essential. After all, if we look at many entrepreneurial and managerial success stories, we see how success is often linked to the ability of humans, by following their instinct, to decide independently, sometimes even despite objective evidence. These are not just Italian stories but stories worldwide in which humans have maintained their centrality in decision-making and strategic processes. Those were different times, and things are more complex now. I disagree. Management must maintain its subjective component without leaving inappropriate technological and objective spaces. Humans must govern the processes and use the technology, not vice versa. This is especially true today, where the importance of technology is increasing with the digital transition.

References

Alabdullah, T. T. Y. (2022). Management accounting insight via a new perspective on risk management-companies profitability relationship. *International Journal of Intelligent Enterprise, 9*(2), 244–257.

Buchanan, J. M. (1991). Opportunity cost. In: J Eatwell, M Milgate & P Newman (Eds.), *The world of economics*. The New Palgrave. Palgrave Macmillan. https://doi.org/10.1007/978-1-349-21315-3_69

Buchanan, J. M. (2008). Opportunity cost. In: S. N. Dur- lauf & L. E. Blume (Eds.), *The New Palgrave dictionary of economics* (2nd ed.). Palgrave Macmillan. http://www.dictionaryofeconomics.com

James, D., & Predo, C. D. (2015). Principles and practice of cost–benefit analysis. In D. James, & H. A. Francisco (Eds.), *Cost benefit studies of natural Rresources management in Southeast Asia* (pp. 11–46). Springer. http://dx.doi.org/10.1007/978-981-287-393-4_2

King, D. R., Meglio, O., Gomez-Mejia, L., Bauer, F., & De Massis, A. (2022). Family business restructuring: A review and research agenda. *Journal of Management Studies, 59*(1), 197–235.

Le Breton-Miller, I., & Miller, D. (2022). Family businesses under COVID-19: Inspiring models–Sometimes. *Journal of Family Business Strategy, 13*(2), 100452.

Oxford English Dictionary. (2010). *Opportunity cost*. http://www.oed.com

Pareto, V. (1919). *Manuale di economia politica*. Società Editrice Libraria.

Sen, A. (2000). The discipline of cost-benefit analysis. *The Journal of Legal Studies, 28*(S2), 931–952. https://doi.org/10.1086/4681006/468100

Spiller, S. A. (2011). Opportunity cost consideration. *Journal of Consumer Research, 38*(4), 595–610. https://doi.org/10.1086/660045

Zuboff, S. (2019a). *The age of surveillance capitalism: The fight for a human future at the new frontier of power: Barack Obama's books of 2019a*. Profile Books.

Zuboff, S. (2019b). Surveillance capitalism and the challenge of collective action. *New Labor Forum, 28*(1), 10–29.

CHAPTER 4

Assessing the Vulnerability of a Business: The State of Its Health

It may seem unusual to use the term "immune system"—which occurs in the specific context of the physical health of individuals—about companies. Indeed, being economic actors with a life of their own and destined to last over time, companies have their own "immune system" that is well reconciled with the organicist and mechanistic vision introduced in Italian economic-business science by Aldo Amaduzzi.

The role of the "immune system" for the company is significant, considering the high market turbulence and high complexity in contemporary socioeconomic systems worldwide. For these reasons, in this chapter, we highlight the main accounting tools that allow the assessment of the company's state of health along three integrated dimensions: asset composition, financial correlation, and economic performance. Asset composition and financial correlation are related to the balance sheet analysis, whereas economic performance is related to the profit and loss statement (P&L) analysis.

A. Capocchi, *Vulnerability and the Corporate Immune System*,
https://doi.org/10.1007/978-3-031-30254-1_4

Vulnerability and the Immune System

The vulnerability linked to higher market turbulence requires companies to strengthen their "immune system" over time. It may seem unusual to use the term "immune system," which occurs regarding the health of individuals, to refer to companies. Indeed, companies are economic actors with a life destined to last over time (Giannessi, 1970). They have their own "immune system" well reconciled with the organicist and mechanistic vision introduced in Italian economic-business science by Aldo Amaduzzi.

> *The company appears to be a cell of the economic and social fabric, a minor organism that is a component of the overall economic system. The field of study of our discipline thus appears marked by the economic system established and governed given the purpose that the company proposes, a system that is part of the socio-economic system, for which it will, in any case, inform its purpose. The company looks almost like a system, with parts bound together by constraints and stresses. The components of the system are economic forces, that is, personal energies, material economic means, and immaterial economic factors. The system must be considered in its motion (...).* (Amaduzzi, 1948: 11 and 12)[1]

Companies and individuals—men or women—must strive to preserve and strengthen their immune systems.

Vulnerability is "*the exposure of an economy to exogenous shocks, arising out of economic openness*" (Briguglio et al., 2008: 1).

The dimension of vulnerability already studied in the literature regarding economic systems is, today, even after the COVID-19 pandemic and the conflict in Ukraine, an integral part of corporate systems—as is the dimension of risk. Risk mainly concerns the external dimension of the company, being linked to the company's specific and/

[1] Translated from Italian: "L'azienda appare una cellula del tessuto economico-sociale, un organismo minore componente del sistema economico complessivo. Il campo di studio della nostra disciplina appare così segnato dal sistema economico istituito e retto in vista del fine che si propone il soggetto aziendale; sistema che è parte del sistema economico-sociale, al fine del quale informerà in ogni caso il fine suo proprio. L'azienda si presenta quasi come un sistema, con un insieme di parti componenti avvinte tra loro da vincoli e da sollecitazioni. Le componenti del sistema sono forze economiche e cioè energie personali, mezzi economici materiali, fattori economici immateriali. Il sistema va considerato nel suo moto (...)." (Amaduzzi, 1948: 11 and 12).

or potential exposure to hostile events (Lee et al., 2022; Price et al., 2022). The vulnerability concerns the internal dimension of the company, i.e., the greater or lesser predisposition of the company itself to suffer a potentially damaging effect resulting from a hostile event.

The dimension of risk—being mainly external to the company system—places the burden on the company itself to build static tools to mitigate the likelihood of an event occurring, where possible, or mitigate its effects. The dimension of vulnerability being almost exclusively internal to the corporate system is closely connected to the corporate immune system. It leads the company to activate concrete and dynamic policies to strengthen its immune system and reduce the possible effects of a hostile event.

The relationship between vulnerability and risk is controversial in the literature and needs to be consistently recognized. However, this relationship is sure to exist within corporate systems, where precise interrelationships are often created between the two dimensions. The direct correlation between the dimension of vulnerability and the immune system within corporate systems is also certain.

> *Vulnerability regarding corporate business systems can be defined as the physiological or potential exposure of the corporate business system to even sudden and unexpected events that can attack the corporate business system, placing its survival into question.*

The company's behavior in addressing the vulnerability dimension is like that which any human being must undertake to protect their health. The metaphor of health for the human being is very fitting, especially considering the effects of the COVID-19 pandemic within the business environment and after having registered growing turbulence in the environmental system to which companies belong.

After all, business economics has constantly developed lines of study to analyze the state of health of the company system, even with quantitative tools. At the international level, there are numerous studies on the prevention of crisis states and the implementation of effective alert systems aimed at avoiding them (Balcaen & Ooghe, 2006; Beaver et al., 2010, 2012, 2019; Keasey & Watson, 1991; Platt & Platt, 2002; Sharma & Mahajan, 1980; Zavgren, 1983; Zmijewski, 1984).

Assessing the State of Health of the Company

The verification of the state of health of the company takes place using analysis tools that mainly concern three interlinked, albeit independent, management dimensions:

1. Asset composition
2. Financial correlation
3. Economic performance.

The three dimensions are summarized within the year-end financial statements or administrative reports as the main output of the accounting system. The financial statements represent companies not only a legal obligation to protect their stakeholders but also an essential tool for controlling company management along the three dimensions. The financial statement, or administrative report, represents the company's health at the end of each financial year. Therefore, the financial statement or administrative report is the document that interrupts management activity at the end of each financial year to allow its verification and assessment: in other words, it summarizes the company's state of health (Awdeh & El-Moussawi, 2022).

The annual administrative report contains two interrelated statements: the balance sheet and the income statement, or the profit and loss statement.

Therefore, both form an instrument that periodically converts company dynamics into figures and, in turn, economic trends, combining and summarizing the company's management's past, present, and future. The evidence highlighted by financial statements is related to the management acts during the reference period (as recorded in the accounts), the assessments made, and the assumptions used by those in charge of the statements. Financial statements are not intended to determine the exact results as economic performance attributable to the management; instead, they provide the entrepreneur and management with a tool that enables a more in-depth analysis of the company's equilibrium conditions.

Financial statements cannot determine objective results. The statements and results they contain are subjective and linked to the assumptions underlying the evaluation processes used by their drafters.

The Asset Composition

The first document worthy of attention is the balance sheet. The company's composition is represented in two sections: assets on the left and liabilities on the right. The balance sheet has opposing sections, and the statutory scheme following Italian civil law must be represented and classified as shown in Fig. 4.1.

The balance sheet unites the most recent financial years in line with the unitary and systematic nature of the management, allowing the forward transfer over time of balance sheet items that comprise the company's capital. The assets that existed at the end of the previous year, i.e., at the time of the previous financial statements' preparation, are carried forward at the beginning of the following year thanks to the liaison role exercised by the balance sheet.

The balance sheet to assess the company's state of health must be reclassified from the mandatory civil statutory scheme to one more

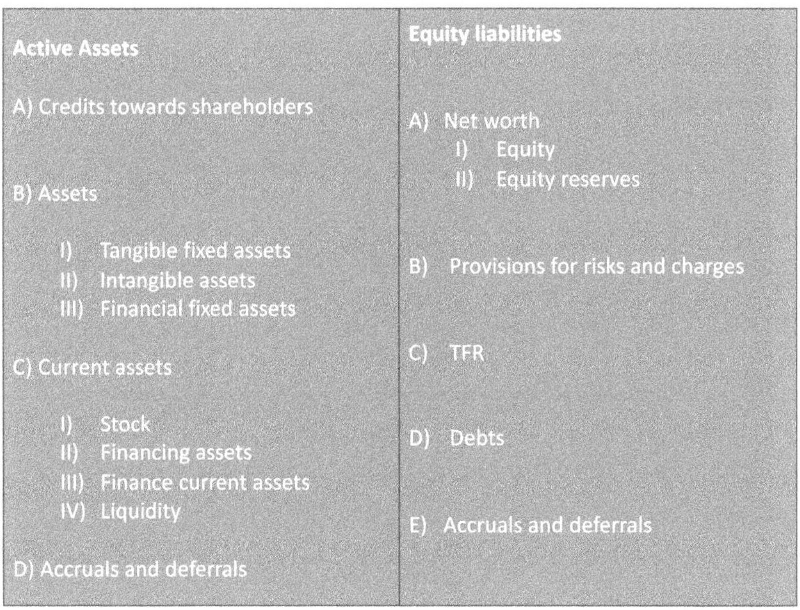

Fig. 4.1 The balance sheet regulated by Italian civil law

suited to analysis and interpretation needs. Although the reclassification processes need not be considered in depth here, it is important to underline how it facilitates reading of the balance sheet, as illustrated in Fig. 4.2.

The reclassified scheme of the balance sheet is more suitable for analyzing the company's state of health. The first section (left section) of the balance sheet distinguishes between fixed assets (FA) and current assets (CA) based on how long the asset remains within the business. Fixed assets include, for example, productive factors with long expected usefulness (long economic life). In contrast, examples of current assets include productive factors of shortly expected usefulness (short economic life) in the warehouse, unsold finished products, trade credit expiring in the following year, and existing liquid assets in cash and bank or postal deposits.

However, in the reclassified balance sheet, operations that the company intends to carry out in the following year must also be considered when drawing this distinction. For example, if the company has a machine that it has decided to dispose of in the next financial year, it must be recorded as a current rather than a fixed asset.

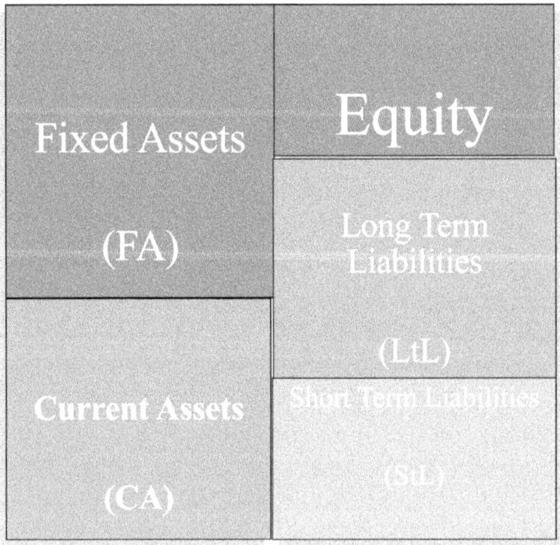

Fig. 4.2 The reclassified balance sheet

The second section of the balance sheet (right section) distinguishes between equity, long-term liabilities (LtL), and short-term liabilities (StL).

Equity is represented by the items that make up the shareholders' equity—except for item IX, which represents the profit (loss) for the year. Where the company makes an annual profit, it may be transferred to the shareholders through a dividend payment; alternatively, it may be allocated to the reserve according to a self-financing policy. Item IX, therefore, assumes a temporary nature, reporting the profit or loss for the year pending the company's decision on its destination. In the event of a transfer, the profit exits the business; in the event of reserve allocation, the profit is capitalized and included in the reserves. Hence, in the financial statements, assets do not include the profit for the year because the destination is unknown. The profit will be treated accordingly if the destination is determined in the reclassification process.

Long-term liabilities (LtL) are represented by the debts a company owes to third-party creditors that are payable more than 12 months in the future. This distinguishes them from current or short-term liabilities (StL), debts a company must pay within 12 months. The balance sheet reports both long-term liabilities and short-term liabilities. LtL and StL considered together, represent everything a company owes. Payment of these debts is always mandatory.

How to Read the Balance Sheet to Assess the State of Health of the Company

The reclassified scheme of the balance sheet is the first step in assessing the state of health of the company, investigating both the asset composition and the financial correlation.

The asset composition of the company is assessed by vertically reading the balance sheet and the financial correlation by horizontally reading the balance sheet.

Vertical reading of the balance sheet occurs using specific composition indicators, and the assets and liabilities are considered separately. Figures 4.3 and 4.4 provide some examples of the component indicators.

Adding equity to long-term liabilities expresses the permanent (long-term) capital, i.e., the means of financing that remain in the company beyond the following year. Adding long-term liabilities to short-term liabilities expresses third-party capital, i.e., financial resources from third

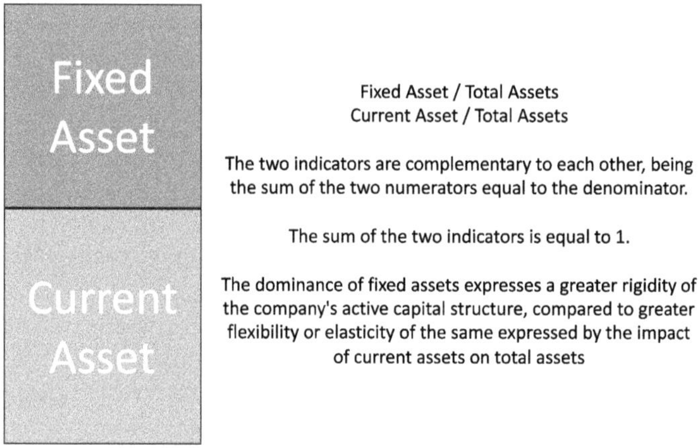

Fig. 4.3 Vertical reading of positive assets composition in the balance sheet—left side

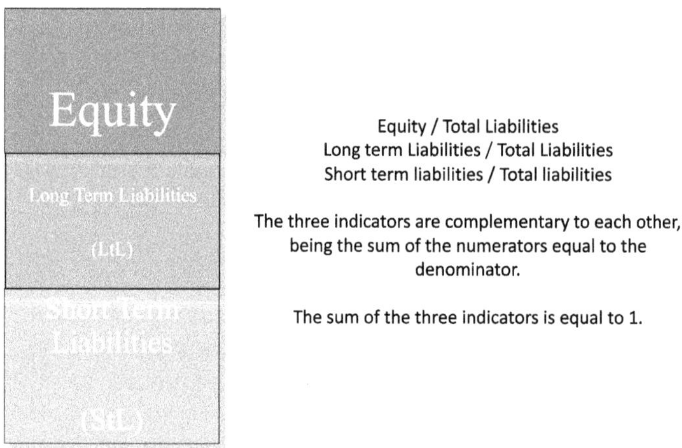

Fig. 4.4 Vertical reading of the liabilities and equity assets in the balance sheet—right side

parties concerning the company's corporate structure or borrowed financial resources. The composition of the financial structure of the company—the right section of the balance sheet—is very important for assessing the company's state of health.

In this direction, the following indicators are handy:

$$(\text{Equity} + \text{LtL.}) / \text{Tot. Liability}$$

$$\text{StL} / \text{Tot. Liability}$$

The first indicator expresses the presence and impact of permanent capital on the total sources of financing. In contrast, the second indicator expresses the impact of short-term liabilities on the total sources of financing.

Particular attention is given to analyzing the company's level of indebtedness, expressed through the indebtedness (or "leverage") index:

$$(\text{LtL} + \text{StL}) / \text{Equity}$$

This indicator measures the direct relationship between own resources and third-party sources or debt. If equity equals the sum of liabilities, the indicator has a value equal to one; if equity is more significant, the indicator assumes a lower value between one and zero (non-inclusive); if liabilities are more remarkable, the indicator assumes a value greater than one. This can be represented as follows:

if Equity = LtL + StL

$$\frac{(\text{LtL} + \text{StL})}{\text{Equity}} = 1$$

if Equity > (LtL + StL)

$$0 < \frac{(\text{LtL} + \text{StL})}{\text{Equity}} < 1$$

if Equity < (LtL + StL)

$$\frac{(\text{LtL} + \text{StL})}{\text{Equity}} > 1$$

It is evident that, from a theoretical point of view, the optimal situation consists of having a financial structure entirely financed by equity.

However, this is not possible, so it is crucial to determine the relationship between equity and debt—that is, third-party capital.

It is not easy to establish the best relationship because this relationship should also consider other variables. However, a value of 2 is generally the optimal value for this ratio.

Suppose the ratio between third-party capital and equity is 2. In that case, this means that equity accounts for one-third, and third-party capital accounts for two-thirds, of the total sources of financing (right section of the balance sheet). In practice, a value of 2 for this ratio is considered sustainable for the company without prejudicing the company's state of health.

The Asset Correlation

The financial correlation is represented by reading the balance sheet horizontally, using specific correlation indicators that summarize and highlight the links and relationships between sources of finance and investments. The following equality expresses the first relationship:

$$(\text{Total Assets}) = \left(\text{Total Liabilities} + \text{Equity}\right)$$

The distribution of financing sources concerning investments must also be verified as appropriate; this distribution is expressed through the analysis of correlations.

The analysis of the correlation between investments and sources of financing must involve verification of the correct financial coverage of the investments themselves. Correct coverage is achieved when the duration of the investment—the pay-back period—is consistent with the duration of the source of financing, i.e., with the maturity/extinction of the source of financing.

The purchase of production factors with a rapid use cycle can occur with short-term liabilities. In contrast, purchasing production factors with a slow use cycle must be covered by permanent (long-term) capital, i.e., equity or long-term liabilities. The financial correlation aims to verify the proper coverage of loans or sources.

To measure the correct correlation of the financial dimension, various margin indicators compare the values of the active assets with those of the passive assets. The correlation indices can be margin indices or quotient indices: margin indices are the absolute difference between the single classes of asset and liability items. Quotient indices are calculated as the ratio between the single classes of asset and liability items. From the point of view of significance, there is no significant difference between calculating an indicator as a margin or a quotient, except for the reading of the value deriving from the indicator itself. In the case of the margin index, the values range from – infinity to + infinity; in the case of the quotient index, the values range from zero to + infinity. When the margin index assumes a value equal to zero, the quotient index assumes a value equal to 1.

Correlation indicators are divided into four families:

- Primary Structure—Indicates the "degree of coverage" of long-term investments through equity (ideal situation):

  a. The margin of primary structure

$$\text{Equity} - \text{Fixed Assets}$$

  b. Primary structure quotient

$$\text{Equity} / \text{Fixed Assets}$$

- Secondary Structure—Indicates the "degree of coverage" of long-term investments through long-term liabilities ("physiological situation"):

  a. The margin of secondary structure

$$(\text{Equity} + \text{Long-term Liabilities}) - \text{Fixed Assets}$$

  b. Secondary structure ratio

$$(\text{Equity} + \text{Long-term Liabilities})/\text{Fixed Assets}$$

- Current assets—Indicates the "degree of coverage" of short-term liabilities by current assets:

  a. Working capital

$$\text{Current Assets} - \text{Short-term Liabilities}$$

b. Availability quotient

$$\text{Current Assets} \,/\, \text{Short-term Liabilities}$$

- Secondary treasury—Indicates short-term liabilities' "degree of coverage" using immediate and deferred liquidity.

  a. Secondary cash margin

$$(\text{Immediate Liquidity} + \text{Available Liquidity}) - \text{Short-term Liabilities}$$

  b. Secondary cash ratio

$$(\text{Immediate Liquidity} + \text{Available Liquidity}) / \text{Short-term Liabilities}$$

Among the indices summarized above, working capital is the main one in terms of reporting value. Working capital is an indicator with a very high reporting value that verifies and measures the consistency between uses and sources. In detail:

$$\text{Working Capital} = \text{Current Assets} - \text{Short-term Liabilities}$$

Working capital needs to have a positive value. Suppose working capital has a value greater than zero. In that case, this shows that the fixed capital or fixed investments have been financed with permanent (long-term) capital or from equity and long-term liabilities. If working capital is positive, a part of the permanent (long-term) capital also covers current uses. This does not lead to an imbalance, having financed short-term investments with medium/long-term funding sources.

If working capital has a value equal to zero, the permanent (long-term) capital, i.e., equity and long-term liabilities, fully covers the fixed assets. From this, the current assets were financed entirely with short-term liabilities.

If working capital assumes a negative value lower than zero, the permanent capital, i.e., equity and long-term liabilities, is insufficient to finance the fixed assets. From this, it follows that a part of the fixed assets was financed with short-term liabilities, causing the company to suffer a severe imbalance, having financed long-cycle recovery loans with short-term financing sources. In this case, the company has financed a long-term asset with a short-term financial resource: the financial imbalance originates from the fact that the repayment of the loan must take place in advance of the recovery of the investment itself. This is the basis of a structural financial imbalance and is not attributable to mere financial equilibrium.

In calculating working capital, all the following items that make up current assets are considered:

- Warehouse
- Financial activities
- Credits
- Cash and cash equivalents.

Two items that make up current assets may be susceptible to incongruity: the inventory concerning closing inventories and receivables. For the warehouse, it is noted that sometimes companies can have an accounting warehouse that differs from the authentic warehouse. For operating receivables, it is noted that companies can sometimes maintain uncollectable amounts of receivables in their financial statements, which should have been written down, leading to a loss.

For these reasons, it is advisable to calculate working capital by carrying out a prior detailed analysis of the composition of the items contained in current assets. Alternatively, the calculation of working capital can be assumed on two levels:

- Level I Working Capital

$$\text{Current Assets} - \text{Short-term Liabilities}$$

- Level II Working Capital

$$(\text{Current Assets} - \text{Warehouse}) - \text{Short-term Liabilities}$$

A positive level II working capital demonstrates the absolute solidity of the structure of the company's finance.

The State of Health of Two Companies: GAMMA and DELTA

To better understand the importance of analyzing both the asset composition and the financial correlation, consider two companies with two different financial structures, as shown in Fig. 4.5. In Fig. 4.5, the two companies are represented by their reclassified balance sheet.

Figure 4.5 illustrates the state of health of the two companies GAMMA and DELTA. Given the information in Fig. 4.5, which company has a more solid financial situation?

Regarding asset composition, vertical balance sheet analysis does not indicate issues for both companies. In the first section (left side), the asset composition is quite the same for the two companies. In the second section (right side), it is possible to highlight a different balance between

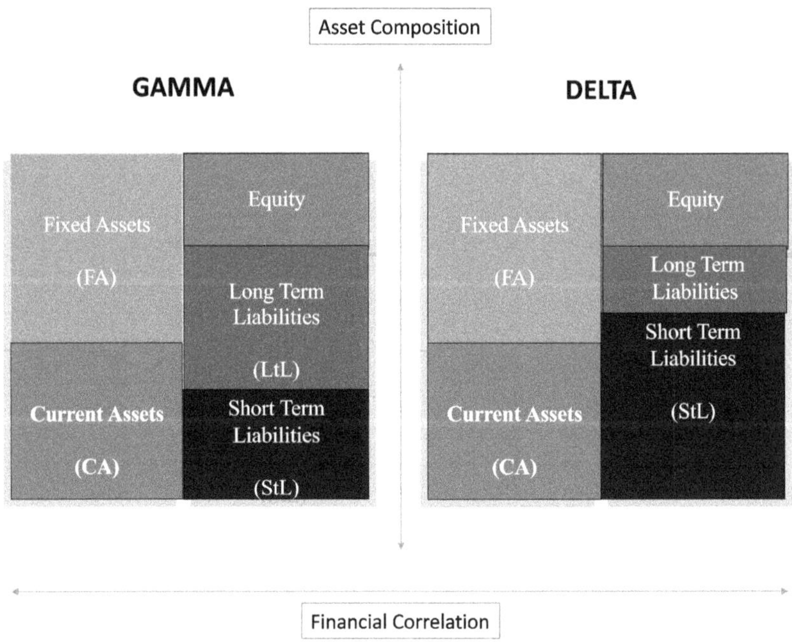

Fig. 4.5 Asset composition and financial correlation of two companies

Long-term Liabilities (LtL) and Short-term Liabilities (StL): no criticality is to be highlighted for higher or lower vulnerability.

What is more significant for the analyzed companies' health is the financial correlation between funding sources (right side) and uses (left side) represented in the balance sheet. In this direction, it is necessary to consider.

- the reported sources and uses
- the composition of sources
- the composition of uses.

The GAMMA company's reclassified balance sheet conveys an excellent financial structure and a strong correlation between the sources of financing and investments. Fixed assets are less than the sum of own resources (equity) and long-term liabilities, which means that fixed assets are covered by permanent (long-term) capital. This is consistent because fixed assets are those whose usefulness is recovered by the company in the medium to long term and certainly beyond the following year. Permanent capital comprises financial resources that will be repaid in the medium and long term, i.e., beyond the following year. Hence, the GAMMA company exhibits a good correlation between medium and long-term loans and medium-long-term sources of financing.

The GAMMA company's short-term liabilities are lower than its current assets. This means that the current assets are hedged by short-term liability sources (i.e., those expiring within the next financial year) and permanent (long-term) capital. Covering part of the current assets with permanent (long-term) capital is not problematic for the state of health. This does not alter the correct correlation of sources of use because, within the current assets, a warehouse sometimes has a minor rotation concerning the following year. Its capital (equity) is in the permanent (long-term) capital. So, it is possible to suppose that the long-term capital contributes to covering the warehouse as a part of the current asset.

The DELTA company's reclassified balance sheet conveys a poor financial structure and weak correlation between the sources of financing and investments. Fixed assets are higher than the sum of own assets and long-term liabilities, which means that fixed assets are not covered by permanent capital. With permanent capital insufficient to guarantee the coverage of fixed assets, the remaining portion of the latter is covered by short-term liabilities.

Covering part of the fixed assets with short-term liabilities represents a severe alteration of the correlation between sources and uses because the time limits for extinguishing liabilities are shorter than the recovery time of investments. This is a risk in terms of vulnerability for the company's state of health.

Therefore, the company will be unable to repay its loans and third-party capital soon, not having recovered its investments or uses. The difference between the time limits for extinguishing short-term liabilities and the recovery time for fixed assets is a fundamental prerequisite for the company's financial imbalance.

In line with what has been outlined above regarding the DELTA company, Fig. 4.5 shows that current assets are lower than short-term liabilities and, therefore, are entirely covered by short-term funding sources. This does not constitute an alteration of the correlation sources of assets; instead, this alteration involves covering part of the fixed assets with part of the short-term liabilities.

Analysis of the company's state of health through analysis of the structure of its balance sheets reveals a solid financial imbalance in the DELTA company, deriving from an unsustainable debt structure. It means that the DELTA company lacks a vigorous state of health, and its vulnerability is higher than that of company GAMMA.

The financial imbalance may assume a great relief and significant gravity. In the DELTA company's higher vulnerability, it is reasonable to expect a significant incidence of financial charges related to the high short-term indebtedness. The DELTA company is likely to work with many poorly rated credit institutions and will be forced to chase through its financial cycle all the deadlines ending in the short term. This is another reason for the higher vulnerability of DELTA company.

In this situation, the financial cycle takes over the economic cycle and consumes all the wealth the latter produces. The DELTA company sells to cash in and meet deadlines: if an expected outcome does not materialize, the company risks insolvency. In short, the DELTA company is more exposed to risk having a higher vulnerability than company GAMMA.

Is It Possible to Reduce the Vulnerability of Company DELTA, and If So, How?

In the face of the critical issues that emerge from the analysis of the state of health of the company DELTA, is it possible to reduce the level of vulnerability of the company?

In this case, the correct answer to the question above is not that "it depends," but that "yes, it is possible." It is essential to determine *how* it is possible to reduce vulnerability. On the one hand, it is indeed possible; on the other hand, simply recognizing this is certainly not the achievement of the result.

The DELTA company's situation can be improved through two closely related actions. The first consists of shareholder capitalization, whereby members contribute new own resources. Own assets can be created through (i) increasing the share or stock capital, (ii) the entry of new shareholders, or (iii) establishing or strengthening reserves.

In practice, in challenging situations such as that of the DELTA company, it is difficult for shareholders to capitalize on the company by adding their own money. New potential members are unlikely to be willing to join the company. This means that although it is not impossible, it is difficult because the level of vulnerability is very high, and the consequent risk of default is not negligible.

The second action consists of restructuring debt by increasing long-term and reducing short-term liabilities. The restructuring of debt transforms short-term liabilities into long-term liabilities. Debt restructuring requires the availability of financial institutions. In a situation such as that represented by the DELTA company, it seems unlikely that a new bank would be willing to take on the risk of providing medium- or long-term loans. A more feasible alternative is for a credit institution to which the company is already indebted to convert its debt from short-term to long-term liability. As a rule, the credit institution that is most exposed and has the least security may be the most willing to help the DELTA company because it will otherwise suffer significantly if it becomes insolvent.

Referring to Fig. 4.5, a company's financial correlation can be assessed and analyzed by calculating the simple net working capital (Working Capital) indicator. Net working capital is the difference between current assets, CA (left side), and short-term (or current) liabilities, StL (right side):

$$\text{Working Capital} = \text{CA} - \text{StL}$$

From which it is derived that:

$$\text{Working Capital} = 0 \text{ if CA} = \text{StL}$$

$$\text{Working Capital} > 0 \text{ if CA} > \text{StL}$$

$$\text{Working Capital} < 0 \text{ if CA} < \text{StL}$$

A company's net working capital should be higher than or equal to zero: short-term liabilities StL are equal to or less than current assets CA, and current assets CA are partly financed with permanent capital. This is the case in the GAMMA company (Fig. 4.6).

Suppose the net working capital is negative, as in the DELTA company (Fig. 4.7). In that case, short-term liabilities cover current assets and part of the fixed assets, thereby seriously damaging the correlation between sources and uses.

A final observation concerns the calculation of net working capital. Traditionally, this includes stock as part of the current assets. Sometimes,

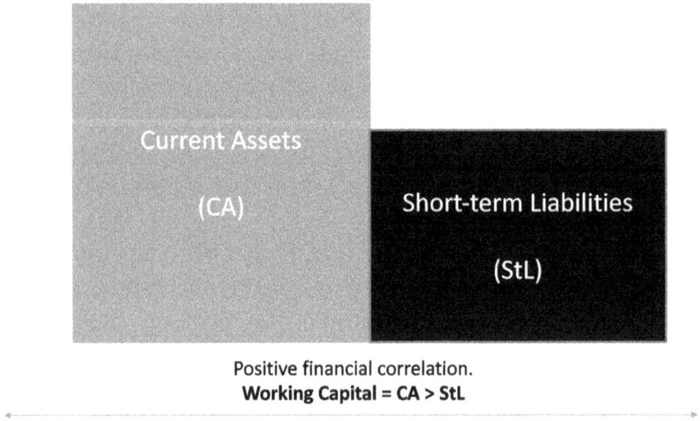

Fig. 4.6 Positive financial correlation

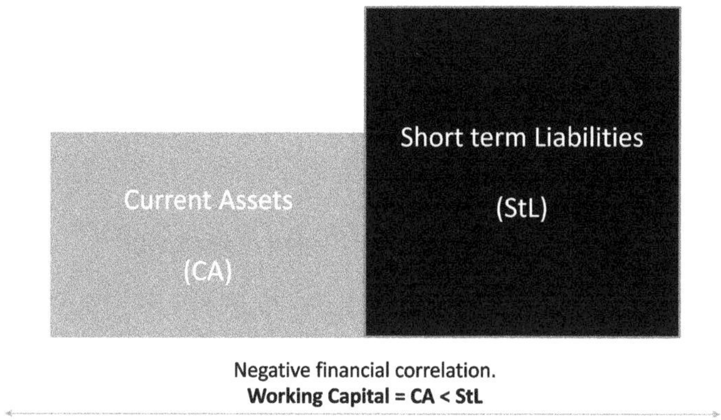

Fig. 4.7 Negative financial correlation

the accounting value of the stock does not correspond to its actual value. For this reason, it may be helpful to calculate the net working capital without including stock as part of current assets, CA. This exclusion allows for a more prudent analysis of the correlation between sources and uses through the second-level net working capital:

$$\text{Working Capital} = \text{CA} - \text{StL}$$

From which:

$$\text{Working Capital} = (\text{Warehouse} + \text{Credits} + \text{Financial assets} + \text{Liquidities}) - \text{StL}$$

From this, the following is derived:

$$\text{Working Capital II level} = (\text{CA} - \text{Inventory}) - \text{StL}$$

Excluding stock from the calculation of net working capital also responds to the need to neutralize the effect of the presence of the stock on the analysis, both because its accounting value may not correspond to its actual value and because the company must always have stock available to deal with unforeseen requests or to avoid production bottlenecks.

If the company's second-level working capital is higher than or equal to zero, its financial situation can be highly positive. If the working capital is higher than or equal to zero, but the second level of working capital is negative, the company's financial correlation is still positive; however, in this scenario, the analysis requires greater caution and attention.

The Economic Performance

The third dimension to assess the state of health of the company is related to its economic performance. This dimension is expressed in the profit and loss statement (P&L), which represents and summarizes the economic dynamics of company management through the contraposition of positive and negative economic components—revenues as positive economic components and costs as negative economic components.

The profit and loss statement (P&L), income statement, or statement of operations is a financial report that summarizes a company's revenues, expenses, and profits/losses over a given period. The P&L statement shows a company's ability to generate sales, manage expenses, and create profits. It is prepared based on accounting principles that include revenue recognition, matching, and accruals, which makes it different from the cash flow statement.

Although the complexities of the P&L statement need not be considered in depth here, it is important to underline how the scheme adopted by the Italian Civil Code has a scalar structure and follows the configuration of the production value by contrasting it with production costs, as represented in Fig. 4.8.

The scalar scheme of the profit and loss statement allows dynamic analysis of the economic net result's formation process. This is important to assess the state of health of the company.

The economic performance assessment is based on several key indicators used to measure economic value creation at different management levels.

The first indicator expresses the difference between the production value and production cost. This indicator is referred to as earnings before interest and tax (EBIT); it conveys the economic result that the company achieves due to its operational management area.

The significance of EBIT lies in allowing the formulation of judgments on the company's ability through its operational management area (i.e., through its core business) to create economic value.

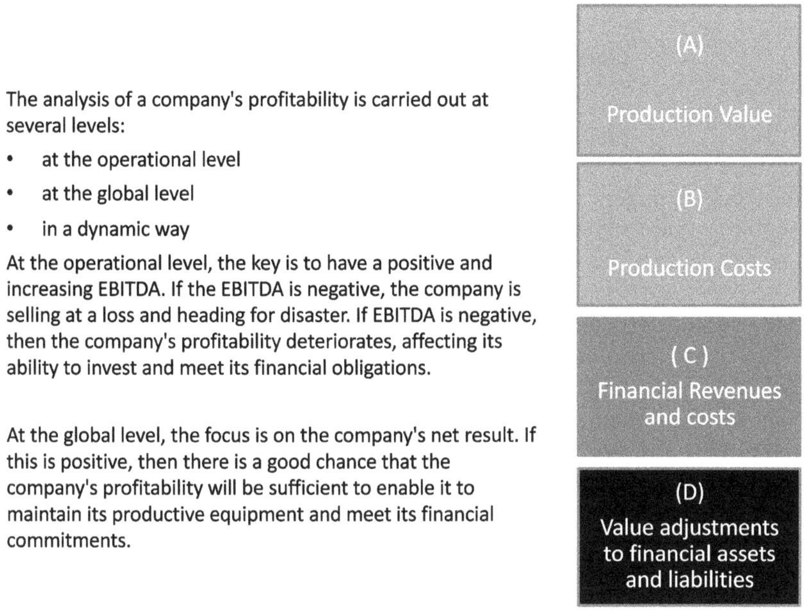

Fig. 4.8 The profit and loss statement regulated by the Italian civil law

If EBIT is positive, then the company's primary operations can create economic value; if negative, then the company cannot carry out its productive activities in conditions of economic efficiency, perhaps because it lacks technical efficiency, for example. In the statutory scheme, the company's pre-tax economic result for the year is calculated as the difference between EBIT and the results of the financial management area. The latter is determined by juxtaposing revenues from financial investments, financial costs, and value adjustments with financial assets. In short, the process of determining the economic result can be represented as follows:

(A − B) EBIT

−

Result of the financial management area

=

Profit before tax

$$-$$

Corporation Tax

$$=$$

Net Income

The P&L statement required by the Italian Civil Code is a good starting point for understanding a company's economic dynamics. Sometimes, however, it may be helpful to reclassify the P&L statement to allow a more profound analysis of these dynamics and, more precisely, diagnose the formation processes of economic value.

From the business economics perspective, the configuration of the P&L statement and the production value are flanked by the configurations of sales value and added value. Without wishing to elaborate on reclassifying the P&L statement, exploring the analysis of what happens within the operational management area (through different classifications of costs is especially important). On the one hand, about value production, the statutory P&L statement enables the operational management area to be isolated from the financial management area; on the other hand, it does not allow the dynamics of the economic value creation to be shown in greater depth within the operational management area.

In this direction, it may be helpful to distinguish between variable costs and fixed costs within production costs. A variable cost is a corporate expense that changes in proportion to how much a company produces or sells. Variable costs increase or decrease depending on a company's production or sales volume. Fixed costs are expenses that remain the same regardless of production level. Whether a firm makes sales or not, it must pay its fixed costs because they are independent of the production level. There is also a category of costs that falls between fixed and variable costs, known as semi-variable costs (or semi-fixed or mixed costs). These costs are composed of a mixture of both fixed and variable components.

The difference between sales revenues and variable costs provides an extremely useful indicator to support decision-making processes within the company and better understand economic value creation dynamics. This indicator is called contribution margin (CM) and is calculated as follows:

$$\text{CM} = \text{Sales Revenues} - \text{Variable Costs}$$

The contribution margin is the number of proceeds a company collects after using sales proceeds to cover variable costs. Every dollar of CM goes directly into paying for fixed costs; once all fixed costs have been paid for, every euro of contribution margin contributes to profitability. For this reason, variable costs are required for companies trying to determine their break-even point. In addition, the identification of variable costs is necessary to determine sale targets for a specific profit target.

The contribution margin expresses the extent to which sales revenues cover fixed costs. The difference between sales revenues and variable costs measures how revenues contribute to covering fixed costs after covering variable costs.

If the CM is equal to or less than zero, the sales revenues cannot contribute to the fixed cost coverage. Conversely, sales revenues cover variable and fixed costs if the CM exceeds zero. This does not mean the company will have a positive net income or operating margin: the latter depends on fixed costs and the CM. The higher the CM, the greater the contribution to covering fixed costs. If fixed costs are lower than the CM, the company will have a final positive net income and a positive operating income. The usefulness of the contribution margin is understood both upwards and downwards—upwards or toward variable costs and sales revenues; downwards or toward fixed costs:

Sales revenues

–

Variable Costs

=

Contribution margin

–

Fixed costs

=

EBIT

The relationship between the CM, variable costs, and sales revenues is useful for increasing the percentage of contributions and company profitability. Because the CM is the difference between the sales revenues and variable costs, the two levers to increase the company's ability to cover fixed costs and create wealth are the variable revenues and costs:

$$\text{CM} = \text{Sales Revenues} - \text{Variable Costs}$$

From which:

$$\text{CM} = \Sigma \text{pi} \times \text{qi} - \text{Variable Costs}$$

Sales revenues are the sum of the quantities sold for sales prices. If the company wants to increase the CM, it can increase the quantities sold, increase sale prices, reduce variable costs, or pursue all three options in combination. Increasing the CM leads to an increase in company profitability.

Other valuable indicators include added value (AV) and earnings before interest, taxes, depreciation, and amortization (EBITDA) to deepen economic value creation and company profitability. Added value is the difference between sales revenues and the costs of purchasing productive factors from outside the company; EBITDA is the difference between sales revenues and the costs of productive factors with a fast use cycle:

$$\text{AV} = \text{Sales Revenue} - \text{Costs of inputs purchased from outside}$$

$$\text{EBITDA} = \text{Sales Revenue} - \text{Costs of productive factors with a fast use cycle}$$

By integrating these indicators in the P&L statement, a reclassification scheme can be introduced that aims to deepen understanding of the processes of economic value creation and diagnose the company's status in terms of its economic and income dynamics. Changes in the inventories of finished products are not considered below for simplicity:

Sales revenues

–

Variable Costs

=

Contribution margin

–

Fixed costs for factors purchased outside

=

Added Value

−

Fixed costs due to factors within the company

=

EBITDA

−

Depreciation and amortization

=

EBIT

Personnel costs can be considered among the fixed costs for factors within the company, though there is no unitary doctrine on treating these costs. It is debatable whether personnel costs can be considered variable or fixed costs. Finally, depreciation and amortization are deducted from EBITDA to determine EBIT.

References

Amaduzzi, A. (1948). *Ragioneria Generale*. Casa Editrice Dott. Luigi Macrì.

Awdeh, A., & El-Moussawi, C. (2022). Capital requirements, institutional quality and credit crunch in the MENA region. *International Journal of Emerging Markets, 17*(8), 1909–1925.

Balcaen, S., & Ooghe, H. (2006). 35 years of studies on business failure: An overview of the classic statistical methodologies and their related problems. *The British Accounting Review, 38*(1), 63–93.

Beaver, W. H., Correia, M., & McNichols, M. F. (2010). Financial statement analysis and the prediction of financial distress. *Foundations and Trends in Accounting, 5*(2), 99–173. https://doi.org/10.1561/1400000018

Beaver, W. H., Correia, M., & McNichols, M. F. (2012). Do differences in financial reporting attributes impair the predictive ability of financial ratios for bankruptcy? *Review of Accounting Studies, 17*, 969–1010. https://doi.org/10.1007/s11142-012-9186-7

Beaver, W. H., Cascino, S., Correia, M., & McNichols, M. F. (2019). Group affiliation and default prediction. *Management Science, 65*(8), 3559–3584. https://doi.org/10.1287/mnsc.2018.3128

Briguglio, L., Cordina, G., Farrugia, N., & Vella, S. (2008). *Economic vulnerability and resilience concepts and measurements*. WIDER Research Paper, No. 2008/55, ISBN 978-92-9230-103-3, The United Nations University World Institute for Development Economics Research (UNU-WIDER), Helsinki.

Giannessi, E. (1970). *Appunti di economia aziendale*. G. Pellegrini.
Keasey, K., & Watson, R. (1991). Financial distress models: A review of their usefulness. *British Journal of Management, 2*(2), 89–102.
Lee, C. K., Wiklund, J., Amezcua, A., Bae, T. J., & Palubinskas, A. (2022). Business failure and institutions in entrepreneurship: A systematic review and research agenda. *Small Business Economics, 58*(4), 1997–2023.
Platt, H. D., & Platt, M. B. (2002). Predicting corporate financial distress: Reflections on choice-based sample bias. *Journal of Economics and Finance, 26*(2), 184–199.
Price, S., Wilkinson, T., & Coles, T. (2022). Crisis? How small tourism businesses talk about COVID-19 and business change in the UK. *Current Issues in Tourism, 25*(7), 1088–1105.
Sharma, S., & Mahajan, V. (1980). Early warning indicators of business failure. *Journal of Marketing, 4*(4), 80–89.
Zavgren, C. (1983). The prediction of corporate failure: The state of the art. *Journal of Accounting Literature, 2*, 1–37.
Zmijewski, M. E. (1984). Methodological issues related to the estimation of financial distress prediction models. *Journal of Accounting Research, 22*(Suppl.), 59–86.

PART II

Corporate Immune System

CHAPTER 5

The Immune System

This chapter defines the company's immune system and describes its composition and the dynamics that allow it to be strengthened over time.

The immune system consists of the defenses with which the company mitigates the effects of hostile and/or harmful events. The immune system does not exclude the possibility of the event but mitigates its impact on the company's economic, equity, and financial situation.

For these reasons, the immune system is essential in reducing corporate vulnerability and supporting the company's survival in full compliance with the going concern principle.

The immune system is a dynamic system that varies over time, strengthening or weakening. Noteworthy are the company policies that, over the years, can favor the strengthening or weakening of the immune defenses. This chapter describes the dynamics that favor strengthening the corporate immune system.

Going Concern Principle

The company, as a productive combination of different assets endowed with its own life and destined to last over time (Amaduzzi, 1948; Giannessi, 1970), in line with the principles of Italian economic-business science and with international accounting principles, has been endowed

A. Capocchi, *Vulnerability and the Corporate Immune System*, https://doi.org/10.1007/978-3-031-30254-1_5

since its inception—establishment—with its immune system. The company's immunity can be traced back to its ability to deal with critical situations and unforeseen events without losing the conditions that allow it to survive, even if it suffers economic damage. The company's survival as a productive combination, on the one hand, and as an economic actor, on the other hand, has been recognized and embodied in the going concern principle for many years (Humphreys & Trotman, 2022).

> *Accountants are generally agreed that the assumption of the going concern is an essential accounting convention or "principle."* (Storey, 1959)

The company is an economic actor that must, at any moment, protect its survival through the principle of continuity or going concerned. This protection can only be achieved by pursuing certain management conditions through which the company guarantees itself the ability to deal with critical issues and turbulence. The going concern concept is a fundamental principle of accounting. It assumes that a company can continue its trade during and beyond the following administrative period, meeting its financial obligations. It is an assumption that the company can run its business and that the value of its assets will endure. This principle is also known as the continuing concern concept.

The going concern principle is the assumption that an entity will remain in business for the foreseeable future—this means the entity will *not* be forced to halt operations and liquidate its assets in the near term at what may be meager fire-sale prices. The essential point is that an entity is assumed to be a going concern without significant information to the contrary (Madonna & Cestari, 2015; Marasca et al., 2020; Menon & Williams, 2010).

The concept of going concern was introduced by Lawrence R. Dicksee in his book on Auditing, published in London in 1892. It was a strongly contextualized concept at the time of writing:

> *It being the primary object of most ordinary undertakings to continue to carry on operations, it is fair that the assets enumerated in a Balance Sheet be valued with that end in view.* (Dicksee, 1902: 179)

Numerous definitions have been proposed in the literature over the years, with meanings that only sometimes coincide, according to the different applications and areas of reference. Following the analysis by Lombardi (2021), Yeh et al. (2014) define the going concern principle as follows:

> *one of the most important accounting assumptions in the preparation of financial statements. According to this principle, an entity or organization will continue its operations into the foreseeable future, at least, or in perpetuity.* (Yeh et al., 2014: 98)

Although there is a tendency to consider the going concern synonymous with business continuity, as Lombardi observes, the two meanings do not always coincide. Specifically, Lombardi observes that:

> *The business continuity is not strictly connected to the accounting perspective: it is recognized in the operativity and strategy of the corporate systems, especially in providing goods and services to the markets. It reflects strategic decision-making having effects on the future of companies.* (Lombardi, 2021: 11)

The principle of going concern, on the other hand, Lombardi observes, is closely linked to accounting principles and related regulation (Sterling, 1968). Lombardi goes further to describe the going concern as follows:

> *In the context of managerial discipline, the going-concern is a foundation of the management operations. (…) The going-concern must be considered as a conclusive judgment based on evidence and not as an assumption. Therefore, a potential issue to investigate is if the going-concern is confirmed when the company is probably going to continue its activity indefinitely. Thus, the way to follow can change.* (Lombardi, 2021: 12–13)

The accounting standards also govern their implications on the reporting of the financial statements. For example, US GAAP states that:

> *the continuation of a reporting entity as a going concern is presumed as the basis for preparing financial statements unless and until the entity's liquidation becomes imminent. Preparation of financial statements under this presumption is commonly referred to as the going concern basis of accounting. If and when an entity's liquidation becomes imminent, financial statements should be prepared under the liquidation basis of accounting in accordance with Subtopic 205–30, Presentation of Financial Statements—Liquidation Basis of Accounting.* (FASB, 2014: 1)

On this point, Lombardi (2021) also observes the importance of the managerial perspective for the identification of the conditions and events that can endanger the survival of the company:

> *In the management perspective, a key point is related to the identification of conditions or events that raise substantial doubt about an entity's ability to continue as a going-concern. Thus, management should also consider whether its plans could mitigate those relevant conditions or events, alleviating their substantial doubts.* (Lombardi, 2021: 18)

Without going into accounting aspects, what is relevant is the link between this principle and the need for the company to build an effective immune system. On this point, we note the impact of the COVID-19 pandemic and how many governments had to intervene to suspend verification of the ability of companies to last over time through accounting documentation (Brennan et al., 2022): verification that in many cases—due to the effects of the COVID-19 pandemic on companies' balance sheets—would have given a negative result, posing significant problems for the entire system (Ho et al., 2023).

> *In this context, the Italian Legislator provides a specific exception to the verification of the assumption of the business continuity to approve the financial statements on 31 December 2019 and ensure the flow of information to the stakeholders. Article 7 of the Legislative Decree of 8 April 2020 No. 23 (so-called Liquidity Decree) establishes that to prepare the financial statements of the financial year 2019, the valuation of the items of the financial statement in the perspective of business continuity can (in any case) be carried out if it exists in the financial statements closed on a date before 23 February 2020. Such a rule allows accounting assessments to be made as if there is continuity, even when it was in doubt due to the COVID-19 pandemic. The Legislator, therefore, offered a sort of sterilization of the effects of the economic crisis, applicable in the event of the existence of business continuity before 23 February 2020.* (Lombardi, 2021: 21)

The Immune System: The Level of Capitalization

The corporate immune system is embodied mainly, but not exclusively, in the company's capitalization level. Company capitalization is measured at the balance sheet level—i.e., through balance sheet analysis—as the ratio between company financing from shareholders' means and third-party sources of finance (Upreti et al., 2022).

Own means or own capital are mainly represented by equity, and third-party means or third-party capital are represented by the liabilities the company owes to third parties, regardless of their maturity.

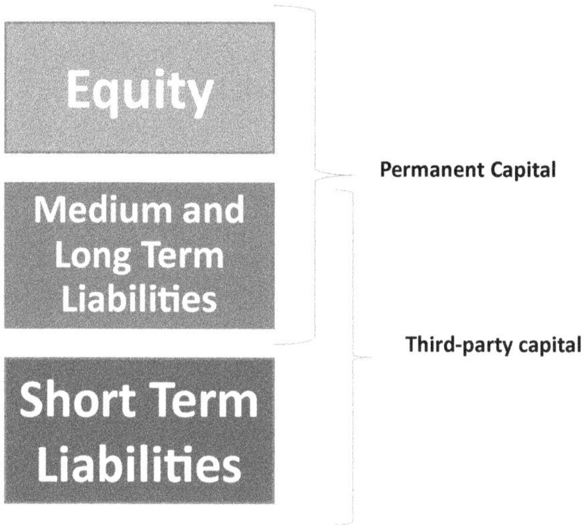

Fig. 5.1 The capital structure of funding sources

The capital structure is considered with reference only to the sources of financing, as shown in Fig. 5.1.

Figure 5.1 represents the capital structure of the sources of financing where the sum of own means or own capital and consolidated liabilities identifies the permanent capital, i.e., the capital that remains within the company for a medium to long-term period. In the case of non-equity, there is a deadline for repayment of the invested capital; in the case of consolidated liabilities, the maturity is medium or long-term.

The sum of consolidated and current liabilities represents the borrowed capital, i.e., the sources of financing that the company has acquired from third parties and must necessarily repay. Three distinctive elements characterize third-party capital:

- It has a deadline by which it must be returned
- There is an obligation to repay it. The company can only succeed in returning it if the management is performing.

- It has a cost represented by interest. It is provided in return for consideration. Also, concerning the cost, the company must bear it regardless of the management trend.

Equity capital, in contrast, is not subject to maturity, has no repayment obligations, and has no cost. It can be remunerated by payment of dividends, whose amount and distribution depend on the economic result the company achieves and on the company's policies. The remuneration of own capital occurs with the distribution of profits through dividend payments to the shareholders.

The company's capitalization level is the ratio between its own and third-party capital. The higher the company's capitalization level, the greater its immunity. The lower the company's capitalization level, the weaker its immune defenses. Weak immune defenses of the company result in greater corporate vulnerability and, consequently, greater risk for the company should hostile events occur.

The level of company capitalization is measured using an indicator called the "debt ratio":

Debt Ratio

is

Third-Parties Capital / Equity

or

(Consolidated Liabilities + Current Liabilities) / Equity

Consolidated liabilities and current liabilities constitute all company payables. Equity is represented by share capital and reserves.

The level of company capitalization and, therefore, the strength of its immune system vary over the company's life cycle based on management performance and company policies.

At the time of the company's establishment, own means are represented by the capital subscribed by shareholders or by the share capital. At the time of incorporation, a capital reserve, known as the share premium reserve, may be present if the shareholders—in addition to subscribing to the nominal value of the share capital based on their share of ownership—also pay a more significant amount as a share premium to strengthen the capital structure of the company. A share premium reserve is a form of available capital reserve. The shareholders can also request and obtain repayment of the share premium reserve during the company's life. The distribution of the share premium reserve to shareholders requires the prior condition that the value of the legal reserve has reached 20% of the share capital value.

At the time of the company's establishment, the debts or third-party capital represent all the resources that the company has acquired from third parties to finance its business start-up, given the limited funding provided by shareholders at this stage.

There is no absolute value at which the level of company capitalization can be considered adequate. The adequacy of the level of capitalization depends on many internal and external factors of the company. Among the latter is the sector to which the company belongs and the type of activity it carries out.

In general, however, it is believed that an optimal value of the debt ratio is equal to 2, i.e., that:

$$\text{(Consolidated Liabilities} + \text{Current Liabilities) / Equity} = 2$$

If the debt ratio equals two, equity capital accounts for one-third of the company's total capital structure, and third-party capital accounts for two-thirds. Scholars consider this ratio the optimal ratio to guarantee the company a sound financial structure based on a good level of capitalization, as shown in Fig. 5.2.

The relationship between equity capital and debt capital within the company is also measured using another indicator called the "Leverage Index":

$$\text{Leverage Index is } (\text{Equity} + \text{Third-party Capital}) / \text{Equity}$$

or

$$(\text{Equity} + \text{Medium- and Long-term Liabilities} + \text{Short-term Liabilities}) / \text{Equity}$$

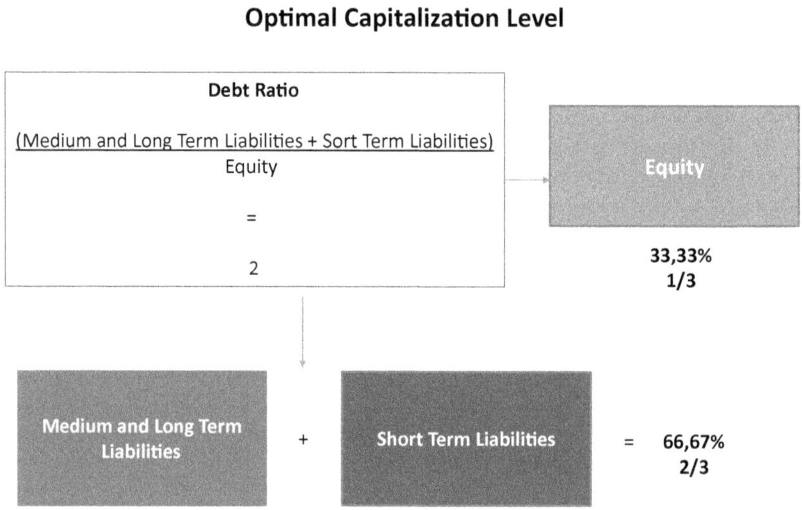

Fig. 5.2 Optimal level of capitalization

The leverage index can take on different values, which are usually interpreted as follows:

- If it is equal to 1, the company has no debts. This means that all sources of financing are equity capital. This is the perfect value. The company can finance its activities without asking for loans from third parties.
- If it is between 1 and 2, the equity capital is greater than the debt capital. This situation occurs often and means that although the company is in debt, its resources are a substantial source of its financing.
- If it is equal to 2, it means that own capital and third-party capital are equal, i.e., that the company uses equal amounts of the two sources of financing.

Index	Value			
Debt Index	0	1	2	>2
Leverage Index	1	2	3	>3
Meaning	No Debt	Equity = Third-Party Capital	Equity = 1/3 and Third-Party Capital = 2/3	More Debt than Equity

Fig. 5.3 Debt index and leverage index

- If it is greater than 2, the debt capital is greater than the equity capital, which could represent a risk factor. In this scenario, the company may be "undercapitalized."

It appears evident that for values greater than 2, a company undercapitalized has weaker immune defenses and a greater vulnerability. For values between 1 and 2, the company has an excellent immune defense system and a lower vulnerability.

Figure 5.3 represents the correlation that exists between the two indicators. When the company finances itself only by means, the debt index equals zero, and the leverage index equals 1. When the company has used equity and third-party capital equally, the debt index equals 1, and the leverage index equals 2. When the debt index equals 2, i.e., when the company has recourse to equity capital for one-third of its sources of financing and to third-party capital for two-thirds, the leverage index equals 3. When the company has used third-party capital more, the debt index is higher than 2, and the leverage index is higher than 3. Values of the leverage index and debt index greater than 2 and 3 represent a growing vulnerability for the company due to its significant reliance on borrowed resources.

The Immune System: Provisions for Risks and Charges

The corporate immune system is not only based on the level of capitalization, as described so far but is also made up of provisions for risks and charges, which represent liability items in the balance sheet and represent funds that the company can use against events of a specific nature.

Although such events will not necessarily occur with certainty, they represent a concrete risk for the company, i.e., the company's exposure to a specific and well-identified risk factor connected to a hostile event. Establishing a provision for risks and charges must be connected to an event of a specific nature because the company cannot provide such provisions for generic events and/or for events that do not represent a concrete and practical risk to it. If the company is not exposed to a risk, it cannot create a provision for risks and charges in its capital structure concerning the event linked with the risk (Chen & Lee, 2023).

Provisions for risks and charges are therefore created for events of a specific nature for which:

- It has yet to be discovered if or when the event will occur. On the contrary, it is hoped that the event will not occur.
- The quantum (i.e., the damage the event could cause to the company) is unknown.

Provisions for risks and charges are represented within the company's capital structure among the sources of financing because their creation is initiated through company self-financing policies (de Villiers et al., 2022).

Indeed, these are improper self-financing policies because the company sets aside an economic value represented by a non-monetary cost.

"Improper" does not have a negative meaning in this context. The improper term only wants to identify a method of self-financing different from self-financing based on the non-distribution of dividends and the consequent capitalization of the profits produced.

The provision for risks and charges represents a non-monetary cost and does not entail an immediate financial outflow. Therefore, the resources set aside using non-monetary costs remain absorbed and stored within the company and will be used when the event occurs for which the provision was set up and fed into over time: the use of the provision will allow the company to which the event occurs to totally or partially cover the damage suffered by the event itself.

By way of example, suppose there are two companies, company A and company B. Company A behaves similarly to a grasshopper and does not set aside anything in the provision for flood risks and charges. Company B behaves similarly to an ant and creates a flood risk fund within its capital structure to mitigate the possible damage from a hostile event—in this scenario, a flood.

Suppose that in December 2022, the two companies in the same area suffered a flood, causing the same economic damage to each company of 500,000 euros. Over the years, company B has set aside resources for risks and flood charges amounting to 350,000 euros.

At the time of the damage, company B, as shown in Fig. 5.4, does not record the amount of the damage, 500,000 euros, as a loss in its income statement but records the part of the damage that exceeds its provision for risks and charges, i.e., 150,000 euros. Company B also uses its provision for risks and charges for floods, 350,000 euros, to cover the loss incurred, up to the amount of the provision itself—in the present case, up to 350,000 euros.

At the time of the damage, company A, as shown in Fig. 5.5, records the entire amount of the damage, 500,000 euros, as a loss in its income statement because it cannot mitigate the effect of the adverse event—represented by the damage suffered—by using a provision for risks and charges.

Company A's non-recognition of the need to provide against risks and charges results in the company having greater exposure to risk and therefore having greater vulnerability to a hostile event of a specific nature when it occurs and when the damage that such an event could cause to the company is unknown.

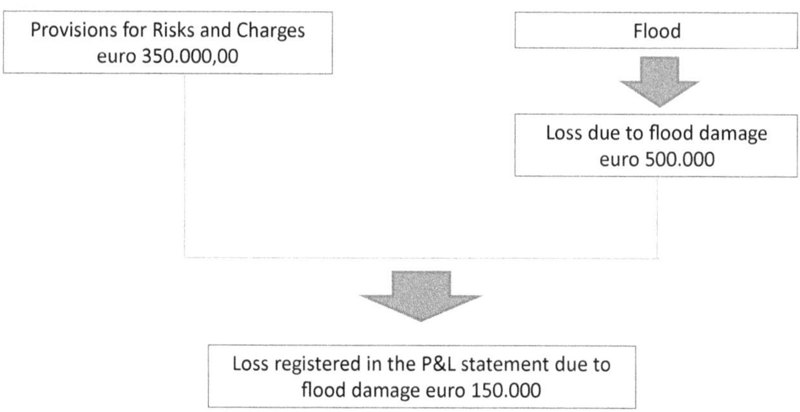

Fig. 5.4 Company B

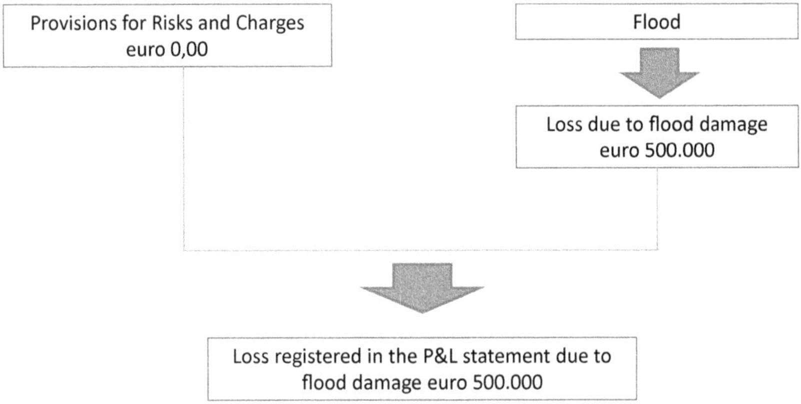

Fig. 5.5 Company A

Therefore, a company's provision for risks and charges results from responsible and farsighted behavior compared with the behavior of ants relative to grasshoppers. Company B, like the ants, regularly ringfences part of its wealth by storing it internally for when the adverse event arrives, i.e., winter. In contrast, company A, like the grasshopper, does not care about what may happen in the future and lives daily, exposing itself to the risk of loss.

The absence of the provision for risks and charges exposes the company to risk because the loss cannot be mitigated by the presence of the provision for risks and charges; it will be fully accounted for in the income statement and balance sheet and may affect all or part of the company's assets. If the loss significantly affects the company's assets, the company is exposed to the risk of non-continuity, i.e., cessation of its activity.

It is therefore evident that because company management must guarantee business continuity and business continuity is linked to the company's economic results during individual administrative periods, the behavior of company A is irresponsible, putting the company's survival at risk.

Company B's behavior is far more responsible, which creates the provision for risks and charges and creates conditions for mitigating possible and eventual damages deriving from the hostile event due to proper self-financing, protecting the survival and continuity of the company. From what has been said, the vital link between the company's immune system, corporate vulnerability, and the principle of continuity should be evident.

Strengthening of the Immune System

The immune system can be strengthened during the company's life through appropriate company policies. Three company policies enable the immune system of a company to be strengthened:

1. Capitalization of the company by increasing the amount of share capital that is paid up
2. Self-financing
    (a) Own
    (b) Improper.

As already written, the term improper does not have a negative meaning in this context. The improper term only wants to identify a method of self-financing different from self-financing based on the non-distribution of dividends and the consequent capitalization of the profits produced.

Capitalization of the company involves an increase in equity. Growth can take place through increased share capital. However, not all increases in share capital lead to a strengthening of the immune system.

Increases in share capital can be paid or free. Paid increases in share capital occur when existing or new shareholders contribute new resources. When paid share capital increases, the book values of share capital and shareholders' equity increase accordingly.

Free share capital increases occur differently, with the use of available reserves. The company uses one or more available reserves to increase its share capital: in this case, the book value of share capital increases, but the book value of shareholders' equity remains unchanged because the book value of the used reserve or reserves decreases. In cases of free increases, therefore, there is an increase in the value of share capital offset by a decrease of the same amount in the book value of the available reserve used, with a balance—in terms of change in the book value of the shareholders' equity—equal to zero.

From here, it is evident that only paid increases in share capital will increase the company's capitalization level and strengthen its immune system. Free capital increases have no benefit for the company's immune system.

Self-financing, another policy to strengthen the corporate immune system, may be proper or improper.

Self-financing benefits the company's capitalization and an immune system like paid share capital increases. Self-financing entails the allocation of profits to reserves instead of distributing the profits to shareholders: the profit produced by management is held internally within the company and recorded in reserves. The allocation to shareholders' equity causes retained earnings to increase, thus increasing the overall value of equity.

Own self-financing is a slow-growth policy for increasing the corporate capitalization level and represents responsible behavior—akin to the behavior of ants. With self-financing, the company sets aside wealth produced without distributing it to shareholders. In addition to strengthening the immune system, this wealth produced and set aside can be used for virtuous purposes, for example, to make investments, pay the company's employees, and create barriers to entry by competitors.

Improper self-financing entails setting aside wealth through non-monetary costs to retain and store wealth within the company.

As already seen, provisions for risks and charges fall into this category. To these must be added another company policy, depreciation.

Being a non-monetary cost, even depreciation is a form of improper self-financing. Indeed, there is no financial output in the case of depreciation because this had already occurred when the production factor was purchased. With depreciation, the company intends to recover the wealth used in purchasing the production factor with a long-term cycle of repeated use or a slow cycle of use to replace it when necessary. This protects the company's competitiveness, which is increasingly linked to the availability of innovative and technologically advanced production factors.

However, depreciation as an improper self-financing tool is also considered imperfect because the depreciation charge, which represents the non-monetary cost, is calculated on the historical cost of the slow-cycle production factor. Sometimes the historical cost is heavily penalized by the increasing price trend in the market. For the company, this determines—at the end of the amortization period—the recovery of the initial wealth used to purchase the slow-cycle production factor. However, said wealth is insufficient to replace the goods because prices have increased in the market.

In any case, once again, a company that invests in and practices amortization policies is a company that protects and strengthens its immune system.

Immune System and Corporate Profitability

To understand how the company strengthens its immune system through self-financing, it is necessary to describe the functioning of the company itself by examining the management cycle.

Entrepreneurship is a phenomenon that occurs over time, intending to create transformation from an economic perspective. Entrepreneurship is based on adherence to the business cycle.

> *The business cycle for a company is like the perfect functioning of the automatic gear of a Swiss watch when the watchcase is opened.*

As a unitary phenomenon, the business cycle represents a system that consists of all the economic transactions the company puts in place to achieve its goals.

Figure 5.6 articulates the business cycle in five integrated phases. Phase 1 concerns collecting the capital required to start the production process from an economic perspective.

Capital can have a dual origin: own capital (equity), risk capital contributed by shareholders, or third-party or debt capital acquired through financial institutions. Before starting a new business or when a new investment is planned, it is essential to understand the total amount of capital the business requires. The total amount of capital required depends on several factors: the nature of the business; the sector in which

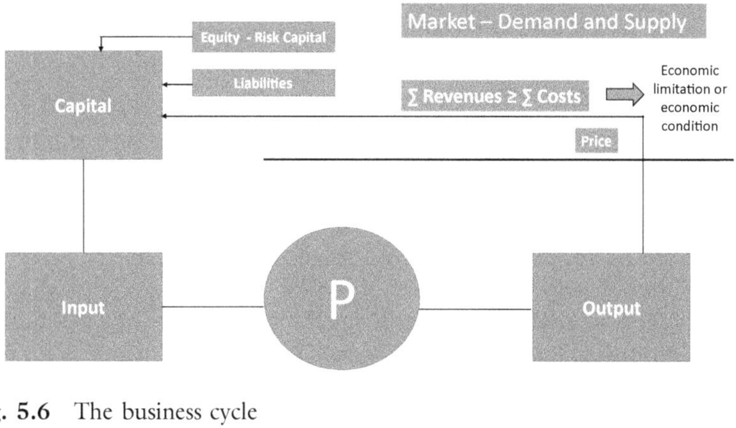

Fig. 5.6 The business cycle

the company operates; the duration of the production process (in particular, the lead time); proximity to the outlet market; and, finally, the payment conditions.

A simulation using the business plan managerial tool is necessary to understand the total amount of capital required. The business plan should answer two main questions. (1) Is the business sustainable? (2) If yes, how much capital must be activated?

Once the required amount of capital has been determined, shareholders must verify their underwriting capacity. The amount the shareholders may underwrite represents the risk capital, also called equity. The difference between the total amount of capital required and the equity available represents the amount of capital that debt must provide.

$$\text{Capital} = \text{Equity} + \text{Debt}$$

Three main elements differentiate equity and third-party capital: (1) third-party capital is subject to an obligation to repay, whereas for own capital—being risk capital—there is no obligation to repay; (2) third-party capital is subject to expiry, whereas own capital does not have a repayment deadline because there is no repayment obligation; and (3) third-party capital is subject to the payment of interest, whereas remuneration for own capital is linked to the performance of the company's management and the policies adopted by the shareholders.

Equity remuneration requires the achievement of a profit by the company's management, and the shareholders decide how to distribute the profit. Shareholders may also decide not to distribute the profit but to capitalize it in reserves, a virtuous self-financing process.

The company requires capital to buy all the production's productive factors (or inputs). Production factors can have either a slow or rapid cycle of use.

Production factors (phase 2) with a slow cycle of use will be used by the company several times and participate in the production process for more than one cycle and administrative period. For this reason, they are also referred to as production factors classified as fixed assets.

Production factors with a rapid cycle of use (or fast-cycle production factors) might only be used by the company once as part of a production cycle because they lose their effectiveness after use. For this reason, they are also referred to as production factors with simple fertility.

The difference between production factors with a slow or rapid cycle of use is essential when accounting for the purchase cost. In the first case, the purchase cost is recorded in the balance sheet, and an annual depreciation cost is recorded in the income statement. In the second case, the purchase cost is recorded in the income statement, among the other costs accumulated during the year.

The production factors acquired by the company are combined in the production process (phase 3). The production process comprises two aspects worthy of attention: (1) the meaning of the process and (2) the economic prospects of the process. The meaning of production differs by type of company. In a manufacturing company, the production process represents the transformation of inputs into outputs. Manufacturing companies may be industrial or craft companies. In the past, industrial companies were based on a capital-intensive model and required investment in their production structure. In contrast, craft companies were based on a labor-intensive model, with the center of production represented by a workforce factor.

Today, this distinction has lost its relevance because, even in artisan enterprises, investment in technology has become necessary as a distinctive competence for competitiveness, and artisan enterprises have become capital-intensive models. Therefore, the difference between industries and craft enterprises is based on the organizational model and the quantity and quality of production. In these industries, there is large-scale production, which is standardized and of inferior quality. In artisan businesses, smaller quantities of higher-quality outputs are produced.

Among manufacturing companies, where the production process involves the transformation of inputs to outputs, there are service companies and commercial (or trade) companies. Service companies produce intangible outputs. In commercial (or trade) companies, the production process involves the transfer of goods in time and space.

In all cases, the production process must be conducted from an economic perspective. This means that output is obtained at the end of the production process. The output (phase 4) is destined to be sold. The sales process presupposes the existence of an outlet marketable to receive the product that is either tangible or intangible, transferred in time and/or space.

When the output enters the market at an economic level, the relationship between supply and demand determines the price.

The price, as shown in Fig. 5.6, represents, on the one hand, the economic value determined by the relationship between supply and demand. On the other hand, it represents the value necessary to close the economic cycle by allowing the initial capital to be recomposed as outputs and the consequent continuation of the business cycle (phase 5). From an economic perspective, price is simply an indicator expressing the market relationship between supply and demand. From the business-economic perspective, the price is a lever to recompose the initial capital at the end of the management cycle, guaranteeing productive continuity.

For the price to allow the recomposition of the initial capital, the business cycle must respect the economic equation of business. The economic equation of business presupposes that the price is higher than or equal to the sum of all costs.

$$\text{Price} > \sum \text{Costs}$$

At the end of the business cycle, three different situations can occur:

1. Capital at the beginning of the cycle is equal to capital at the end of the cycle. This means the price is equal to the sum of the costs. In this situation, although the business has yet to create profit, the company can continue its business.
2. Capital at the beginning of the cycle is lower than capital at the end of the cycle. This means the price is higher than the sum of the costs, and the economic equation of business is positive. In this situation, the business has created a positive profit. Profit can be invested in the company and/or distributed to shareholders.
3. Capital at the beginning of the cycle is higher than capital at the end of the cycle. This means the price is lower than the sum of costs, and the economic equation of business is negative. In this situation, the business has created a negative profit (loss): at the end of the cycle, the company has less capital than at the beginning. To recompose the capital necessary for the business cycle, the shareholders can capitalize on the company by paying new capital through equity, or the banking system can be asked to intervene. It is conceivable that the shareholders would only be willing to replace the money lost by re-capitalizing the company. However, it is also possible that the banking system would not be willing to take responsibility for the loss and would therefore require the shareholders to express their trust in the company's business and its ability to generate wealth.

In all cases, the business cycle should close with the reconstitution of the initial capital to give continuity to the management. The recomposition of the initial capital is linked to the company's ability to respect economic conditions (or economic constraints), and, therefore, the price must cover the sum of the costs.

Compliance with the economic conditions of management depends on internal conditions within the company and external conditions such as market conditions.

The Meaning of Price

Following the business-economic approach, the price may have three meanings, as shown in Fig. 5.7.

Traditionally, the price has always been considered a static quantity through which an asset's specific value is attributed. Since the late 1970s, some economic sectors (e.g., air transport and hotel services) started to see price not as a static quantity but as a dynamic value. Today, new technologies have facilitated real-time comparisons of prices in markets, leading to changes in consumer behavior, and the dynamicity of prices has increased even in more traditional sectors.

Moreover, the same economic theory indicates that the price of an asset is closely linked to the intrinsic value of the asset itself as well as time and space dimensions.

The price of a half-liter bottle of water can be used as an example. The price leaves the factory is, at most, 0.12 cents. The price at which it can

- Economic Meaning of Price – Price is an indicator that shows when there is a match between Supply & Demand in the market

- Managerial Meaning of Price – Economic Condition «$\sum$ Revenue ≥ $\sum$ Cost»

- Business Meaning (Creation of Value) of Price – M. E. Porter Theory, where Price is the way to measure the capacity of a business to create economic value. The economic value for Porter is the capacity to satisfy (potential) customers. To measure value creation, Portcr aims to consider the maximum price a customer can pay at a specific moment and in a particular place to buy a specific product/service. The WILLINGNESS TO PAY.

Fig. 5.7 The meaning of the price

be purchased from a university vending machine is 0.20 cents. The same water bottle can be purchased from a bar inside the university for 0.55 cents and at a bar outside the university for €1. Finally, the same water bottle on a low-cost flight can be purchased for €3.50.

This example demonstrates how the price of a simple half-liter mineral water bottle is highly variable and dynamic depending on where it is purchased. The same considerations can be made concerning other goods, not only the spatial and time dimensions. For example, a similar principle applies to the advance purchase of a flight or hotel-room booking.

Price can therefore have a meaning in terms of an economic dimension, a business-economic dimension, or a social dimension.

In the economic dimension, price is an indicator that measures the relationship between supply and demand in each market. The relationship between supply and demand generates an economic value (price) that expresses not just the value of the goods involved in the transaction but the value of the transaction itself.

In the business-economic dimension, price expresses the economic condition of the business, i.e., the company's ability to cover all its costs with the price, guaranteeing the continuity of the business cycle as indicated in Fig. 5.6. Price is closely linked to the structure of company costs, which often represents a fundamental constraint on the company's ability to create value.

The social dimension of price is of intermediate significance between the economic and economic-business dimensions. In the social dimension, according to the economic theory formulated by Porter, price is the maximum value that, at a given moment and in a specific place, the consumer (or potential consumer) is willing to pay to buy a particular asset.

According to Porter's theory, the business can create value if the customer is satisfied. The economic level of satisfaction of the customer is measured by the maximum price that the customer is willing to pay at that specific moment and in that specific place to buy a specific asset. According to Porter, price is dynamic and is different for each customer (or potential customer), and is not related to the company's cost structure but is more influenced by the customer's perception of value.

Many fashion companies create two product lines. One line has a high-added value and a very high price. These are products aimed at a few select customers. A much cheaper line, usually called "Sport" and cannot be considered economical, is expensive for a low-quality product aimed at a vast market. Customer is typically willing to pay a high price for a low-quality product because they are attracted by the product brand rather than the quality of the product.

The high-added value product is aimed at a qualified customer who can recognize the product's quality and has the economic ability to purchase it. The low-quality product sold at a high price is aimed at a customer who does not consider quality and is often unable to verify it or is otherwise disinterested. The customer aspires to the brand and the recognition provided by the product. It is no coincidence that fashion products of this type are strongly branded and recognizable.

The situation for a company that produces wine is very different. The investment required to increase quality and, consequently, the price has implications for the production process and is often remarkably high. There is also a very long time required to obtain the expected results from the investment, and there is a need to educate the consumer to understand the process and, therefore, to recognize the more excellent value of the product—leading to a propensity to pay a higher price.

It is evident that, for a company, the aim is not just to sell but to sell at the maximum price a customer is willing to pay at a given moment and in a particular place. A fashion company can achieve this goal by investing in advertising, communication, and marketing. It is more difficult for a company that produces wine to achieve the same result because the latter would have to invest in technology and new production processes and wait much longer before reaching the expected result.

In all cases, prices are becoming increasingly dynamic. Companies must, on the one hand, try to keep their costs low to have greater profitability and, on the other hand, increase customers' willingness to pay. This would increase the price by creating economic value, which is consistent with the teachings of Porter.

Porter's theory on creating value through the maximum price the customer is willing to pay has resulted in the most recent revenue-management tools aiming to maximize company profitability through the willingness to pay lever.

The Life Cycle of a Company: Accounting Period

An element worthy of attention within the dimension of time and the theme of the measurement of management relates to the company's life cycle. A company can be likened to a living organism (a cell) with its life cycle in business management. The company's life does not necessarily coincide with the life of the founder or an entrepreneur. There are companies whose life cycle has involved many generations of entrepreneurs and other companies whose life cycles have been shorter than that of their founder or entrepreneur.

Suppose it is true that the business life cycle must be considered unified and systematic. In that case, it is also true that the measurements and needs related to the analysis of the business dynamics require certain activities to be performed periodically—hence the need to scan the business life cycle, identifying time intervals referred to as administrative periods.

The accounting period is the time interval that marks the passing of corporate life. The company's life cycle consists of the sum of multiple accounting periods. The number of accounting periods that comprise the business life cycle is ongoing.

The accounting period typically lasts twelve months but may be shorter (e.g., seasonal activities) or longer (e.g., for specific crops). In Italy, the accounting period typically coincides with the calendar year. If the accounting period coincides with the calendar year, it begins on the 1st of January and ends on the 31st of December of the same calendar year.

The duration of the accounting period is determined following the business' nature and the production process's length. If a company is established during a calendar year—for example, on the 15th of June—it could decide to make its first accounting period shorter than twelve months; in this case, from the 15th of June to the 31st of December. Alternatively, it could have a longer first accounting period—in this case, from the 15th of June to the 31st of December of the following year. Within each period, the company carries out transaction management. An exercise is the set or system of management operations that the company puts in place over a given accounting period. The exercise represents the content of the operations determined by the administrative period's time interval. The exercise and administrative period are closely connected, even if, in practice, they almost always use one year as the reference time interval. At the end of each financial year, companies should draw up a document in the form of a financial report, referred to as a financial statement.

Within the life cycle management of the company, measurements are made in the different dimensions and used to inform the unified business management. The first dimension worthy of attention is the time dimension. The measuring process needs to address the time dimension because it is less tangible and less noticeable, with few exceptions. However, the time dimension is of primary importance for business management because it indicates the time spent in a particular phase of a company's life cycle. When considering how to measure the work of human resources, remuneration policies, the operation of machinery, production cycles, investment policies, and periods of supply needs in terms of storage and warehouse space, the time dimension expresses the vitality of the economic, financial, and productive systems of the company.

> *Time is "one of the most essential conditions necessary to characterize the phenomenon of business and is more significant than other types of economic activities (...) isolated, unsystematic."* (Franceschi Ferraris & Cavalieri, 2005: 26)[1]

The phenomenon is based on the effect of the time dimension on the company and creates opportunities and threats to the survival of the company. The time dimension is present throughout the company's life cycle, marks the course of operations, directs the management, and determines efficiency and effectiveness. The time dimension affects the entire corporate system and can be considered a resource, with the company's success depending on the exploitation.

Considering the time dimension, attention should be focused on measuring time inside and outside the company system. A company's business and life cycle can only be designed considering time. The company does not exist for a single moment but can be considered part of a system of company time. It is through the time dimension that all companies can be summarized in a unified manner, and it is the time dimension expressed when company time is considered.

The company can provide a time or can manage time. A company that manages time or effectively controls the time dimension is like an orchestra's conductor during a performance. The conductor combines and synthesizes all the musical instruments but must also give attention to their details and sounds or accentuations and adjust them to the environment in which the act is performed. A company that manages the overall time dimension has less control of all the individual elements—in our

[1] Translated from Italian Language: "una delle condizioni essenziali del fenomeno aziendale necessarie a caratterizzarlo rispetto ad altri tipi di attività economiche (...) isolate, asistematiche."

analogy, of the musical instruments that make up the orchestra—in other words, the company combines corporate activity and all the processes within the business.

Time assumes a critical role and should be kept carefully under control when analyzing the capacity of the management cycle for the company to sustain itself and ensure its continuity.

References

Amaduzzi, A. (1948). *Ragioneria Generale*. Casa Editrice Dott. Luigi Macrì.

Brennan, N. M., Edgar, V. C., & Power, S. B. (2022). COVID-19 profit warnings: Delivering bad news in a time of crisis. *The British Accounting Review, 54*(2). https://doi.org/10.1016/j.bar.2021.101054

Chen, S., & Lee, D. (2023). Small and vulnerable: SME productivity in the great productivity slowdown. *Journal of Financial Economics, 147*(1), 49–74.

de Villiers, C., Jia, J., & Li, Z. (2022). Are boards' risk management committees associated with firms' environmental performance? *The British Accounting Review, 54*(1), 101066.

Dicksee, L. R. (1902). *Auditing: A practical manual for auditors*. Gee and Co.

Financial Accounting Standards Board. (2014). Presentation of financial statements—Going concern. Financial Accounting Series. Disclosure of uncertainties about an entity's ability to continue as a going concern, No. 2014–15. www.fasb.org. Accessed 31 Mar 2021.

Franceschi Ferraris, R., & Cavalieri, E. (2005). *Economia Aziendale* (Vol. I). Giappichelli.

Giannessi, E. (1970). *Appunti di economia aziendale*. G. Pellegrini.

Ho, K.-C., Huang, H.-Y., Pan, Z., & Gu, Y. (2023). Modern pandemic crises and default risk: Worldwide evidence. *Journal of International Financial Management & Accounting*, 1–32. https://doi.org/10.1111/jifm.12172

Humphreys, K. A., & Trotman, K. T. (2022). Judgment and decision making research on CSR reporting in the COVID-19 pandemic environment. *Account Finance, 62*, 739–765. https://doi.org/10.1111/acfi.12805

Lombardi, R. (2021). *The going-concern-principle in non-financial disclosure: Concepts and future challenges*. SIDREA Series in Accounting and Business Administration. Springer. https://doi.org/10.1007/978-3-030-81127-3

Madonna, S., & Cestari, G. (2015). The accuracy of bankruptcy prediction models: A comparative analysis of multivariate discriminant models in the Italian context. *European Scientific Journal, 11*(34), 106–133.

Marasca, S., Montanini, L., D'Andrea, A., & Cerioni, E. (2020). The how and why of integrated reporting in a public health care organization: The stakeholders' perspective. *Business Strategy and the Environment, 29*(4), 1714–1722.

Menon, K., & Williams, D. D. (2010). Investor reaction to going concern audit reports. *The Accounting Review, 85*(6), 2075–2105.

Sterling, R. R. (1968). Going concern: Examination. *Accounting Review, 43*(3), 481–502.

Storey, R. K. (1959). Revenue realization, going concern and measurement of income. *The Accounting Review, 34*(2), 232–238.

Upreti, V., Adams, M., & Jia, Y. (2022). Risk management and the cost of equity: Evidence from the United Kingdom's non-life insurance market. *The European Journal of Finance, 28*(6), 551–570.

Yeh, C. C., Chi, D. J., & Lin, Y. R. (2014). Going-concern prediction using hybrid random forests and rough set approach. *Information Sciences, 254*, 98–110.

CHAPTER 6

The Immune System and Corporate Vulnerability

In this chapter, we focus on the corporate immune system's role in risk management policies and strategies, not by eliminating the probability that a hostile event may occur but by mitigating its effects to protect the principle of business continuity.

The immune system is a tool to mitigate corporate crises and/or crises of entire production sectors. Hence, implementing tools within complex systems, namely business, and production, for continuous monitoring of the progress of the immune system to exercise a control function is especially important given the turbulence of current production systems.

This chapter also highlights a case study that, over the years, has assumed importance in terms of corporate crises and how the tools identified to monitor the efficiency of the corporate immune system can also be used at a macro level to compare different production sectors to determine those most vulnerable and most exposed to risk. In this chapter, it is crucial to understand how strengthening the immune system is a necessary, albeit not sufficient, condition to mitigate the effects of adverse events on the individual company and entire production sectors.

A. Capocchi, *Vulnerability and the Corporate Immune System*,
https://doi.org/10.1007/978-3-031-30254-1_6

The Role of the Immune System in Risk Management

The corporate immune system does not eliminate the risk of interruption of business continuity or, worse, of non-survival for the company. As in the case of human beings, even if companies have an excellent immune system, over time, they can run into crises that end their existence. After all, the company's end must not be experienced as an extraordinary event because the future, as the beginning, is a phase consistent with the company's existence, understood as a productive combination (Birkinshaw & Ridderstråle, 1999).

Numerous situations can cause the end of the company. Some may be attributable to circumstances within the corporate system, such as poor investments, incorrect decisions, management's inability to understand and anticipate changes, and so on. Other situations can be attributable to factors outside the corporate system, such as sudden market changes, technological overruns, or innovation processes that wipe out entire markets (Lawrence, 1954; Miller, 1983).

In both cases, what is certain is that the company's end is rarely concluded in the short term—it is a process that takes time and may even begin in a distant era concerning the manifestation of the first symptoms. In the analysis of the corporate purpose, the similarities with the human being are numerous. Even for companies, the end does not typically manifest itself when the crisis starts—the process can sometimes remain latent for many years and manifest itself when it is already too late to be remedied. For this reason, it is essential to use all the tools that management has at its disposal to periodically check the company's health to avoid losing control and to govern within the complexity in which companies operate (Schwenk, 1988; Pfeffer, 1992).

Returning to the corporate immune system role—it plays a decisive role not in mitigating the probability that an event may occur but rather in mitigating the harmful effects the event may have on the company. Excellent and appropriate immune system functioning helps reduce the company's vulnerability, preventing it from entering a state of crisis, manifest or silent.

Corporate Vulnerability and Crisis

The phenomenon of corporate crisis has economic, social, cultural, and legal implications. It must be well framed to analyze it correctly and identify the most effective tools for reducing its effects or even preventing its manifestation. In this regard, the company crisis can be classified by following the twofold classification schematically represented in Fig. 6.1.

Figure 6.1 highlights how company crises can be classified based on two dimensions: the first dimension concerns the cause of the crisis and allows us to distinguish (i) the economic crisis from (ii) the non-economic crisis; the second dimension concerns the extent of the crisis and allows us to distinguish (i) the company crisis from (ii) the sector crisis (Chen & Lee, 2023).

The simplification contained in the dual classification represented in Fig. 6.1 also allows the dynamics of the crisis itself to be highlighted through the dials: a dynamic as a result of which the sector crisis can lead to one or more corporate crises or severe crises of the company can lead to an industry crisis. Likewise, a non-cyclical crisis can lead to a cyclical crisis if the state of crisis continues over time (de Villiers et al., 2022).

The classification of corporate crises in the two dimensions represented above makes it possible to identify four quadrants: within each quadrant, it is possible to indicate a degree of "severity" of the crisis, even prospective, and to identify specific intervention tools.

The dynamics of the company crisis can be represented in Fig. 6.1 by verifying the connections between the different quadrants. On the one hand, the company crisis itself usually manifests itself in times that are not too close to the moment of its origin; on the other hand, it

Framing of the corporate crisis phenomenon

Company Crisis Framework Matrix		Breadth of the Crisis	
		Corporate crisis	Sectori crisis
Causes of the crisis	Economic crisis	First Quadrant	Second Quadrant
	Non-cyclical crisis	Third Quadrant	Fourth Quadrant

Fig. 6.1 Framing of the corporate crisis phenomenon

is appropriate to implement a methodology suitable for identifying, in a preventive manner, the vulnerability of an economic sector, a geographical area, and/or a company, to enable intervention with support tools before the crisis manifests itself and/or reaches levels of no return.

The Case of Blockbuster[1]

The description of this case study is extracted from what was written by João Clérigo de Almeida in 2011 (de Almeida, 2011). "An interesting case of how the market can change rapidly is represented by the giant Blockbuster and the dynamics that led to its rapid rise and equally rapid decline. Blockbuster's founder David Cook opened his first video rental store in Dallas in 1985. The video-rental industry at that time was highly fragmented. The rental sector was locally developed, with thousands of small, privately owned stores. This model comprised thousands of stores—small stores with limited numbers of available titles and restrictive policies in terms of the use of videotapes.

Blockbuster was different, and with its business model in that period, it represented a revolutionary innovation: each store had more than 8000 titles available for rent, the positioning of the stores was family-friendly, with bright and colorful stores that did not carry adult films, and they introduced the "take from the shelf to the counter" concept.

The experience that Blockbuster wanted to create for the consumer was significant: in the stores, it was possible to buy popcorn, soft drinks, sweets, and so on, allowing the customer to reproduce the cinema experience in their own home. By 1987, Cook had already opened 19 Blockbuster stores and wanted to grow his business further, but he needed more capital. That was when Cook thought of inviting Harry W. Huizenga to invest in the business, the man who had previously grown Waste Management Inc. from a single-route garbage truck business into a Fortune 500 company,

Despite initial doubts, Huizenga bought a majority stake in Blockbuster and started Blockbuster's growth spree, with 250 stores already operating in 1988. By then, Cook had already left due to acquisitions policy diverging. In the following years, Blockbuster experienced

[1] The description of this case study follows what João Clérigo de Almeida wrote in 2011. J. C de Almeida, *The Fall of a Giant*, Catolica Lisbon School of Business & Economics, 2011.

incredible growth by focusing on national marketing campaigns, positioning Blockbuster as "America's Family Video Store." Moreover, under Huizenga's leadership, the company adopted a diversification strategy, entering TV studios and music and play-center businesses.

By 1994, Blockbuster had more than 4000 stores worldwide and was still under Huizenga's leadership. Later that year, the media company Viacom Inc. bought Blockbuster in a deal valued at $8.4 billion. This merger aimed to create a large company capable of seizing new business opportunities and strengthening both companies' operational performance. As a result of the merger, Huizenga stepped down. The 1994–1997 period was volatile for Blockbuster. With increased competition from other channels, a maturing video-rental industry, CEO successions, and a relocation back to Dallas that caused many vital people to leave the firm, Viacom sold 20% of Blockbuster in 1999. Blockbuster's 1999 post-IPO value was $2.9 billion. Viacom had also stopped Blockbuster's product diversification and scaled down the business.

One of the most significant changes for Blockbuster in 1997 was the arrival of a new CEO. Blockbuster hired John Antioco as its new president and CEO because of his reputation as a turnaround specialist, first at 7-Eleven Inc. and then at Taco Bell. Antioco's 10-year tenure as CEO would be one of the most challenging in Blockbuster's history, as he would have to deal with several highly complex business decisions.

In recent years, the American giant has begun to collide with the spread of the Internet. The Internet rapidly changes consumer habits, favoring the use of content first by renting online videos and then directly in streaming mode. Indeed, streaming comes after peer-to-peer, which allows consumers to share video content through unique platforms. In more detail, with the advent of the Internet, anyone could go online and order a DVD conveniently from their home PC and wait for delivery. Blockbuster had to compete with general mass retailers such as Amazon.com and specialist DVD retailers like Express.com and Reel.com in this new framework.

Blockbuster already had an online presence through its website, which it did not use to sell merchandise or rent DVDs. The company had always been in a traditional "bricks-and-mortar" business, only renting and selling VHS tapes and DVDs through its stores. In late 1999, Blockbuster's CEO John F. Antioco commented on Blockbuster's first move at the online environment: "[Blockbuster will] continue to focus on growing market share in the growing VHS/DVD rental category through our retail store base and increasingly through blockbuster.com." The idea was to turn blockbuster.com into a "vibrant e-commerce engine for selling DVD, VHS (video tapes), music, and movie-related products."

Because Blockbuster was essentially a retailer, it needed more resources and capabilities to become an electronic player successfully. To address these deficiencies, Blockbuster took several steps:

- First, Blockbuster outsourced the order and fulfillment processes for blockbuster.com to Order Trust Inc., a move which, according to Blockbuster executives, would allow them to focus on marketing and branding instead of technology and infrastructure.
- Second, Blockbuster signed a deal with TeleTech Holdings Inc., where TeleTech would provide customer and technical support to blockbuster.com users to achieve high customer service.
- Third, Blockbuster created two new senior-level positions—President of New Media, occupied by Santo Politi, a former Matsushita and Panasonic engineer, and manager who would pursue new media opportunities—and Senior VP of e-Commerce. Shellye Archambeau, an IBM veteran with positions in marketing and management, would be in charge of executing Blockbuster's Internet strategy.
- Finally, Blockbuster entered a multi-year partnership with AOL in which it would gain access to AOL's customer base of almost 20 million and would be allowed to sell movies on AOL's platform. AOL would also invest $30 m in blockbuster.com to further develop it. In exchange, Blockbuster would promote AOL's services and software in their stores.

Unfortunately, Blockbuster's strategy was insufficient to compete in the new digital environment.

In the middle of 2000, Blockbuster's leading rival, Hollywood Entertainment, had just decided to shut down Reel.com due to its inability to profit. Forrester Research analysts were predicting waves of consolidation and failures among online retailers, "with companies that sell DVDs, videocassettes, and CDs solely online being some of the first to go," according to senior analyst Joe Sawyer.

Besides e-commerce, an additional threat came from Internet-based firms that offered to bring rental movies to their customers' homes. Kozmo.com was the most renowned company of this kind.

Blockbuster executives knew that the promise of delivering rentals to customers' homes had immense potential, appealing to more than 90% of active renters. Blockbuster negotiated a deal with Kozmo.com in which they would provide the inventory, and Kozmo would deliver and receive around $1 for each rental delivery. This deal did not go forward, so Blockbuster turned to Streamline.com, a Kozmo.com rival, to deliver their rentals directly to customers' homes. Even though the partnership worked, Streamline had to shut down in late 2000 due to a failure to find financing to keep operations running. Eventually, Blockbuster tried another home delivery partnership, this time with Food.com, an Internet-based meal delivery service with 16,000 partner restaurants and closed to one million members in 2000. The companies would both receive orders from clients and then the Food.com delivery personnel would drop by a local Blockbuster to get the movie, go to the restaurant to pick up the meal and deliver the order. Eventually, when the Internet bubble burst in 2000, most Internet-based delivery services were forced to shut down, mainly because, although they held much promise, they had faced a challenging time turning their vision into a profitable business.

A third threat that the Internet posed for Blockbuster's business model was Internet-based subscription services.

The leading company behind this idea was Netflix Inc., which employed a disruptive business model. A Netflix subscriber would pay a $20 monthly fee; in return, the subscriber would receive up to three DVDs simultaneously in his mailbox. Once the subscribers returned the DVDs, Netflix would send them the following DVDs in their online "rental queue"—their movie wish list. This model meant that subscribers could keep the movies for as long as they wanted and eliminated unpleasant late fees. Furthermore, Netflix paid for the DVD transportation costs (the DVDs were sent via first-class mail by the United States Postal Service).

Initially, Blockbuster executives dismissed Netflix as a threat because they believed the DVD-by- mail business would appeal to only some renters and that it would only capture a small fraction of the rental market. However, by 2002, Netflix was already listed on a public stock exchange; its revenues had doubled since 2001, and had close to one million subscribers, even though its net income was still negative. Blockbuster's first indirect reaction came in mid-2002 when the "Movie Freedom Pass" was unveiled. Under this subscription-based offering, Blockbuster customers would pay a monthly fee of between $25 and 30, be able to take three DVDs or tapes home at a time without due dates or late payments, but would still have to go to a Blockbuster store pick up and drop off movies.

To address the growing VOD market, Blockbuster signed a three-party deal in mid-2000 with DirectTV and the now defunct Enron Corp. Blockbuster would provide the movies, DirectTV would deliver them to households via their satellites, and Enron would provide the broadband. The deal caused some excitement in the industry but fell apart some months after being signed due to commercial difficulties. Later in 2003, Blockbuster tried another incursion into the VOD business, delivering online content as legal downloads. To do this, Blockbuster acquired a majority stake in Cinemanow.com to test the viability of this practice.

Despite all the technological threats looming over Blockbuster's rental business in the early twenty-first century, the company was well positioned at the end of 2003. Blockbuster was the leading movie rental company with almost 9000 stores worldwide and nearly $6 billion in revenues.

With the rental business shrinking due to the new economic challenges and competitors that the DVD and the Internet brought, Blockbuster was searching for a way to expand and diversify its business.

Finally, in their 2003 annual report, Blockbuster announced that it would enter the online market aggressively in 2004 to grow its business by bringing back customers lost to Netflix and attracting new customers who would like to enjoy the convenience of a "clicks and bricks" strategy. Blockbuster executives also announced that they were willing to suffer short-term losses in developing their online business.

Blockbuster Online would work as an internet rental subscription business by running an online platform that would look very similar to what Netflix was offering regarding site design and subscription model but differentiate itself from Netflix by integrating the online business with the physical business.

In March 2007, after a decade leading Blockbuster, John F. Antioco declared that he would leave the company after a disagreement regarding his 2006 bonus award. Blockbuster hired James W. Keyes, a former chairman, and CEO of 7-Eleven Inc., an international chain of convenience stores, to replace him.

Keyes' strategy for Blockbuster was to "move in our customers' minds from a video-rental store to one that provides entertainment content." This meant fulfilling customers' needs in-store, managing the online DVD subscription business, and building capabilities that allowed Blockbuster to deliver movies via Internet streaming or download.

In July 2007, Keyes started with a substantial downsizing of Blockbuster Online's marketing budget to stop the losses the program was inflicting on the company. Additionally, the prices for Total Access were reviewed upwards, with the pricing plan allowing clients to keep three DVDs simultaneously and raising unlimited free DVD exchanges at stores from $17.99 to 24.99. The cheaper plans were also revised, especially the policy allowing unlimited free DVD exchanges at stores. 2009 was marked by poor quarterly performances, with losses in every quarter. In this period, Blockbuster entered multiple deals with several companies, such as Sonic Solutions, a digital platform provider, telecom companies, and TiVo, to consolidate their position as a multichannel content provider. There were some early signs of financial distress, with rumors of bankruptcy as early as March.

In 2010, Blockbuster went through severe cost-cutting programs and experienced difficulties in securing financing, selling assets to pay the debt, missing bond payments, de-listing from the New York Stock Exchange, and ultimately filing with the SEC for Chapter 11 protection to avoid liquidation.

In short, Blockbuster Inc. went from being the world's leading and most profitable company in the video-rental business to a bankrupt company in less than a decade. Following the above sequence of events, it is easy to understand the reasons behind Blockbuster's crisis.

It is particularly essential to highlight how Blockbuster has contributed to the closure and bankruptcy of many small video-rental stores and then collapsed with the advent of the Internet."

Monitoring of the Corporate Immune System

As we have already observed, the corporate immune system does not enable avoidance of the state of crisis. Still, it highlights the vulnerability of a company and/or a sector by monitoring some simple indicators (Capocchi, 2018; Gallati, 2022).

Two indicators summarize the company's state of health:

1. The capitalization index or debt ratio
2. Working capital.

The debt ratio, as already observed, is given by the ratio between borrowed capital and equity:

(Consolidated Liabilities + Current Liabilities) / Equity

As already described, the level of company capitalization and, therefore, the strength of the company's immune system varies during the life cycle of the company itself, also based on management performance and company policies:

- At the time of the company's establishment, the own means are represented by the capital subscribed by the shareholders or by the share capital. At the time of incorporation, a capital reserve may be present—called share premium reserve—if the shareholders, in addition to subscribing to the nominal value of the share capital based on their share, also pay an additional amount as a share premium to strengthen the capital structure of the company. The share premium reserve is an available capital reserve. The shareholders can also request and obtain its return during the company's life. The distribution of the share premium reserve to shareholders requires the prior condition that the legal reserve has reached 20% of the value of share capital. At the time of the establishment of the company, the debts or third-party capital represent all the resources that the company has acquired to finance the start-up of its business because it cannot obtain these resources from the shareholders;
- At the time of operation of the company, i.e., immediately after its establishment, the corporate immune system is naturally nourished by the effect of capitalization, i.e., of its self-financing and improper self-financing. Own self-financing consists of the allocation to reserves of the profits produced in particular administrative periods. Profits are created and not distributed to shareholders by way of dividends. Improper self-financing consists of the depreciation and provisions that the company makes in the provisions for risks and charges. Depreciation and provisions for risks and charges represent non-monetary costs that absorb wealth from revenues and

keep it within the company because they are not costs connected to financial outgoings.

As already observed, no value can cause the level of company capitalization—its debt ratio—to be considered adequate: the adequacy of the capitalization depends on many internal and external factors. Among the latter is also the sector to which the company belongs and the type of activity carried out. In general, however, it is believed that an optimal value of the debt ratio is equal to 2, i.e., that:

$$\text{(Consolidated Liabilities} + \text{Current Liabilities) / Equity} = 2$$

Suppose the debt ratio is equal to two. In that case, equity capital accounts for one-third of the total capital structure of the sources of financing, and borrowed capital accounts for two-thirds. Scholars consider the one-third and two-thirds ratios optimal to guarantee the company a sound financial structure based on good capitalization.

Working capital allows analysis of the company's state of health in the financial dimension. The balance sheet, in analyzing the correlation between loans and sources of financing, allows us to understand whether the company's financial structure is solid or vulnerable.

As already noted, it is worth remembering that working capital is given by:

$$\text{Working Capital} = \text{Current Assets} - \text{Current Liabilities}$$

Working Capital, as already highlighted, should take a positive value. Suppose working capital has a value greater than zero. In that case, the fixed capital and fixed investments have been fully financed with permanent capital or from equity and consolidated liabilities. If working capital is positive, a part of the permanent capital also covers current assets. This does not lead to an imbalance because short-term investments have been financed with medium/long-term funding sources.

If working capital is zero, the permanent capital, i.e., equity and consolidated liabilities, fully covers the fixed assets. From this, the current assets were financed entirely with current liabilities.

If working capital has a negative value—i.e., lower than zero—the permanent capital, i.e., equity and consolidated liabilities, is insufficient to finance fixed assets. From this, it follows that some of the fixed assets are financed with current liabilities, causing the company to suffer a severe imbalance, having financed long-cycle recovery loans with short-term financing sources. In this case, the company has financed a long-term asset with a short-term financial resource, and the financial imbalance originates from the fact that the repayment of the loan must take place in advance of the recovery of the investment itself. This is the basis of a structural financial imbalance and is not attributable to mere financial equilibrium. In calculating working capital, all the items that make up current assets are considered:

- Warehouse stock
- Financial activities
- Credits
- Cash and cash equivalents.

As noted, two items that make up current assets may be susceptible to incongruity: the inventory concerning closing inventories and receivables. For the warehouse, it is noted that sometimes companies can have an accounting warehouse that differs from the authentic warehouse. For operating receivables, it is noted that companies can sometimes maintain uncollectable amounts of receivables in their financial statements, which should have been written down, leading to a loss.

For these reasons, it is advisable to calculate working capital by conducting an initial detailed analysis of the composition of the items in current assets. Alternatively, the calculation of working capital can be assumed on two levels:

- Level I Working Capital

$$\text{Current Assets} - \text{Current Liabilities}$$

- Level II Working Capital

(Current Assets − Warehouse stock) − Current Liabilities

A positive amount relating to Level II Working Capital highlights the complete structural solidity of the company's financial dimension with a very positive impact on the company's state of health.

Monitoring of the company's immune system and the state of health of the company must be carried out periodically. The periodicity of the monitoring makes it possible to collect a historical series of values relating to the two indicators, which allows the evolution of the company dynamics to be represented in a meaningful way.

Why Are Health and Immune System Monitoring Performed with Only Two Indicators?

Monitoring the degree of efficiency of the company's immune system can be performed with only the two indicators described above because they enable the state of health of the company to be summarized as follows:

1. The two indicators summarize the company's equity situation regarding capitalization and financial structure.
2. The balance sheet links business management across periods. Management is assessed at the end of each administrative period but must be considered a unit. The balance sheet represents the link between the years, attributing unity and systematicity to company management.
3. The debt ratio expresses the solidity of the corporate capital structure by measuring the ratio between own capital and third-party capital.
4. Working capital expresses the consistency between loans and funding sources by measuring their correlation and the structural balance of the financial dimension.

The combined analysis of the two indicators and their periodic monitoring is sufficient for the company to monitor its health effects.

The only limitation of using the two indicators identified above is the time delay in reporting: to be significant, the two indicators must be calculated based on balance sheet data at the end of the administrative period. The balance sheet data at the end of the administrative period are not available in real-time but are available after a time delay. This represents a criticality in the monitoring process because events that put the company at risk can occur in the time interval between the end of the administrative period and the moment in which the balance sheet data are available. Also, for this reason, it is recommended that a periodic monitoring system be implemented annually. In any case, it can enrich the analysis of the last reference period with trends showing the dynamics of the company's state of health.

The Corporate Vulnerability of Italian Companies: A Practical Case

The two indicators can be used to monitor the immune system's efficiency in a single company or even in an entire sector.

By way of example, let us assume that we use the AIDA database (Bureau Van Dijk) and examine some productive sectors. In Italy, productive sectors are codified using ATECO codes. For the analysis, we consider companies with more than 250 employees belonging to the following ATECO codes:

- 10 Food Industries
- 15 Leather Industries
- 16 Wood Industry
- 17 Tissue and Paper Industry
- 24.1 Iron and Steel Industry
- 24.2 Pipe Manufacturing Industry
- 30 Construction of ships and boats
- 31 Furniture Manufacturing
- 41 Building Construction.

From the AIDA database (data extraction performed on 3 August 2022), there are four thousand three hundred fifty-eight companies in Italy with at least 250 employees (based on the latest approved financial statements as of 31 December 2021). The numbers for the ATECO codes analyzed are shown in Fig. 6.2.

Figure 6.2 shows the number of ATECO codes analyzed for companies with 250 or more employees.

NUMBER

ATECO		NUMBER OF COMPANY WITH MORE THAN 250 EMPLOYEES
10	FOOD INDUSTRY	81
15	LEATHER INDUSTRY	30
16	WOOD INDUSTRY	4
17	TISSUE AND PAPER INDUSTRY	22
24.1	IRON AND STEEL INDUSTRY	12
24.2	PIPE MANUFACTURING INDUSTRY	8
30	CONSTRUCTION OF SHIP AND BOATS	5
31	FORNITURE MANUFACTURING	18
41	BUILDING CONSTRUCTION	14
TOTAL		194

Fig. 6.2 Number of companies with 250 or more employees analyzed based on ATECO code

The overall strength of the immune system within a single sector—as indicated by the ATECO code—with reference only to companies with more than 250 employees is represented by determining the median value, as shown in Fig. 6.3.

Figure 6.3 highlights the median values of the data analyzed for each sector or ATECO code, making it possible to compare the various sectors and identify sectors with higher capitalization levels, those more exposed to debt, and so on.

ATECO	Turnover	Employees	Equity	Short Term Liabilities	Medium and Long Term Liabilities	Total Asset	Current Asset	Provisions for risks and charges
10	176.382 €	462	64.280 €	68.081 €	7.145 €	164.576 €	82.998 €	2.288 €
15	120.504 €	403	36.757 €	39.120 €	2.243 €	102.059 €	76.182 €	873 €
16	132.834 €	353	63.961 €	27.591 €	45.305 €	173.553 €	66.675 €	4.044 €
17	175.593 €	437	85.728 €	70.676 €	17.512 €	178.716 €	101.490 €	1.996 €
241	599.837 €	950	363.751 €	271.188 €	59.411 €	705.441 €	403.538 €	7.403 €
242	261.654 €	337	71.723 €	113.201 €	3.997 €	213.836 €	170.561 €	413 €
30	186.054 €	366	92.898 €	128.390 €	59.114 €	237.580 €	149.969 €	4.244 €
31	96.599 €	303	35.431 €	34.486 €	11.108 €	100.229 €	59.549 €	1.207 €
41	49.881 €	319	12.131 €	33.005 €	1.539 €	54.287 €	41.691 €	831 €
TOT	167.501 €	426	61.673 €	59.038 €	7.852 €	152.355 €	87.198 €	1.470 €

The numbers in euros are expressed in thousands of euros with regard to the 2021 financial statement

Fig. 6.3 Representation of median values by ATECO code

The mean values—arithmetic mean and median—are represented in Fig. 6.4, which allows the identification of the sectors most exposed to risks for greater vulnerability.

In detail, if the analysis focuses on the value of the mean, it can be easily seen from Fig. 6.4 that the sectors with a more fragile immune system are as follows:

- The food sector has, on average, a very high debt ratio, with positive but low average working capital. Analysis based on the median value allows us to normalize the representation because 50% of the companies in this sector have a debt index lower than 2.
- The situation is different for the construction of ships and boats and building construction sectors which report a debt index higher than 2, both in terms of average value and median value; for the building construction sector, this is also accompanied by a working capital value lower than the overall for all companies across all ATECO codes median value.

The purpose of the two indicators, as already stated, is not to analyze the state of crisis of a company or sector but to identify the most vulnerable companies and/or sectors most exposed to possible future crises.

AVERAGE AND MEDIAN VALUES

Average value			Median value		
ATECO	Debt Index	Working Capital	ATECO	Debt Index	Working Capital
10	13.69	38,033	10	1.35	8,459
15	5.27	64,466	15	1.29	31,178
16	1.21	60,955	16	0.91	39,084
17	1.66	32,842	17	1.30	21,259
241	2.00	111,505	241	1.11	95,893
242	6.92	116,300	242	1.08	26,784
30	7.97	159,088	30	4.35	44,858
31	1.77	26,040	31	1.22	20,063
41	4.45	26,412	41	3.88	9,857
TOT	7.84	50,848	TOT	1.42	18,337

Fig. 6.4 Average and median values for ATECO code

Future crises may be determined by adverse events such as the COVID-19 pandemic or the war conflict in Ukraine.

The comparison in terms of vulnerability between the various analyzed sectors, as represented by their ATECO codes, is graphically represented in Fig. 6.5.

Figure 6.5 allows the positioning of the single ATECO codes to be represented comparatively within a Cartesian plane. In detail, the Cartesian plane was constructed by placing on the abscissa axis (X) the debt index, whose values range from 0 to plus infinity, and on the ordinate axis (Y) the working capital, whose values range from 0 to plus infinity.

Representation on the Cartesian plane makes it possible to consider the sectors positioned closest to the origin concerning the debt ratio and with the highest working capital values to be less vulnerable and therefore endowed with a more efficient immune system; in Fig. 6.5, the least vulnerable the food sector (10). The sectors positioned further to the right concerning the origin based on debt ratio and lower in respect to the ordinate axis concerning working capital are more vulnerable and therefore equipped with a less efficient immune system; in Fig. 6.5, these are the building construction (41) and construction of ships and boats (30) sectors.

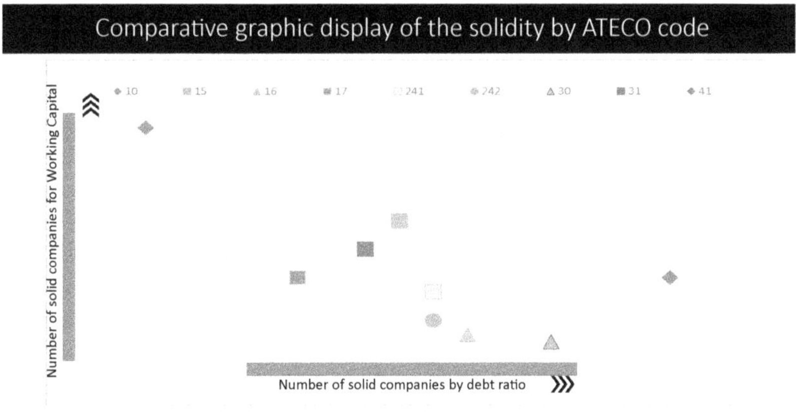

Fig. 6.5 Positioning of the ATECO code in terms of vulnerability

Summary Considerations

At the end of this chapter, we point out some synthesis elements worthy of attention that summarize our discussions so far:

1. For a business, the corporate immune system serves the same purpose as the immune system in living beings. The company should strengthen its defenses against potential dangers that put its continuity at risk.
2. The corporate immune system does not eliminate the possibility that an adverse event could occur and "infect" the company or even an entire production system. However, the immune system helps mitigate the consequences of the "infection" to protect business continuity. For this reason, it is crucial, especially in times of instability and turbulence, to encourage company policies aimed at protecting and strengthening the company's immune defenses through policies such as (1) asset capitalization, (2) reducing debt exposure, and (3) strengthening the efficiency of the corporate financial structure.
3. A company equipped with an efficient immune system protects its survival and the entire production sector to which it belongs, with significant positive economic and social consequences for the economic system as a whole.
4. The efficiency of the corporate immune system is built over time, in line with the organic vision of the company as an economic actor with its own life and continuity.
5. Hence, it is essential to implement tools for continuously monitoring the efficiency of the company's immune system within modern management systems; these should be simple, easily accessible, and usable tools to build integrated information systems.

The efficiency of corporate immune systems must become a priority for managers who hold roles of responsibility within companies, but also for national governments, which must encourage the strengthening of immune defenses throughout the company's life through specific industrial and fiscal policies to prevent future criticalities (Kanter, 1982; Hamel, 1996).

For these reasons, the concept of the corporate immune system must increasingly become an area of focus in management planning and risk management systems.

References

Birkinshaw, J., & Ridderstråle, J. (1999). Fighting the corporate immune system: A process study of subsidiary initiatives in multinational corporations. *International Business Review, 8*(2), 149–180. https://doi.org/10.1016/S0969-5931(98)00043-2

Capocchi A. (2018). *Economic value and revenue management systems: An integrated business management model*. Palgrave Macmillan.

Chen, S., & Lee, D. (2023). Small and vulnerable: SME productivity in the great productivity slowdown. *Journal of Financial Economics, 147*(1), 49–74.

de Almeida J. C. (2011). *The Fall of a Giant*. Catolica Lisbon School of Business & Economics.

de Villiers, C., Jia, J., & Li, Z. (2022). Are boards' risk management committees associated with firms' environmental performance? *The British Accounting Review, 54*(1), 101066.

Gallati, R. R. (2022). *Risk management and capital adequacy*. McGraw-Hill.

Hamel, G. (1996, July–August). Strategy as revolution. *Harvard Business Review*, 69–83.

Kanter, R. M. (1982, July–August). The middle manager as innovator. *Harvard Business Review, 60*, 95–105.

Lawrence, P. (1954, May–June). How to deal with resistance to change. *Harvard Business Review*, 49–56.

Miller, D. (1983). The correlates of entrepreneurship in three types of firms. *Management Science, 29*, 770–791.

Pfeffer, J. (1992). *Managing with power: Politics and influence in organizations*. Harvard Business School Press.

Schwenk, C. (1988). The cognitive perspective on strategic decision making. *Journal of Management Studies, 25*(1), 41–55.

CHAPTER 7

Operational Risk and Immune System

This chapter will focus on the relationship between the corporate immune system and value creation.

The efficiency of the corporate immune system is fueled over time thanks to self-financing policies. Proper and improper self-financing represents the natural and physiological tool for strengthening the company's immune defenses throughout the life and functioning of the company itself.

An implicit assumption of any corporate self-financing policy is the company's ability to operate in conditions of value creation. The creation of value is an essential condition for any self-financing policy. But how can the company guarantee itself functioning in conditions of value creation?

The creation of value is not an issue of an economic nature. Value creation is closely linked to business operations and the business combination of production. Therefore, it is essential to address the issue of value creation by paying attention to the relationship between economic and technical efficiency. This relationship is well explored in this chapter.

A. Capocchi, *Vulnerability and the Corporate Immune System*,
https://doi.org/10.1007/978-3-031-30254-1_7

To Be Profitable

The business purpose in the case of a company consists in the creation of economic value with which, in compliance with the business cycle, the company, at the end of each administrative period, reconstitutes the initial capital ensuring continuity of management (Sneddon, 2022).

The creation of economic value is closely linked to the condition of economic equilibrium, where (Amaduzzi, 1948; Giannessi, 1970; Bertini, 1990):

$$\text{Total Revenue} \geq \text{Total Costs}$$

$$\text{Total Revenue} \geq \text{Variable Costs} + \text{Fixed Costs}$$

Simplifying and supposing that the company (i) produces only one good/service, (ii) sells all the quantity produced, (iii) that the unit price is constant, (iv) that the variable unit cost is constant, and that (v) there are no limits to the capacity productive:

$$\text{Total Revenue} \geq \text{Variable Costs} + \text{Fixed Costs}$$

$$P * Q \geq \text{VC} * Q + K$$

where

P is the constant price
Q is the quantity produced and sold
VC is the variable cost per unit
K is the fixed cost.

The creation of economic value, as the company profitability, is linked to the following levers (Capocchi, 2019): (i) the selling price; (ii) the quantity produced; (iii) the variable unit cost; (iv) fixed costs.

The price depends on company policies and market conditions. Therefore, the price driver is strictly linked to constraints external to the company. The quantity produced also depends on the market conditions, understood as the ability of the market to absorb the amount offered and requirements within the company. The internal needs of the company that affect the quantities produced pertain to the production capacity of the company or its productivity. The variable unit cost depends on the company's ability to exercise its contractual power with suppliers for better purchasing economic conditions. The variable cost per unit is closely linked to the company's ability to access competitive supply markets (Jevons, 1871; Walras, 1874; Menger, 1976).

The fixed costs are closely linked to the company's economic efficiency, which in turn depends on the technical efficiency of the same. Technical efficiency is the company's ability to exploit its maximum production capacity.

Considering that

$$P * Q \geq \mathrm{VC} * Q + K$$

$$P * Q - \mathrm{VC} * Q \geq K$$

$$Q * (P - \mathrm{VC}) \geq K$$

$$Q \geq K/(P - \mathrm{VC})$$

It is possible to understand that profitability depends on the following primary drivers: (i) Fixed costs, which means technical efficiency, and (ii) contribution margin expressed by the denominator given by the difference between the unit sale price and unit variable cost. At ongoing fixed costs, company profitability can be increased by acting on the contribution margin or the value spread between the unit sale price and the unit variable cost. This range can be increased by increasing the sale price, reducing the variable cost per unit, or with both solutions.

The Production Capacity

The conditions of cost-effectiveness over time are closely related to the company's ability to make the most of the potential of its production capacity. The production capacity expresses the productive potential regarding the volume of activity available to the company. It is closely linked to the resources that the business combination has at its disposal. The concept of production capacity involves the study of quantitative relationships between the input and output of production processes, between the different factors and the different products. The production capacity can be defined as "*the ratio between the physical quantity of the product obtained (obtainable) and the physical quantity of every single factor consumed (consumable) to make the product.*"

The business combination has a limited endowment of resources (production factors), from whose employment a specific volume of activity arises according to the following function:

Place α the limited supply of productive resources available to the company at a given moment *t'* where α is the Σ of the productive factors $f1, f2, \ldots, fn$.

The productive capacity Y at the moment *t'* is a function of α

$$Y = f(\alpha)$$

where f represents the organizational and management methods combined with the resources.

A mere sum of available resources cannot measure the productive potential of the company system, being also a function of how the company's resources, be they the organizational, technical structure, the plants, the equipment, and the fast, productive factors cycle of use, are combined from an organizational and management point of view. With the same resources, two companies may express a different productive potential. In this regard, think about the importance of technology, how company processes are identified and regulated, and how human resources are used.

More than the production capacity as the productive potential of the company system, the focus must be on the maximum production capacity, understood as the maximum amount of activity that the company in each period/instant can produce/sell using the limited supply of resources available.

The definition above requires two clarifications:

- The maximum production capacity can be referred temporally to as a time interval or an instant of company life. For some companies, the maximum production capacity at a time interval is worth mentioning. For other types, the reference must be made at every moment of the company life.
- The maximum production capacity can be referred to as the phenomenon of production or sales. Indeed, the two phenomena can also coincide. For some companies, the maximum production capacity for the production phenomenon is worth mentioning. For other types, the reference must be made to the sales phenomenon.

Maximum production capacity is a vital reference for measurement processes within the business combination (East, 2022). The company as a productive combination must pursue as its purpose the exploitation of its maximum production capacity: the exploitation of the maximum production capacity must be the "technical end" of the company on which to base the "economic end" of the company itself (Nimmy et al., 2022). The company must know its maximum production capacity and the productive factors from which the combination comes out. The knowledge of the maximum production capacity is a prerequisite for measuring the degree of exploitation of the same by the business combination concerning its policies and decisions.

Technical Efficiency and Economic Efficiency

The degree of exploitation of the maximum production capacity is measurable, among others, by determining so-called technical efficiency. Technical efficiency is the relationship between a given output level and a certain input level. The output is represented by the level of activity realized or achievable; the input is represented by the level of resources used or usable. Technical efficiency is measured through "physical quantities" of output and input levels.

Having taken this relationship, technical efficiency has a double meaning depending on the perspective of analysis and reading:

- The maximum output level is achievable with a limited budget and input date.
- The minimum level of input that can be used to obtain a given output level.

The two meanings are interrelated: each company can deal with the theme by indifferently following one or the other perspective of observation. The choice of one in place of the other affects the measuring instruments.

The measurement of technical efficiency is closely related to the measurement of the economic conditions of the company: from the technical efficiency springs the economic efficiency of the same company where the output and input quantities are replaced by the economic values of the output obtained o obtainable and inputs used or usable. Technical efficiency is a necessary condition for achieving economic efficiency.

Economic efficiency is represented by the ratio between the output value obtained or obtainable and the value of the inputs used or usable. The value is expressed in economic terms, that is, in terms of economic value produced and economic value absorbed. Similarly to what is claimed for technical efficiency, economic efficiency has two closely related meanings:

- The maximum output value can be reached with the data value of the inputs used.
- The minimum input value can be used to obtain a given output value.

The company can only achieve its economic efficiency if it has reached its technical efficiency. The achievement of technical efficiency requires the exploitation of all of its production capacity The accomplishment of technical efficiency and, therefore, the exploitation of all production capacity is necessary, but more is needed for the company to achieve its economic efficiency. Achieving economic efficiency is a prerequisite for guaranteeing the company's cost-effectiveness over time.

Economic efficiency, in addition to being strictly related to technical efficiency, is also related to economic variables and their variation due to internal and external variables of the company system: think, among others, of price fluctuations on the markets.

The achievement of economic efficiency is necessary, but more is needed for the achievement of the economic conditions of the company in each period.

The economy is a short-term measure measured by the correlation between revenues and costs. In the financial statements system, the correlation between revenues and costs is guaranteed within the income statement through the accrual principle.

Economic efficiency must be projected over the medium to long term in the company's search for stable or lasting equilibrium conditions.

There needs to be more than the achievement of technical efficiency to guarantee the company's economic efficiency: a company can maximize the exploitation of its production capacity but not achieve economic efficiency conditions because of its policies to purchase inputs or own sales output policies.

Technical efficiency is a medium-long-term objective that all business combinations must tend asymptotically at any moment. If, from a purely theoretical point of view, the non-technical efficiency should lead to economic inefficiency for the company, the observation of the company phenomenology highlights many cases in which technically inefficient companies can maximize their economic value, taking positions of economic efficiency, and achieving very positive company performances. On the other hand, technically efficient companies—that is, very close to exploiting their maximum production capacity—can have negative business performances and do not respond to economic conditions.

What is certain is that the lack of technical efficiency has a cost in economic terms for the company: the cost of technical inefficiency is represented by the higher incidence of costs of the unused production structure on the unit product/service. Although challenging to highlight this cost in the income statement, it impacts the company balance sheet even when situations that are particularly favorable to the company make it possible to optimize the creation of economic value.

The cost of technical inefficiency is twofold and consists of the following:

- The cost of the unused productive capacity or idle overhead costs, the component of which can easily be determined.
- Opportunity cost, whose component is not readily determinable.

In manufacturing companies, the production capacity depends on the structure and facilities available to the company. These are usually so-called capital-intensive companies. In service or commercial companies, production capacity depends on the company's available human resources. These are typically so-called labor-intensive companies.

The resources available to the business combination define the maximum production potential, i.e., the maximum volume of activity. What appears essential is the construction through a system of measurement of a correlation between a system of technical measurement of the production capacity and its exploitation level and an economic measurement system of the company's performance.

The "Kreislauf"

The link between the technical measurement system of the company's production potential and the economic measurement system of company performance recalls the relationship between volumes, costs, prices, and revenues. The relationship between volumes of costs, prices, and revenues was dealt with in the Italian economic-business doctrine by Egidio Giannessi in the study that led to the publication of the "Kreislauf" (Giannessi, 1982).

The starting point of the problem is related to cost behavior and price behavior:

> *while costs cannot be determined without knowing the size of the production volume, strictly dependent on price trends, they find their meaning in the economic conditions that oversee the detection of costs. The summary of the "Kreislauf" is expressed in terms of "costs-prices-revenues" and is based on the volume of production volumes.* (Giannessi, 1982: 4)[1]

In other words, the observation of the company phenomenology has led Egidio Giannessi to criticize the approach—pervasive in the fifties and sixties—of J. M. Clark that the problem of the economy of companies is attributable to the full exploitation of the production capacity prepared, without to consider the economic conditions under which the exploitation of the productive capacity itself takes place.

Clark linked the company's profitability to the exploitation of production capacity, conducting an incomplete analysis of the cost formation process and the correlation of cost prices: Clark's study classified costs into variable and constant costs. The classification was analyzed and promptly criticized by Giannessi, also concerning the contribution contained in the studies of Eugen Schmalenbach. While Clark bases its observations on the elimination of unused production capacity to reduce the incidence of constant costs on unit costs, Schmalenbach analyzes all the cost components and, with the creation of a series of classes, attempts to represent the

[1] Translated from Italian Language: "(…) mentre i costi non possono essere determinati senza conoscere l'entità del volume della produzione, strettamente dipendente dall'andamento dei prezzi, questi ritrovano il loro significato nelle condizioni economiche che sovrintendono alla rilevazione dei costi. La sintesi del 'Kreislauf' si esplica sul piano 'costi-prezzi-ricavi' ed ha per base l'entità dei volumi di produzione" (Giannessi, 1982: 4).

cost dynamics against the production considered in a state of normalcy, in a state of over-employment and a form of underemployment (Clark, 1923; Schmalenbach, 1956).

Giannessi observes that the problem of company profitability is not a problem of mere exploitation of production capacity. Instead, it is necessary to measure the impact in economic terms of the exploitation of production capacity and, therefore, of the convenience or non-profitability to maximize exploitation itself, through an economic measurement system, concerning the prices to which the products/services are offered on the market. In other words, Giannessi observes the need to investigate whether the output resulting from the greater exploitation of production capacity is traded on the market at a remunerative price, that is, at a price able to improve the economic equilibrium conditions of the company.

The economic impact cannot be measured with the distinction between variable and fixed costs. Still, it must also consider the marginal cost and the concept of marginal utility. Suppose the price of the additional output unit obtained with increased production capacity utilization is higher (remunerative price). In that case, the rise in cost borne by the company to produce the same output unit is convenient. Otherwise, it has no convenience. To determine the convenience or not convenience also through marginal utility, it is necessary—observes Giannessi—to consider the loop created because (1) production costs depend on the production volume, (2) production volume depends on price trends, and (3) prices depend on production costs.

If the problem is studied considering—similarly to Clark—costs classifiable in variable and constant costs, it seems easy to reach the same conclusions as Clark: increasing volumes means reducing the incidence of constant costs to benefit company profitability. In this way, exploiting production capacity becomes the main lever to improve company profitability.

Indeed, Giannessi analyzes the weaknesses of Clark's thinking concerning the uncertainties related to the behavior of costs and the uncertainties regarding the behavior of revenues. For both economic components (costs and revenues), the uncertainties can be:

- Uncertainties of "entity" regarding determining the measure of the economic component.

- "Distribution" uncertainties regarding allocating the economical components to the "groups" or accounting aggregates with them.
- "imputation" uncertainties concerning the impossibility of applying uniform criteria in the reference of "groups" or accounting aggregates to unit and production class costs.

The uncertainties described above determine the creation of an area of evanescence within which it is not possible to establish to what extent an increase in production can benefit the economy of the company or damage it:

> This *area also prevents establishing when that by reducing the offer price, we simply give up the profit margin we hoped for, when we start to no longer cover the constant cost components and when, finally, the non-coverage of variable cost components begins.* (Giannessi, 1982: 45)[2]

In this context, Kreislauf is inserted: if a company intends to strive for its technical purpose by exploiting the maximum production capacity, how can it evaluate the convenience or non-profitability deriving from the possible increase in activity volumes?

To perform this assessment, it is necessary to determine company costs accurately and compare them with the corresponding price formations. To assess company costs accurately, it is essential to know the measure of constant costs and their impact on unit and production costs. The volume of activity is necessary to understand the incidence of constant costs. The volume of activity is, however, linked to prices. As a result of the uncertainties mentioned above, the Kresilauf is formed:

> Without *knowing the production volume, it is impossible to determine the ratio of incidence of constant cost components to unit and production class costs. Without knowing this relationship, it is impossible to speak of*

[2] Translated from Italian Language: "tale zona impedisce anche di stabilire quand'è che riducendo il prezzo d'offerta si rinuncia semplicemente al margine di profitto sperato, quando si comincia a non coprire più i componenti di costo a carattere costante e quando, infine, ha inizio la mancata copertura dei componenti di costo a carattere variabile" (Giannessi, 1982: 45).

> *exact production costs or, at least, sufficiently exact to be used to formulate expediency judgments.* (Giannessi, 1982: 47)[3]

Costs tend to adapt to prices even if their size is closely related to the volume of activity. The volume of activity also depends on the company's sales policies, linked to the recognition of costs. Prices tend to adjust to costs, but costs depend on the activity volume, which, in turn, is linked to price levels. The dynamics described above are inserted into a loop whose solution appears complex. However, searching for the solution is essential to allow companies to leave the evanescence area resulting from the Kreislauf, created in the relationship between costs, prices, and revenues.

The solution identified by Giannessi does not have an objective nature, is subjective, and is based on the logic that the company must consider in all its decision-making processes. The solution is based on an evaluation process, which cannot be exhausted by applying mathematical formulas but must consider all the elements that can enter direct and indirect relation with the judgment of convenience. These elements may be internal to the company but may also be external to the company:

> *The theory of use "at any cost" of the plant's production capacity must be reviewed and replaced with the theory that requires the evaluation of all internal circumstances and external, economic and non-economic, particular and general, which influence the formulation of judgments of convenience.* (Giannessi, 1982: 61)[4]

Giannessi's observations on the relationship between volumes, costs, prices, and revenues are very relevant today, given the complexity of the competitive dynamics.

[3] Translated from Italian Language: "Senza conoscere il volume della produzione è impossibile determinare il rapporto di incidenza dei componenti di costo a carattere costante sui costi unitari e di classe di produzione. Senza conoscere questo rapporto è impossibile parlare di costi di produzione esatti o, almeno, sufficientemente esatti da essere utilizzati nella formulazione di giudizi di convenienza" (Giannessi, 1982: 47).

[4] Translated from Italian Language: "La teoria dell'utilizzazione 'ad ogni costo' della capacità produttiva degli impianti deve essere riveduta e sostituita con la teoria che impone la valutazione di tutte le circostanze, interne ed esterne, economiche e non economiche, particolari e generali, che influenzano la formulazione dei giudizi di convenienza" (Giannessi, 1982: 61).

The Risk of Being Inefficient

Technical efficiency has an impact on company profitability. Technical efficiency is linked to the degree of exploitation of the maximum productive capacity and the behavior of company fixed costs. Greater technical efficiency within the limits of total production capacity positively impacts corporate profitability by reducing the incidence of fixed costs.

The issue of technical efficiency is vital for all companies. But it is most felt in companies that produce services because they cannot stock the output. They cannot store the production because, in services, company output is intangible.

From a management perspective, the possibility to stock the output allows the transfer over time and space of inputs waiting to be used in the production process and outputs (products) waiting to be traded on the market. This possibility can be reached thanks to the warehouse. Although the warehouse may generate costs, it fulfills a fundamental role for the entire company system management. The lack of warehouses in service companies has led some companies to create a virtual warehouse to make the management of technical inefficiencies more flexible. In airlines, for instance, the virtual warehouse is called overbooking. So, when does a company risk being inefficient?

A company risk being inefficient whenever the production volumes in each time interval do not reach the maximum productive capacity. The reasons for the non-reach of the maximum production capacity in each time interval can be different:

- Reasons of a technical nature attributable to the non-opportunity of exploiting the potential to the maximum.
- Economic reasons, such as a temporary increase in the prices of raw materials or production costs, caused, for example, by increased energy costs for contingent reasons such as a war conflict.
- Reasons internal to the company include the desire to invest in enhancing or making production more efficient or the need to carry out maintenance that temporarily does not allow maximum productivity use.
- Reasons external to the company related to a specific market, political, social, or other contingencies.

The state of technical inefficiency is physiological in a company's life cycle, especially in specific periods, and need not necessarily cause concern. Concern must be aroused when inefficiency is or becomes "pathological," i.e., deriving from organizational problems within the company or unfavorable market conditions; it does not assume a temporary nature but persists over the years, becoming a real risk for business continuity.

For these reasons, the company must adopt a system for constant monitoring of its technical inefficiency to understand when it exceeds the physiological level and assumes a pathological nature.

A state of uncontrolled technical inefficiency not only causes costs to be borne by the company that damages company profitability and compromise the immune system but also poses a real risk to business continuity.

The Double Cost of Technical Inefficiency

To understand how much technical inefficiency costs the company and the impact it produces on the company's immune system, refer to a service company and an airline company. Indeed, the problem remains the same in economic terms for a manufacturing company. Still, as will be better seen later, the issue is more felt by companies that produce services since they cannot—as already stated—store their outputs.

Within the tourism industry, recent decades have been characterized by the birth and development of the low-cost phenomenon in air transport due to deregulation in the sector. The low-cost phenomenon has contributed significantly to recent changes in tourism, particularly in the behavior of tourist consumers, with a cultural and behavioral revolution. These revolutions have made air transport more accessible, driving a rise in passenger traffic and mobility and "reducing the distances" between different countries. Transportation times are shorter by air, and travel frequency has increased due to pricing policies resulting from deregulation and increased competition within the market.

From an economic point of view, those who travel low-cost cannot consider traveling for free, or the airline aims to engage in corporate philanthropy. On a low-cost flight, the average ticket cost—calculated by summing the price paid by all passengers and dividing by the total number of passengers—is in line with the average ticket cost on a non-low-cost flight.

Making:

ni = passenger i
Pi = the price paid by the passenger ni

Then:

$$\text{Average ticket revenue (ATR)} = \Sigma Pi/\Sigma ni$$

where:

ΣPi is the total revenue from ticket sales to passengers
Σni is the number of passengers on board the aircraft.

In a low-cost flight, the airline sustains two types of costs: variable costs and fixed costs. Variable costs vary with the number of passengers, such as fuel consumption or aircraft cleaning costs. Conversely, fixed costs do not change as the number of passengers varies; they include the cost of onboard personnel, aircraft amortization, and maintenance costs.

Fixed costs are, therefore, stable whether the plane travels empty or full. The airline seeks to fill the aircraft to maximize production capacity and achieve maximum technical efficiency.

Let's have an aircraft with 100 seats in a class that flies daily from Florence to Paris. The airline knows that the aircraft's occupancy rate, i.e., the load factor, averages 65%, meaning that the flight carries an average of 65 paying passengers.

The 35 empty seats represent a cost for the company in the form of technical inefficiency: an aircraft that can accommodate 100 passengers only carries an average of 65.

The occupancy rate represents the exploitation rate of the aircraft's maximum production capacity and, therefore, the technical efficiency rate. This percentage is represented by the ratio between tickets sold (Ts) and available tickets (Ta):

$$\text{Load factor} = Ts/Ta$$

The non-occupancy rate measures the aircraft's technical inefficiency, calculated from the difference between the maximum technical efficiency (reached at 1) and the load factor:

$$\text{Technical Inefficiency } = 1 - \text{ Load Factor}$$

$$\text{Technical Inefficiency } = 1 - (Ts/Ta)$$

From an economic perspective, this inefficiency translates into a cost borne by the airline that is both twofold and "subtle."

The cost of technical inefficiency is twofold because it is expressed in two closely related components:

$$\text{Cost of Technical Inefficiency (CTIn) } = \alpha + \beta$$

Component α represents the missed revenues, while component β represents the higher incidence of fixed costs. The sum of the two components ($\alpha + \beta$ represents the double cost of technical inefficiency.

Missed revenues represent the cost of failing to sell all 100 tickets. The cost to the airline of the 35 unsold tickets is calculated as the product of the number of unsold seats and the price of those seats:

$$\alpha = \Sigma bi \times pi$$

where bi represents an unsold ticket, and the price of each ticket is the same.

The higher incidence of fixed costs is linked to those costs' distribution over the number of seats sold. The fixed costs (Ω) are stable compared to the number of passengers purchasing air tickets. Ω is spread over the number of seats inside the aircraft. The minimum incidence of fixed costs in our example is, therefore, represented by:

$$\text{Incidence Fixed Costs min } = \Omega/100$$

The minimum incidence of fixed costs expresses the aircraft's economic efficiency because of its technical efficiency. The maximum fixed cost incidence is reached when the airline has not sold tickets. In the latter case, the airline will probably cancel the flight and move the passenger to another.

If the airline sells 65 tickets, the incidence of fixed costs increases, as determined by the following ratio:

$$\text{Incidence Fixed Costs 65} = \Omega/65$$

where:

$$\text{Incidence Fixed Costs 65} > \text{Incidence Fixed Costs min}$$

as

$$\Omega/65 > \Omega/100$$

The Economic Impact of Technical Inefficiency on the Immune System

Technical inefficiency always determines a double cost for the company. It is also an expense that is not visible in the P&L. This makes it very dangerous, especially in cases of lack of particular attention from management.

The so-called "cannibalization" effect is the first economic impact of technical inefficiency. The cost that the technical inefficiency determines for the company harms its profitability by reducing it and cannibalizing the margins on the outputs sold. In the example of the plane, the airline has sold 65 tickets at specific prices, imagining it has a certain margin on the ticket sold. Indeed, ex-post margins will be lower precisely because of technical inefficiency and, therefore, the greater incidence of fixed costs. The higher incidence of fixed costs determines a cannibalization effect on the margins expected from actual sales for the company. The higher incidence of fixed costs consumes the margin on tickets sold, reducing overall company profitability.

For this reason, airlines prefer potentially selling all tickets, even at a lower price, rather than having empty seats. The cost of a vacant seat on the aircraft is higher than that of selling the same seat at a lower price.

Suppose the airline sells five tickets that statistically remain unsold at a low-cost price (LCPrice) commensurate with variable costs and a small contribution to fixed costs. In that case, it obtains a double advantage from (1) the increase in revenues—albeit almost totally absorbed by the increase in variable costs and (2) the reduced incidence of fixed costs. The distribution of the same amount reduces the incidence of fixed costs on a 65 + 5 basis, i.e., 70 tickets sold compared to the distribution of 65 tickets.

From here, it is easy to understand that selling at lower prices and low-cost policies represent:

- A management lever to increase technical efficiency and, thereby, corporate profitability.
- A marketing lever attracts many potential customers to seek the lowest-priced ticket despite only five (in the example) being available for the flight. The other passengers will pay a standard fare for their ticket.

The double cost of technical inefficiency is "subtle" because the two components α and β do not appear in the airline's profit and loss statement or within a specific economic report of a single flight. The cost items do not include lost revenue or the greater incidence of fixed costs. However, these components are present and influence economic efficiency and the company's profitability. Hence managers must pay close attention to the technical dynamics that characterize the business and the exploitation degree of maximum production capacity.

Technical efficiency is a condition for economic efficiency. Company profitability is closely linked to the exploitation of maximum production capacity. Otherwise, the company should practice very high pricing policies concerning production costs: this happens in some specific sectors but cannot be the rule.

The cannibalization of corporate profitability also harms the immune system. Lower profitability corresponds to a lower ability of the company to carry out self-financing policies. Lower self-financing results in a lower contribution in economic terms to strengthening the company's immune defenses. As highlighted, this should be fine if the technical inefficiency is physiological and temporary. It must arouse attention and concern if it is "pathological" and long-lasting.

The Warehouse Is a Tool to Mitigate the Risk of Technical Inefficiency

Faced with the risk deriving from technical inefficiency and the economic effects that it produces, companies can mitigate the economic effects through an optimal warehouse policy. The warehouse represents the most accessible tool for all companies to reduce the economic damage from technical inefficiency. Unfortunately, the warehouse is not accessible to all companies: it is in the manufacturing and not the services sectors, where the output is intangible.

For a manufacturing company, a warehouse is necessary to guarantee continuity in the transformation process and the product sales process; similarly, for a commercial company, a warehouse is required to ensure the procurement, marketing, and (in some instances) preservation of goods. By contrast, for a service company—for example, a consulting firm or airline business—the intangible nature of the output means it cannot be stored. However, though service companies may not require a warehouse for their output, their productive factors may need to be warehoused.

Typologies of outputs and inputs concern some characteristics the products and productive factors must require storing. The first is tangibility, understood as the materiality of the output or input, though it is sometimes possible to create a warehouse even for non-tangible (non-material) resources. In this last regard, consider a "time bank": a system that stores intangible resources such as working hours. In addition to tangibility, the outputs, and inputs must be conservable and stored together with the equipment and systems the warehouse must be equipped with. This conservation aims to ensure the maintenance of the inputs and/or outputs and their technical characteristics.

Procurement policies mainly concern the choice of suppliers, the location of suppliers, purchase quantities, purchase methods, and payment methods. If a company's supplier is geographically distant and the transport times are long, or if the price of inputs is highly variable on the market, or to obtain more significant discounts, a company can buy several inputs exceeding its actual need from the programming of the production cycle and store the excess for future use.

Sales policies mainly concern customer identification, customer localization, production quantities, sales methods, and payment methods.

In the face of a particular market or internal conditions, a company may produce a higher quantity of output than the actual demand expressed by the market, storing the residual part for future sale. For procurement and sales policies, the company must consider the cost of money and its degree of debt: both elements define the company's financial structure.

From a management perspective, the warehouse is considered controversial. In some respects, the presence of a warehouse is considered necessary, functional, and positive since it supports the company's management and production processes; in other respects, the presence of even a necessary warehouse is judged negatively and limited to the minimum required to use. This last direction is driven by considerations of the cost of the warehouse and the themes of "just-in-time" and, more recently, lean enterprise explored in various studies.

From a managerial perspective, the importance of the warehouse extends beyond the storage function: it allows the transfer over time and space of inputs waiting to be used in the production process (in the economic sense) and outputs (products) waiting to be traded on the market.

Although this function generates a cost, it fulfills a fundamental role for the entire company system management.

The transfer function in time and/or space is understood if the warehouse is analyzed as an element of the company system, considering its link to its production capacity.

Indeed, the warehouse's importance and managerial utility are perceived when analyzing companies that typically do not have stock, such as service companies or companies operating in specific sectors. From a managerial perspective, if connected to production capacity, the warehouse represents a "shock absorber" of technical inefficiencies in the production processes, procurement, and sales policies. The presence of a warehouse allows the company to transfer inefficiency over time:

- The company can buy more inputs (production factors) than are required by the production plan to take advantage of procurement policies, discounts available from suppliers, or fluctuations in price and/or exchange rates; the quantity not absorbed by the production process is moved forward over time through storage in the warehouse.
- The company may produce more output than required by sales plans to benefit from internal and/or market conditions, transferring the quantity not absorbed by the market through storage in the warehouse.

The transfer function served by the warehouse does not eliminate inefficiencies but allows their effects to be mitigated in economic terms. In some cases, the costs of managing the warehouse can be totally or partially absorbed by the advantages that have guided the company in its policies on supply, production process planning, and sales. The link between the warehouse and the company's production capacity requires the company to develop a measurement system that combines technical and physical measurements with economic-financial measurements.

Overbooking as a Tool to Mitigate the Negative Economic Impact of Technical Inefficiency

Overbooking is an example of a "virtual warehouse" that is very common in the tourism sector but also very effective in other sectors where the output is not tangible (Imai et al., 2023). Overbooking, like the warehouse, is a tool whose use can mitigate the adverse effects of technical inefficiency on company profitability and, therefore, the immune system.

From a business economics perspective, overbooking is the tourism company's virtual warehouse. As in an authentic warehouse, the company must establish the optimal level of stock: for the virtual warehouse, this translates into quantifying the output units not corresponding to the actual production capacity made available on the market.

The term overbooking highlights the will of the tourism company to go beyond its practical limits of production capacity in its booking/order/purchase request policies:

> *Overbooking occurs whenever a seller with constrained capacity sells more unit than he has available. ... The reason that seller engaged in such a seemingly nefarious practice is to product themselves against unanticipated no-shows and cancellation.* (Phillips, 2005: 207)

As Phillips authoritatively asserts, overbooking policies characterize companies with limited production capacity that sell or make available units of output beyond those available, pursuing the goal of protecting the company from possible cancelations of reservations/orders and so-called no-shows. Overbooking policies represent a lever for the company to maximize its profitability in response to certain potential behaviors by customers and to guarantee its technical efficiency.

It is a virtual warehouse because—analogously to what happens in an authentic warehouse—the company uses overbooking to transfer over time its production inefficiencies, which may be characterized by stasis in the production process as demand contracts or a peak in demand caused by an expansion of the demand function itself.

Unlike companies with a physical warehouse for stocking materials and finished products, companies with no warehouse are more oriented to consistently exploiting their total production capacity. By contrast, for companies with warehouses, control over them and production flows can be carried out within a given time interval.

In companies without inventories, the immediate economic manifestation of the cost, deriving from inefficiency in allocating production capacity, justifies the strong orientation toward always maximizing production capacity exploitation. By contrast, companies with warehouses can put in stock the output units produced and not sold.

This fact is noted for service companies such as airlines, theaters, hospitals, or hotels because the quantity produced equals the amount of output sold.

In this direction, and to overcome the lack of stock, overbooking policies represent a preventive response by the company to ensure greater exploitation of its production capacity.

By selling more output units than those available through the production process, the company minimizes the risk of under-utilizing its production capacity due to demand contraction or certain behaviors, such as customer cancelations.

With overbooking, the company realizes a virtual warehouse of output units placed on the market.

As for an authentic warehouse, the company must determine the optimal level of outputs not available to be placed on the market, recognizing that the virtual warehouse poses risks related to forecasting the optimal level of virtual stock.

The company's policy of overbooking has, from a management perspective, economic and legal consequences. Economically, overbooking intends to limit—almost as a form of insurance within the company—the risk deriving from customer behavior, which can damage the company in terms of lost revenue and/or opportunity costs. The risk limitation occurs with the transfer of the same, in whole or part, to the customer, who may be required to pay the penalty or part of the price even if they do not use the output.

The penalty may also vary depending on the time factor. Where the company establishes a penalty to customer Þ, it can be:

$$0 \leq \text{Þ} \leq P$$

where P is the price of the output.

A penalty equal to zero or a meager amount does not absolve the function of discouraging client behaviors potentially harmful to the company. On the other hand, a penalty equal to the price of the output discourages the exercise of the option. Regarding this last point, consider companies that make the customer pay the price entirely in advance, such as low-cost airlines. In these situations, the company transfers the risk to the customer by guaranteeing the advance price payment and not allowing the customer to change the output. In these situations, where the company does not run any risk in economic terms, it may not be helpful to resort to overbooking, thus removing the need for a virtual warehouse. If the economic risk is zero, this does not exclude the non-achievement of the company's total production capacity, which has no economic consequences for the company's efficiency and profitability.

In legal terms, the consequences of overbooking include the risk of breaching contracts with customers: this occurs whenever those who have booked/ordered/requested the output units made available on the market complete the purchase. According to regulations that protect consumers, a breach of contract results in financial penalties for the company: for instance, the company must compensate affected customers for any (actionable) inconvenience caused.

References

Amaduzzi, A. (1948). *Ragioneria Generale*. Casa Editrice Dott. Luigi Macrì.

Bertini, U. (1990). *Il sistema d'azienda*. Giappichelli.

Capocchi, A. (2019). *Economic value and revenue management systems*. Palgrave Macmillan.

Clark, J. M. (1923). *Studies in the economics of overhead costs*. University Press Chicago.

East, T. (2022). Operational risk management. In *Routledge handbook of risk management and the law* (pp. 5–18). Routledge.

Giannessi, E. (1970). *Appunti di economia aziendale*. G. Pellegrini.

Giannessi, E. (1982). *Il "Kreislauf" tra costi e prezzi*. Giuffré.

Imai, M., Sato, T., & Shiina, T. (2023). Revenue management problem in the aviation industry with optimal seat allocation model. *International Journal of Service and Knowledge Management, International Institute of Applied Informatics, 7*(1), https://doi.org/10.52731/ijskm.v7.i1.716

Jevons, W. S. (1871). *The theory of political economy*. Sentry Press.

Menger, C. (1976). *Principles of political economy*. Institute for Humane Studies.

Nimmy, S. F., Hussain, O. K., Chakrabortty, R. K., Hussain, F. K., & Saberi, M. (2022). Explainability in supply chain operational risk management: A systematic literature review. *Knowledge-Based Systems, 235*. https://doi.org/10.1016/j.knosys.2021.107587

Phillips, R. L. (2005). *Pricing and revenue optimization*. Stanford University Press.

Schmalenbach, E. (1956). *Kostenrechnung und Preispolitik*. Westdeutscher Verlag.

Sneddon, J. (2022). Pandemic risk management; protecting people while ensuring business continuity. *Process Safety Progress, 41*(1), 8–13. https://doi.org/10.1002/prs.12302

Walras, L. (1874). *Elements of pure political economy*. Imprimerie L. Corbaz & C. Editeurs.

PART III

Integration, Classification and Risk Management Activities

CHAPTER 8

The Internal Control Risk Management System (ICRMS)

In the management of vulnerability and in policies to strengthen the company's immune system, the risk attitude assumes importance. Risk attitude is the propensity of a company, organization, or socio-economic system to take on risk. The risk attitude translates into the behaviors accepted in the face of risk and decision-making processes. Indeed, the risk attitude dimension does not pertain to the company, organization, or socio-economic system as such but belongs to the individuals who make up the company, organization, and socio-economic system with roles of responsibility and decision-making. Over the years, there have been numerous studies that, from different disciplinary perspectives, have studied the determinants of risk attitude. In this short chapter we want to highlight the main concepts that have marked the dynamics of the studies conducted at an international level to identify today the relationship between the risk attitude and the dimension of vulnerability. This relationship is essential in constructing the integrated risk management and control system.

Risk Perception

Risk perception may be defined as a cognitive process involved in various daily activities which guides people's behavior when faced with decisions involving potential risks. Risk perception involves different dimensions,

A. Capocchi, *Vulnerability and the Corporate Immune System*, https://doi.org/10.1007/978-3-031-30254-1_8

such as both immediate and future consequences and their implications on a rational and objective level and an emotional and subjective level. There is often a discrepancy between the subjective perception of risk and the objective assessment of the risk itself. Sometimes people fear activities that aren't dangerous and don't fear activities that could have very dramatic consequences. Many recent studies have dealt with distinguishing between actual risk and perceived risk. Sometimes real risks are perceived as less than residual risks. This is also not only for socio-political reasons.

The processes of perception and assessment of reality guide and support the decisions of the individual and the community. What falls under our observation are data that do not have a univocal meaning but require a mental work of contextualization and attribution of meaning, which then goes to guide the decision-making and, therefore, the intervention. The perceptual process consists of five phases which are:

- Attention: the data are filtered and selected, only sometimes at a conscious level, to establish the elements that will be accepted for subsequent processing. The intensity, frequency, contrast, novelty, and the subject's needs, beliefs, interests, and expectations influence attention.
- Organization: the information collected is merged and traced back to higher-level abstract concepts, organized into categories and schemes, i.e., cognitive structures.
- Interpretation: the subject who perceives, attributes meaning to the information collected, identifying its causes, foundations, and possible implications. This involves a constant redefinition and rebalancing of one's cognitive assets.
- Recall: much of the selected, organized, and interpreted information is not used immediately but stored in the memory to be recalled having informative and experiential cores about past events.
- Judgment: the processing of information translates into the specific evaluation of an object, an event, a person, or a situation. This evaluation will influence the subject's subsequent perceptions, decisions, and behavior.

Risk perception is personal: we decide to face or avoid the situation subjectively. Our daily activities are based on our perception of risk, resulting from its conscious (or unconscious) evaluation. The perceptive process of risk is strongly influenced by the emotions generated when we discover and learn about a new danger and what possible damage it can cause us.

Individual perception of risk:

- Previous habits and experiences influence it: the individual tends to underestimate the risks associated with work habits, the chances that arise daily, and the low probability.
- It is based on personal experience or that of others.
- It varies the collective acceptability of the risk, which changes over time in places, work groups, and cultures and is related to personal and cultural values, age, and gender.

This perception depends on the following:

- The knowledge of the dangers, thus the feeling of immunity from those familiar with a given situation.
- The immediacy of the damage.
- The freedom to take risks.
- The concentration of the damage over time.
- The harmfulness of the dangers present and their frequency.
- Personal exposure.
- The subjective cost/benefit assessment: if a particular behavior brings another benefit, the risk associated with it will be perceived to a lesser extent.

Risk appetite:

- Decreases if the events are deemed uncontrollable by the subject and dependent on forces or external events.
- It grows if the issue considers the events controllable and depends on external forces.

Risk perceptions can be intuitive and based on how information about the source of risk is communicated, psychological mechanisms for processing uncertainty, and prior experience of danger. Following Ortwin Renn (2004: 104), this thought process results in perceived risk: a collection of notions from which people form their sources of risk relating to the information and their basic common sense.

Risk perception research has identified several perceptions models used to perceive and assess risk:

- Risk is a fatal threat.
- Risk is fate.
- Risk is a test of strength.
- Risk is a game of chance.
- Risk is an early warning indicator.

The perception of risk has always been aimed at rationalizing the risk itself to be able to identify suitable tools to manage it over time.

Risk, Uncertainty, and Ambiguity

Kahneman (2003) and Richard Thaler (2018), Nobel Prize for economics in 2002 and 2017, respectively, observed how individuals in the presence of conditions of uncertainty tend to show an aversion to the risk of loss (Fasone & Puglisi, 2019). Murmann and Sardana (2012) argue that successful entrepreneurs can adapt their decision-making styles by assessing their expertise and ambiguity level in a particular decision-making context. Successful entrepreneurs can change the decision-making process to reduce risk. In their article, they describe the difference between risk and uncertainty.

> *(…) risk is a situation in which all possible outcomes are known, and precise probabilities for each outcome are available to guide decision making (Runde 1998). (…) Uncertainty, by contrast, is a situation where all possible outcomes are known but the probabilities associated with particular outcomes cannot be determined precisely (Runde, 1998). While we follow economists in the use of the term uncertainty, we attach a different meaning to the term 'risk' and employ the term 'ambiguity' to signify a source of ignorance that is not captured in how economists typically use the term 'uncertainty.'* (Murmann & Sardana, 2012: 193)

Ambiguity, following Frisch and Baron (1988), can be defined as "*the subjective experience of missing information relevant to a prediction*" (Frisch & Baron, 1988: 152).

Traditionally, in the management sciences, as Fasone and Puglisi (2019) highlight, the risk is represented following the approach of Dowling (1986):

$$\text{Perceived risk} = \text{Uncertainty} * \text{Adverse consequences}$$

and

$$\text{Perceived overall risk} = \text{Sum of loss probabilities} * \text{Importance of loss.}$$

The concept of uncertainty is related to how Knight expresses (1921) the idea of risk:

> *uncertainty is the possibility of alternative outcome whose probabilities are not capable of measurement. When probabilities are known, adverse outcomes may be insured against. Uncertainty is handled by judgment, an unequally distributed ability.* (Knight, 1921)

Sitkin and Pablo (1992) observed how scholars, over the years, tried to understand which elements may affect individuals' decision-making behavior in risky contexts. For this reason, the issue of risk behavior was introduced as "*the degree of risk associated with the decisions made.*" (Sitkin & Pablo, 1992: 11). In this theoretical framework, they analyzed the different factors that may affect individual risk behavior: (i) characteristics of the individual decision maker; (ii) characteristics of the organizational context; (iii) characteristics of the problem itself.

Following the most dominant literature position, they discussed nine determinants of the three factors affecting risk behavior, as shown below in Fig. 8.1.

Moving from the theoretical framework represented in Fig. 8.1, they proposed an innovative and alternative model of the determinants of risk behavior. In their alternative model, as described in Fig. 8.2, the nine determinants operate indirectly on the risk behavior through the mediating mechanisms of risk propensity and perception.

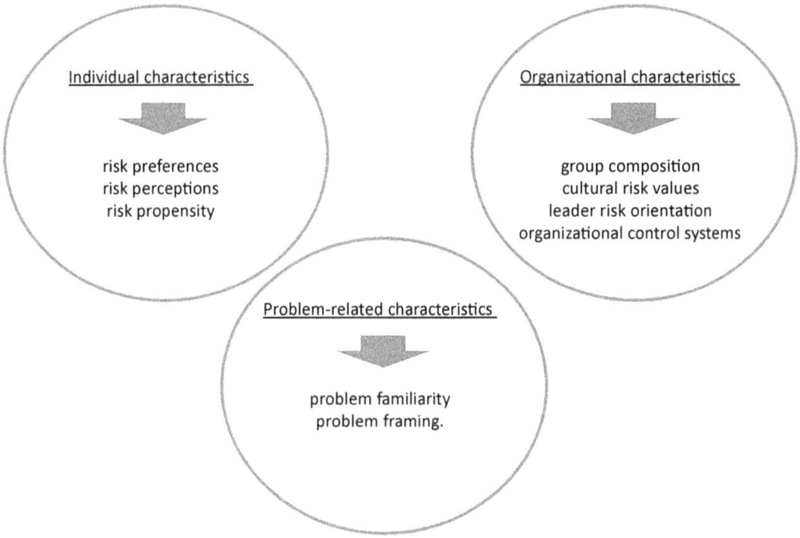

Fig. 8.1 Determinants affecting risk behavior in dominant literature position

At the end of their study, they identify the possible guidelines for future research. Among them, they highlight the vital role of the organizational context. The control systems are inserted within the organizational context. Reference to control systems assumes importance for processing data and information, which are then placed at the basis of decision-making processes.

From Expected Utility to New Models with Descriptive Approaches

The issue of risk attitude has traditionally been linked to the utility function and the need for everyone to maximize it through discretion in decision-making processes. Most classical studies are based on the theory of expected utility formulated by Von Neumann and Morgenstern (1947). The maximization of expected utility guides the individual's choices, also orienting him in the face of risk.

Each decision has a percentage of risk that everyone perceives differently, precisely based on their attitude toward risk. In this approach, risk

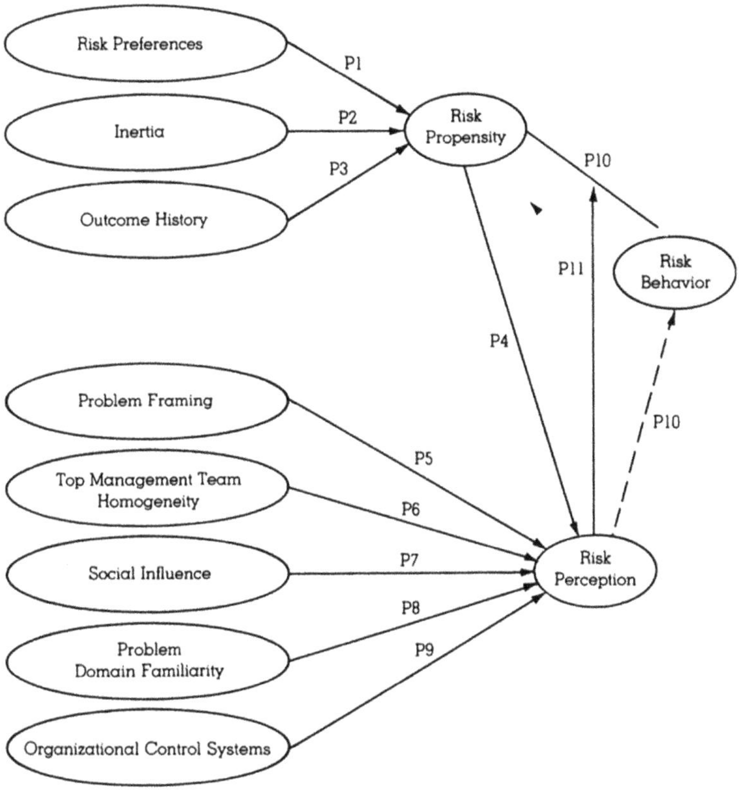

Fig. 8.2 Reconceptualized model of the determinants of risk behavior (Sitkin & Pablo, 1992: 15)

attitude is represented through the derived utility function: a concave utility function expresses risk aversion, while a convex utility function expresses the individual's pursuit of risk.

The theory of expected utility, like a mathematical model, represents an abstraction and simplification of reality and, as such, could be more effective for a complete understanding of the choices of individuals.

Over the years, scholars have tried to build new models with a descriptive approach capable of more precisely anticipating and predicting individuals' preferences.

Kahneman and Tversky (1979) developed the "Prospect Theory." In this approach, three interrelated effects are considered: the certainty effect, the isolation effect, and the context effect.

The certainty effect induces individuals to perceive the specific results as more valuable and instead to underestimate the probable consequences.

The certainty effect fuels risk aversion in contexts characterized by choices between bets with possible returns and certain returns.

The same individuals, having to choose between lotteries in which neither option is sure, are more risk-takers. In situations involving possible losses and certain losses, on the other hand, the choices of individuals tend to be opposite. Kahnemann and Tversky (1979) describe the behavior of individuals through the new "value function" in which the decision maker, instead of weighing the outcomes through probability, does so through the weight each outcome has according to the individual's evaluation.

A further element is represented by the so-called "isolation effect," due to the propensity of individuals to isolate consecutive probabilities instead of treating them. In this way, inconsistent preferences tend to be produced when the same choice is presented in different forms. Lastly, the context effect (called framing), relating to the situation in which the individual finds himself making a choice, also significantly influences the decision. How the problem is formulated affects how the subject perceives the status quo and therefore evaluates the outcomes of his actions.

In 1982 Dyer and Sarin introduced a different definition of risk preference through the concept of risk attitude. With this concept they wanted to separate the marginal value for results from the attitude toward uncertainty. In this way Dyer and Sarin (1982) hypothesized that differences in risk attitudes in terms of expected utility might result from differences in marginal value.

> *The concept of relative risk attitude has several important implications. First, it provides a better description of an individual's attitude to ward risk. Second, it provides a better way to combine preferences of various experts in the context of multicriteria decision making. Finally, it provides a better insight into the implications of some commonly employed preference aggregation rules in group decision making.* (Dyer & Sarin, 1982: 1)

Without reviewing the studies that have characterized the debate on risk attitude from different disciplinary perspectives, here we want to highlight the main factors that characterize it (Andreoni et al., 2019; Apicella et al., 2008; Bonsang & Dohmen, 2015; Booth & Nolen, 2012; Charness & Gneezy, 2012; Cohen & Liran, 2007; Dohmen et al., 2018).

Risk Aversion

Risk aversion is a characteristic that most individuals possess and can dynamically vary in intensity. The dynamism of risk aversion depends on several factors, including temporal and spatial aspects.

Risk aversion translates into the individual's tendency to opt for the safer alternative, i.e., associated with a lower variance than the more uncertain one, even when the latter has a higher expected value. Following this approach, faced with two options having the same expected value, most people will choose the one with lower volatility. Risk aversion can be reduced by increasing the mathematical ability of individuals.

Loss Aversion

Many studies show that individuals fear losses more than they appreciate gains. These studies highlight an asymmetry between the strength of positive and negative expectations and explain this difference with the evolutionary history since the organisms that most fear threats are more likely to survive than the others.

Loss aversion is based on individuals wanting to avoid a specific loss, preferring the option even when the expected value is less than the failures. From this, individuals become risk-takers when all possibilities are perceived as unfavorable.

Recent studies examining the effect of losses in decision-making processes have shown the absence of loss aversion. This has been explained considering that loss aversion may not manifest itself when losses are minimal or that simply because of the concept of "loss attention" (Yechiama & Hochmanb, 2013), being faced with possible losses causes the recourse to a higher-than-average amount of attention. Greater attention in analyzing the options available to choose from seems to cause an increase in risk appetite.

Like risk aversion, loss aversion can be reduced by increasing individuals' mathematical ability.

The Willingness to Risk

Risk management within organizations is closely linked to the concept of risk attitude. Risk attitude is the organization's approach to assessing, pursuing, retaining, or avoiding risk (Hopkin, 2018). A range of possible attitudes can be adopted toward the same situation, resulting in differing behaviors, which lead to both intended and unintended consequences.

As organizations are made up of people, the issue of risk attitude is closely linked to the risk propensity of the managers who lead and govern the organization itself. Indeed, the manifestation of the risk attitude takes place through managerial behavior. Managerial behaviors, in turn, are closely linked to the decisions that management can adopt. The link between risk attitude, managerial behavior, and managerial decision is closely related to the degree of risk perception and the situation toward which the decision and the consequent behavior are directed.

As represented in Fig. 8.3, Risk Attitude is connected to the subjective element of the company management, which directs the company's behaviors and decisions. The personal element of management expresses its willingness to take risks, influencing both behavior and decisions. The willingness to risk filters and translates the risk attitude into managerial behaviors. At the end of the managerial choices comes the organization's risk management, which can influence and change the risk attitude over time. This is in consideration of the fact that the risk attitude is dynamic and subject to constant change.

Risk attitude has been studied extensively in academic and professional settings, and there is a sizable and growing body of knowledge and evidence in this area. Many studies have focused on individuals' gambling behavior and financial investments. The numerous studies conducted over the years have made it possible to understand how the same situation can give rise to different behaviors based on the perception of risk and willingness to risk.

The studies also show how the degree or intensity of uncertainty can change (or through a modified perception), changing the reaction force in the face of risk. In this direction, the organization's external and/or internal variables can constantly influence managerial decisions and behaviors.

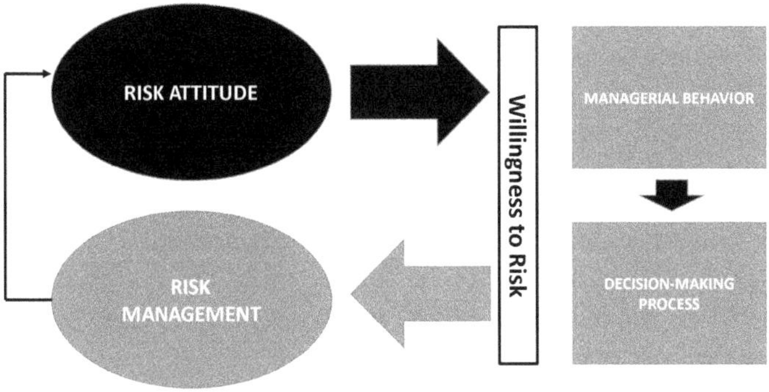

Fig. 8.3 Risk attitude and willingness to risk

The Internal Control and Risk Management System—ICRMS

Companies have many tools at their disposal to deal with risks. Some tools are external to the company; others are internal to it. The set of tools the company can use to manage its risks appropriately flows into the internal control system. The internal control system: more specifically, many companies promptly identify the Internal Control and Risk Management System (ICRMS).

The Internal Control and Risk Management System (ICRMS) is a set of rules, procedures, and organizational structures that allow the identification, measurement, management, and monitoring of the leading company risks, even at a corporate level, if present.

In particular, the ICRMS contributes to ensuring the efficiency and effectiveness of company processes, the reliability of financial information, compliance with laws and regulations, and the company's statute and internal procedures (Vu & Nga, 2022). The ICRMS, therefore, plays a central role in the corporate organization, contributing to the adoption of informed decisions consistent with the propensity for risk and the dissemination of correct knowledge of risks, legality, and corporate values.

The ICRMS is adequate if it allows clear and precise indication of the leading corporate risk factors and allows constant monitoring and correct management to ensure:

- safeguarding the company's assets (strategic objectives)
- the efficiency and effectiveness of company processes (operating goals)
- the reliability of the information provided to the corporate bodies and the market (reporting objectives)
- compliance with laws and regulations as well as with the articles of the company s statute and internal procedures (goals of compliance)

The ICRMS is implemented based on reference models and national and international best practices.

The implementation of the ICRMS can be articulated in different ways. In general, it is considered preferable that the ICRMS reports to the Board of Directors (BoD), with the role of guidance and assessment of the adequacy to be able to involve the following subjects:

- The Directors in charge of the ICRMS are tasked with establishing and maintaining an effective internal control and risk management system.
- The Control, Risk and Sustainability Committee (CCRS), with the general mission of supporting, with adequate investigative activity, the assessments and decisions of the Board of Directors relating to the internal control and risk management system, as well as those relating to the approval of periodic financial reports.

The ICRMS can be implemented through three levels of control:

- Third-level control is exercised by internal bodies of the company, i.e., Internal Audit, or external bodies, i.e., the Board of Statutory Auditors, the Independent Auditors, and the Supervisory Body (in Italy under Legislative Decree 231/2001).
- Second-level control is entrusted to specialist systems such as the Risk Management function, Compliance, the Manager in charge of preparing the corporate accounting documents, the Data Protection Officer, and Management Control.
- Direct line control, entrusted to the individual, organizational units, or Group companies, is carried out on the processes under their responsibility; this control is charged to the Operational Management/Risk owner and is an integral part of every corporate process.

In the international literature and practice, the reference models accompanying the implementation of the ICRMS are different. Among them deserve to be mentioned:

- The framework CoSO Internal Control 1992. The analysis is focused on activities, processes, and organizational units.
- The framework CoSO ERM 2004. An extension of the analysis dimensions to the entire company (legal entities, divisions, business units, and subsidiaries) is made compared to the previous model.

The growing complexity of business structures and greater expectations regarding the effectiveness of corporate governance led the CoSO to publish an update of the original document in May 2013 (Lacković et al., 2022). The update substantially resumes all the main aspects of the initial framework. The most significant changes compared to the original framework are:

- Greater emphasis on the ability of the Internal Control System to prevent fraud.
- Extensive discussion of corporate governance issues, as supervision by part of the Board of Directors and the committees set up within it, is essential for effective internal control.
- Recognition of the relevant role technology plays in implementing Internal Control System.
- Extension of the category of reporting objectives to non-disclosure finance and internal reporting.

The updated version explains 17 application principles associated with the five constituent elements of internal control. The 17 “principles” illustrate the requirements for an effective Internal Control System.

The three levels of control, together with the various players inside and outside the company involved in the risk assessment processes, are shown below in Fig. 8.4.

Figure 8.4 makes it possible to highlight the complexity of the entire control system, the centrality of internal control, and the need for integrated management of the various levels and of the players who participate in the different assessment processes.

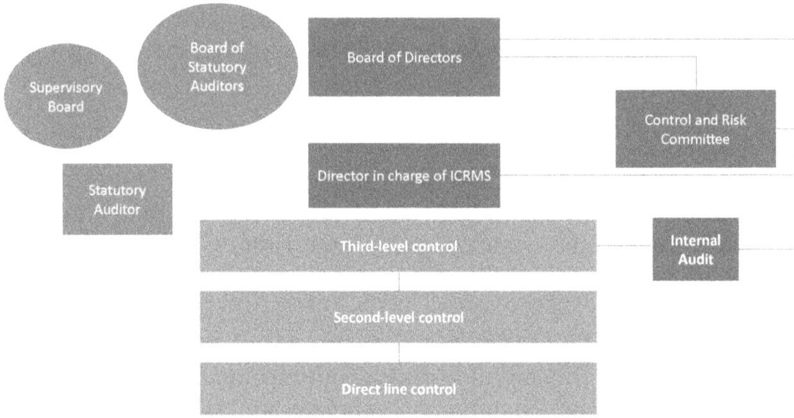

Fig. 8.4 The three level of control

References

Andreoni, J., Di Girolamo, A., List, J. A., Mackevicius, C., & Samek, A. (2019). Risk preferences of children and adolescents in relation to gender, cognitive skills, soft skills, and executive functions. *Journal of Economic Behavior and Organization, 179*, 729–742.

Apicella, C., Dreber, A., Campbell, B., Gray, P. B., Hoffman, M., & Little, A. C. (2008). Testosterone and financial risk preferences. *Evolution and Human Behavior, 29*(6), 384–390.

Bonsang, E., & Dohmen, T. (2015). Risk attitude and cognitive aging. *Journal of Economic Behavior & Organization, 112*(C), 112–126.

Booth, A., & Nolen, P. (2012). Gender differences in risk behaviour: Does nurture matter? *The Economic Journal, 122*, 56–78.

Charness, G., & Gneezy, U. (2012). Strong evidence for gender differences in risk taking. *Journal of Economic Behavior & Organization, 83*(1), 50–58.

Cohen, A., & Liran, E. (2007). Estimating risk preferences from deductible choice. *American Economic Review, 97*(3), 745–788.

Dohmen, T., Falk, A., Huffman, D., & Sunde, W. (2018). On the relationship between cognitive ability and risk preference. *Journal of Economic Perspectives, 32*(2), 115–134.

Dowling, G. R. (1986). Perceived risk: The concept and its measurement. *Psychology & Marketing, 3*(3), 193–210. https://doi.org/10.1002/mar.4220030307

Dyer, J. S., & Sarin, R. K. (1982). Relative risk aversion. *Management Science, 28*(8), 875–886.

Fasone, V., & Puglisi, M. (2019). *Entrepreneur and risk: A systematic literature review with a focus on small business*. Piccola Impresa/Small Business.

Frisch, D., & Baron, J. (1988). Ambiguity and rationality. *Journal of Behavioral Decision Making, 1*(3), 149–157.

Hopkin, P. (2018). *Fundamentals of risk management: Understanding, evaluating and implementing effective risk management*. Kogan Page Publishers.

Kahneman, D. (2003). A psychological perspective on economics. *American Economic Review, 93*(2), 162–168.

Kahneman, D., & Tversky, A. (1979). Prospect theory: An analysis of decision under risk. *Econometrica, 47*(2), 263–291. https://doi.org/10.2307/1914185

Knight, F. H. (1921). Risk, uncertainty and profit. University of Illinois at Urbana-Champaign's Academy for entrepreneurial leadership historical research reference in entrepreneurship. https://ssrn.com/abstract=1496192

Lacković, I. D., & Miloš Sprčić, D. (2022). Three-factor model of enterprise risk management implementation: Exploratory study of non-financial companies. *Risk Management, 24*, 101–122. https://doi.org/10.1057/s41283-021-00086-3

Murmann, J., & Sardana, D. (2012). Successful entrepreneurs minimize risk. *Australian Journal of Management, 38*(1), 191–215. https://doi.org/10.1177/0312896212444114

Renn, O. (2004). Perception of risks. *The Geneva Papers on Risk and Insurance, 29*(1), 102–114.

Sitkin, S. B., & Pablo, A. L. (1992). Reconceptualizing the determinants of risk behavior. *The Academy of Management Review, 17*(1), 9–38.

Thaler, R. H. (2018). From cashews to nudges: The evolution of behavioral economics. *American Economic Review, 108*(6), 1265–1287.

Von Neumann J., & Morgenstern, O. (1947). Theory of games and economic behavior (2nd rev. ed.). Princeton University Press.

Vu, Q., & Nga, N. T. T. (2022). Does the implementation of internal controls promote firm profitability? Evidence from private Vietnamese small- and medium-sized enterprises (SMEs). *Finance Research Letters, 45*. https://doi.org/10.1016/j.frl.2021.102178

Yechiama, E., & Hochmanb, G. (2013). Loss-aversion or loss-attention: The impact of losses on cognitive performance. *Cognitive Psychology, 66*(2), 212–231.

CHAPTER 9

The Classification of Risks and the Activities that Make up Risk Management

There is no unified definition of risk in the business economics literature. Risk derives from the Italian word "risicare," meaning "to dare." In general, it can be stated that risk is any event capable of directly or indirectly compromising the survival of the company.

For this reason, the dimension of risk assumes importance today more than ever in determining the effects that hostile and/or potentially harmful events can create on business continuity. Hence the need to anticipate these events with complex tools to reduce their probability and the adverse effects they can generate on the company. Predicting hostile events is central to decision-making processes and corporate management. To these are added the numerous tools used in practice by companies. Tools that, over the years, have recorded a growing quantitative evolution with an increase in their complexity. Tools that dynamically try to respond to the numerous threats that economic activities may encounter.

In this section, always following an economic-business approach, we want to classify business risks and then highlight the practices that have followed one another over the years and the various activities that distinguish the integrated Risk Management systems. Finally, we want to describe some risk estimation techniques, the use of which helps to strengthen corporate decision-making processes.

A. Capocchi, *Vulnerability and the Corporate Immune System*,
https://doi.org/10.1007/978-3-031-30254-1_9

The Classification of Corporate Risks

The construction of the corporate immune system assumes great importance, but more is needed to allow successful corporate risk management activities. Management must be increasingly integrated at the level of processes and procedures and between the players who contribute internally and externally to guaranteeing business continuity.

The implementation of an integrated risk management system must have the identification of corporate risks as a starting point. There is no single definition of risk in the literature. This is also attributable to the complex dynamics that risks take on in corporate life. It is no coincidence that the numerous approaches that have followed one another in practice at an international level have marked events that have characterized economic cycles over the years. The risk is generally attributable to any event that can directly or indirectly compromise the company's survival. In particular:

Corporate risks are all events that can directly and/or indirectly impact the company's economic, equity, and financial balance.

The manifestation of these events may determine, at the expense of the company:

- An economic imbalance is the company's inability to comply with the economic condition because the sum of revenues must be equal to or greater than the sum of costs.
- Capital imbalance is the determination of a negative shareholders' equity or a sharp reduction of the same even below the limits established by law.
- Financial imbalance is the inability of the company to fulfill its obligations regularly.

Indeed, the three effects briefly described above can also co-occur or can occur at different times, however, progressively making the company unable to continue its business. In this regard, it must be remembered that in the economic-business vision, the company must always guarantee its survival in compliance with the principle of continuity (Gallati, 2022).

Risks can be classified according to various criteria (Hopking & Thompson, 2022). The first criterion distinguishes the risks between external and internal risks.

External risks are attributable to the trend of the economic cycle and to any other macroeconomic variable/of the markets in which the company operates: trend of the financial, raw materials, and outlet markets; the trend of technological cycles; natural events, etc. Management decisions do not directly influence the circumstances that may constitute the sources of such risks.

On the other hand, internal risks pertain to everything concerning the company production cycle: worker safety, operation of the corporate information system, and production efficiency/effectiveness. The events from which these risks originate are influenced, at least partially, by management decisions.

Another classification criterion distinguishes risks between diversifiable risks and systematic risks. By offsetting the relative risks, diversifiable risks can be reduced/eliminated by assuming a multitude of random variables which do not have a perfect linear positive correlation. Diversifiable risks have sub-additive properties; therefore, a business decision's cumulative risk is less than the risk on its own (Tillema et al., 2022).

Systematic risks originate from sources of systematic risk, such as the economic cycle (measurable by observing the trend in GDP), the trend in market interest rates (measurable by following the trend in the reference rates used by banks central to orienting the monetary policy pursued) and inflation (measurable by calculating the YoY trend variation of the consumer price index). Market risk is also one of the systematic risks. Systematic risks have the additive property, and therefore the incremental systematic risk of a management decision is equal to the systematic risk (they add to other company risks as it is impossible to diversify them).

From the additive property that characterizes systematic risks, which therefore makes it impossible to offset these risks with other company risks, it follows that systematic risks have the effect of amplifying a generally positive situation as the company obtains positive results in favorable scenarios of the general economy and to worsen a generally tricky situation since, in the event of a negative trend in the economy, the company would obtain unfavorable results from these risks, in addition to the other difficulties it would present. Hence the belief that other things being equal, the assumption of diversifiable risks (not correlated with the economy and the markets) is preferable to the assumption of systematic risks since the latter is positively associated with the economy and the markets.

A further classification distinguishes risks between pure risks and speculative risks. This distinction is based on the characteristics presented by the random variables: if a negative asymmetry characterizes the random variable due to which the threats of the random variable are more significant than the opportunities, there are pure risks; If the random variable is characterized by symmetry due to which the threats and opportunities appear specular or by a slight positive asymmetry due to which the opportunities are slightly higher than the threats, we have speculative risks.

Pure risks are characterized by the following:

- Sudden realization.
- Immediately observable manifestation.
- Immediate economic effects.
- Possible adoption of suitable initiatives to contain/reduce the damage.

Speculative risks are characterized by the following:

- Progressive implementation.
- Manifestation is not immediately observable but delayed over time.
- Advanced economic effects over time.
- Impossible to adopt initiatives aimed at reducing the economic consequences of events that have already occurred/manifested.

Speculative risks, in turn, can be classified into business and financial risks. Business risks refer to the productive and strategic activity of the corporate core business; financial risks refer to the collection of financial resources, (accessory) investments, and the regulation of contractual relationships.

Business and Financial Risks

Business risks are connected to the company's characteristic management (Power, 2009). Characteristic management represents the company's core business, which expresses the working capital regarding accounting dynamics. Business risks can be divided into operational risks and strategic risks.

The operational risk class includes risks relating to the company's production process. Among them deserve to be mentioned:

- The risks associated with procurement activities include the risk of an increase in the price of raw materials if they are not commodities since, in the latter case, the risk is financial or the risk of scarce availability of raw materials with potential damage to production volumes.
- The risks related to the physical-technical transformation activity, such as the risk of loss of quality and the risks associated with organizational decisions regarding the adjustment, as far as possible, of the production capacity to the actual needs dictated by the production volumes required.
- Risks associated with marketing finished products, such as **production** or delivery times non-compliance.
- The contribution margin and operating income ratio represent risks associated with using leverage. Working leverage makes it possible to seize the risk/opportunity linked to potential changes in company turnover, considering the incidence of fixed costs on turnover.
- Risks associated with the degree of production efficiency.
- Risks Associated with Logistics.
- Price risks—cost for products that represent commodities.

The strategic risks class includes the impacts on the economic, asset, and financial balance produced by strategic decisions taken by management (Wolke, 2017). To this end, decisions regarding the competitive positioning of the company in the reference market, decisions regarding the corporate strategy (e.g., vertical/horizontal integration, i.e., production diversification strategies), and business strategy (cost leadership vs. differentiation) and decisions regarding the choice of the most strategic distribution channels in the case of a company whose production is aimed at the final consumer (B2C). More generally, strategic risks pertain to corporate decisions regarding how the company intends to position itself on the market and compete to achieve, enhance, defend, and develop its competitive advantage. The strategic risks also include the risks related to investments in R&D, made to arrive at a new product to be launched on the market and the risks associated with the assets necessary for carrying out M&A operations aimed at acquiring more outstanding market shares or the acquisition of more significant bargaining power vis-à-vis customers/suppliers (Woods, 2007).

The distinction between strategic and operational risks depends on the type of company and the sector in which it operates.

Financial risks must be identified considering the different areas of company management. In this direction, we can distinguish:

- Financial risks associated with operational management.
- Financial risks associated with financial management.

The following are financial risks associated with operational management:

- Exchange rate risk in the event of international purchase/sale transactions.
- Price risk of commodities traded on the Stock Exchange through financial contracts.
- Risk is linked to ancillary investments not necessarily related to the core business.

The following are financial risks associated with financial management:

- The interest rate risk for the variable rate loans taken out by the company.
- The risk is linked to the effect of financial leverage given by the ratio of financial debt to equity capital, which, like operating leverage, represents a multiplier of volume risks.
- The risk linked to the cost of capital is influenced by the expected value of the return on the reference market and by financing policies, which affects the company's current value.

Within the management of business risks and financial risks, for the determination of the risk profile, the planning and programming activity assumes tremendous importance in estimating the future economic trend. This estimation and analysis activity must be carried out on several scenarios. In particular, at least three scenarios:

- Unfavorable scenario.
- Normal scenario.
- Favorable scenario.

Analyzing the future impact of a business decision through the information acquired from the explicit forecasting activity typically carried out by the business planning activity makes it possible to estimate the synthetic indicators of the random variable in question, i.e., the decision itself. These indicators help evaluate the convenience or otherwise of undertaking a specific decision.

Expansion of Production Capacity

To understand the importance of corporate decisions and their impact on strategic and operational risks, imagine the ALFA company operating in the artisan food production sector.

The ALFA company carries out its activity in a non-modern factory in a town and in where it quickly reaches saturation of its production capacity. The ALFA company can only invest in its headquarters if it complies with the new regulations and has a margin for upgrading its maximum production capacity. Therefore, the owner must decide whether to invest in constructing a new technologically advanced production site capable of reducing technical inefficiencies to maximize company profitability. The cost of building the new production plant is 8 million euros, and the time required for the design/construction and commissioning is 18 months.

The family ownership of the ALFA company is strongly indecisive and cannot decide. This is also in consideration of the total turnover of one's company which amounts to approximately Euro 12 million annually.

The reasons that slow down the decision are:

- Financial risk is linked to the company's lack of ability to support the investment and its repayment.
- Business risk is linked to the owner's fear of being unable to saturate the new production capacity with non-virtuous effects on corporate profitability.
- Market risk is linked, on the one hand, to the trend in raw material prices which affects over 80% of the ALFA company balance sheet, and, on the other hand, to the trend in demand as the product is costly on the market and easily replaceable from lower quality products, different but with much lower market prices.

In 2019, after having carried out numerous analyzes, the ownership of the ALFA company decided not to proceed with the investment. At the end of February 2020, COVID-19 broke out, and the property was convinced that it was right not to proceed with the investment. At the beginning of 2022, the COVID-19 emergency ends, and the war conflict in Ukraine ends with increased energy costs, raw material costs, and logistics costs. A significant increase in construction costs accompanies these increases.

In Early 2023, the situation still needs to be determined. The ALFA company's production volumes have slowed, and the owners have noticed a significant limitation: the ALFA company is an almost single product. Increasing product references requires new production capacity that the company needs to have available.

The owner realizes that if he had built the new production plant today, he could increase his references by decreasing certain risks, such as market risks. However, the property also realizes that if it had started the investment, it would probably have incurred higher construction costs and would be more indebted. The more outstanding debt would have led to the need to create currency to repay the loans taken out with the banks. The need to develop working capital in a period of market contraction due to price increases would have forced the ALFA company to sell at any cost without being able to protect its margins with high risks for maintaining the profitability of the balance sheet.

Considering what has been briefly described above, is it possible to understand whether the ALFA company was right not to invest or whether it should have made it otherwise?

This question needs to be answered. To answer, it is necessary to wait a few more years and understand the macroevolution of the ALFA company's market. However, what is possible to understand concerns the following question: how should the family ownership of the ALFA company set up its business decision?

The business decision is undoubtedly very complex. Therefore, corporate ownership should have tried to reduce complexity using rational analysis tools, including differential ones. Among them:

- A forecast on multiple scenarios of future cash flows that the investment project can generate.
- A quantification of the expected incremental value of the cash flows and the cumulative standard deviation, in such a way as to know the risk profile of the same measured by the total standard deviation and be able to evaluate its convenience or not by calculating the net value present (V.A.N.), starting from the expected value of future cash flows.

If we reasoned in terms of margins, the convenience of the project could be evaluated by comparing the ROI of the project calculated starting from the expected value of the margins that the project can generate and the cost of the financial sources necessary to carry it out determined through the use of the WACC in the case in which the ALFA company decides to finance the investment with its capital and with third-party capital.

Different Approaches to Risk Management

Over the years, risk management has been the subject of an evolutionary process that has seen various approaches. The evolutionary path of risk management can be marked through the following steps:

- Enterprise risk management (ERM).
- Project risk management (PRM).
- Traditional risk management (TRM).
- Financial risk management (FRM).

Enterprise risk management (ERM) considers all corporate risks classified as strategic, operational, financial, and pure. It recognizes the importance of both the threats and the opportunities associated with each type of risk, supporting the decision-making process to create or preserve corporate value. In ERM, all stages of the process and risk management methods are relevant, as ERM deals with all types of corporate risk (Arena et al., 2011; Baxter et al., 2013).

Project risk management (PRM) deals, to a limited extent, with the identification, analysis, and management of risks associated with large company projects, such as, for example, the implementation of a multi-year contract. The objective of the PRM is the project's success, and therefore everything that can compromise its realization is classified as a risk. The realization must take place within the established times. Failure to meet deadlines, in fact, not only jeopardizes aspects of operational management but also delays financial flows with essential effects on the company's financial and equity balance.

Within the PRM, the identification and management of risks through prevention/protection tools assume importance, while risk estimation techniques and management techniques based on hedging transactions accept less importance. Compared to ERM, in which the prevailing statistical-financial/managerial component, in PRM, the technical/engineering component stays (Paape & Speklé, 2012; Farrell & Gallagher, 2015).

Traditional risk management (TRM) has the same objective as ERM, i.e., creating corporate value in favor of shareholders and stakeholders. Still, its range of action is limited to pure corporate risks only. Compared to the ERM, the TRM has a much narrower field of activity. In TRM, all the main phases of the process assume importance, and the management techniques used are prevention/protection measures and coverage through insurance contracts.

Financial risk management (FRM), like Traditional risk management and Enterprise risk management, aims to create corporate value but narrowly focuses on identifying, estimating, and managing corporate financial risks. This approach has acquired increasing importance over the years following the development of the financial market and the derivative instruments we have witnessed. Even for the FRM, the note raised against the TRM remains, i.e., the focus restricted to a single category of company risks leads to making sub-optimal decisions.

The Activities that Makeup Risk Management

Regardless of the approach followed, the risk management system is divided into the following closely related activities:

- Risk Assessments.
- Risk Reporting.
- Risk Treatments.
- Risk monitoring.

The Risk Assessment activity consists of risk assessment and measurement activities. It is divided into five interconnected phases: (1) identification of risks; (2) description of the risks; (3) risk estimation; (4) risk integration; and (5) risk assessment.

The risk identification phase aims to identify the sources of the variables and/or events that can determine unexpected and hostile economic, financial, and equity effects for the company.

There are no specific support techniques capable of minimizing errors due to the failure to identify specific risks, and such errors can sometimes have severe consequences for the company.

In this phase, pure corporate risks are particularly insidious, as they are closely linked to the specific activities and processes of the company. In contrast, the causes of speculative risks are more accessible to identify because of the means of information and the analysis currently available from the company management.

Among the techniques available to company management for the identification and mapping of company risks, the following deserve to be mentioned:

- Analysis of experience, information collected, and experience gained.
- Prompt lists, i.e., the creation of lists of possible corporate risks, starting from historical information and analysis of competitors, help identify the existence of the listed risks.
- Interviews with managers/consultants/professionals help bridge the gap in the skills possessed and identify pure risks of a technical nature.
- Group techniques such as Brainstorming and the management of focus groups help to favor the process of generating ideas useful for the purpose through the involvement of several informed subjects in the decision-making process aimed at identifying risks.
- Analysis of the accounting and technical documentation available.

The accounting and technical documentation available to the company must always be carried out considering the historical series, i.e., the analyzed data dynamics and future projections. Projections often must be based on historical series to make the determinations as prudential as possible in favor of the analysis conducted.

The risk description phase is handy for codifying the identified risks within the company. The coding takes on statistical value over time and allows the company to standardize the dynamics of individual risks over the years. The description of the risks supports the subsequent phases of the process, as it provides detailed—codified—information on the types of risk identified and drawn up based on a methodology previously agreed upon and validated by the company.

The risk estimation phase usually takes place through qualitative/semi-quantitative techniques that lead to a more detailed description of the various random variables and sources of risk previously identified but do not determine the synthetic indicators and quantitative methods which show the determination of the probability distribution of the random variables and the related synthetic indicators.

The risk integration phase consists of estimating the incremental risks linked to the decision-making process and allowing, after aggregating all the identified and assessed risks, to evaluate their impact on the overall company risk.

The risk assessment phase consists of attributing a value to the analyzed random variables, valid for the subsequent treatment or for comparing them where it is necessary to choose between two possible alternatives.

This phase takes on a different form of the techniques adopted in the risk estimation process. Suppose the risk estimation was carried out with qualitative/semi-quantitative techniques. In that case, the subsequent risk assessment phase leads to the expression of a qualitative/semi-quantitative judgment, i.e., a rating or score from which the relevance and extent of the risks are examined. In cases where quantitative risk estimation techniques are adopted, the subsequent evaluation phase leads to attributing a value to the random variables in question. The previously used estimation technique strictly influences how risks are assessed.

The Risk Reporting activity in creating summary reports starting from the information and data collected through the previous risk assessment phase, in such a way as to create a link between this first phase and the phase relating to the management or rather to the treatment of the identified risks, estimated and evaluated risk treatment. Risk Reporting within companies makes up a system that must be well codified through some dimensions that make up the reporting itself: the report's content, the form in which said content is represented, and the frequency with which the information is produced and transmitted. The reporting system builds a language within the company and must be shared at all levels. The reporting coding also depends on the beneficiary of the report and the purpose that the information intends to achieve.

The Risk Treatment activity consists of a set of decisions that contribute to modifying the corporate risk profile.

It is good practice to separate the subjects in charge of assessing the risk from the issues in managing it. This separation is necessary to avoid contaminations that can jeopardize the activities and the skills the two activities require.

Risk management decisions can be ex-ante or ex-post. Ex-ante decisions are all those aimed at minimizing the probability, or the impact, of the hostile scenario of the random variable before it occurs. Ex-post decisions are those taken following the manifestation of the adverse scenario to reduce the effect it can produce to the company's detriment. Among the ex-ante findings can be mentioned:

- Prevention decisions.
- Protection decisions.
- Diversification decisions.
- Coverage or hedging decisions.

Prevention decisions aim to reduce the probability of a hostile event. For example, imagine a stretch of road where numerous accidents occur due to exceeding the speed limits. A preventive measure consists of the decision by the competent body to install a permanent speed camera to discourage the adoption of incorrect behavior by motorists.

Security decisions do not affect the likelihood of a hostile event but their impact on the business.

As an example, always concerning the road section mentioned above, imagine the installation of guardrails capable of cushioning the impact with vehicles, limiting the effects of a possible accident.

The diversification decisions use the standard deviation technique. The overall risk generated by multiple random variables is lower than the sum of the risks considered individually in all cases where these random variables are not positively correlated. Diversification combines very well with financial risks and is often implemented through rational risk allocation decisions.

Covering or hedging decisions lead the company to assume exposure to the risk opposite to the one it wants to manage with a consequent reduction in the overall risk due to compensation mechanisms.

Hedging decisions consist in signing a contract of a different nature with an identified counterparty, such as, for example, the signing of financial derivative contracts to hedge financial risks or the signing of insurance contracts to cover pure risks. Compared to the prevention and protection measures, hedging transactions do not intervene on the risk profile of the original random variable. On a substantial level, we are witnessing the transfer of the economic consequences of the risk to the counterparty of the contract. Among the ex-post decisions can be mentioned:

- Damage containment and reduction measures.
- Financing plans of the economic-financial flows.

Damage containment and reduction measures typically concern pure risks and consist of the actions undertaken following an unfavorable risk scenario to reduce its adverse economic effects. To be effective, these actions must be previously identified and planned, at least as regards the essential aspects.

The financing plans of the economic-financial flows are aimed at identifying (ex-ante) various possible financing channels to be activated following the occurrence of the risk to prevent the economic equity and financial effects produced by the risk itself to the company, are not accentuated by a subsequent liquidity crisis or by the production of substantial economic losses. The financing plans, therefore, make it possible to identify, ex-ante, the actions to be undertaken to avoid making sub-optimal decisions ex-post.

An example is what happened in Italy during the COVID-19 and the opening to companies of access to loans guaranteed by the State to face the liquidity crises and the subsequent recovery of the post-pandemic corporate business.

Among the financial flow financing plans aimed at avoiding corporate crises due to the production of enormous losses, the financing/loss coverage channels that can be activated are, as already partially observed in terms of the corporate immune system:

- Provisions for risks and charges.
- Allocations to equity reserves.
- Divestment of assets that allows for the realization of capital gains.
- Capital injections by shareholders aimed at restoring equity balance.

Among the financial flow financing plans aimed at avoiding situations of a liquidity crisis, the possible financing channels that can be activated are:

- Divestment of readily liquid assets.
- Financial debt.
- Capital contributions by shareholders.

Lastly, the Risk Monitoring activity. It consists of the necessary risk control in the various moments that make up any control system:

- Ex-ante control—planning.
- Feed-forward control—analysis of deviations.
- Ex-post control—final statement.

In addition, to control activities, Risk Monitoring also includes the partial/total recurrence of the risk management process periodically or when conditions change. The validation activities of the effectiveness of the risk management process and any revision of the same, in following the manifestation of unfavorable scenarios, to be able to evaluate the benefits deriving from the process itself.

Risk Estimation

The business risk estimation activities aim to identify the economic equity and financial effects of the possible manifestations of risk and determine the related probability of occurrence. There are three business risk estimation techniques:

1. Qualitative estimation techniques.
2. Semi-quantitative estimation techniques.
3. Quantitative estimation techniques.

The choice of the estimation technique to be used must be conducted considering the cost/benefit ratio with the awareness that quantitative estimation techniques are more complex and require more time, often leading the company to bear higher costs.

In choosing it, it is worth remembering that the first two techniques help describe and classify, in-depth, the company risk classes previously identified. At the same time, the third type—quantitative—allows the determination of synthetic indicators relating to the random variable, source of company risk, and the relative probability distribution.

Qualitative estimation techniques can follow different methodologies. The first methodology is contained in the Australian risk management standards and consists of the "probability/impact" technique.

This technique can be used to estimate pure business risks characterized by only two possible scenarios and is based on the definition of three different qualitative scales representing the probabilities, impacts, and probability-impact combinations that emerge from the risk rating matrix. To establish the attitude toward the estimated risks, it is also necessary to establish the risk rating evaluation criteria in advance. Australian risk management standards suggest using the following rating evaluation criteria that emerge from the "probability/impact" matrix:

- E = Extreme risk, request for immediate action.
- H = High risk, senior management attention required.
- M = Moderate risk, need to specify management responsibilities.
- L = Low risk, ordinary management practices.

Therefore, this qualitative risk estimation technique requires placing/classifying the different types of company risk in the "probability/impact" matrix. Based on the classification, the risks are differently evaluated and treated. The limitations of this technique are represented by the following:

- Non-applicability about speculative risks as these risks also consider opportunities.
- Increase complexity and loss of information if more than two possible scenarios are considered.
- Possible equal treatment of risks with the same risk rating but different summary indicators.
- Not possible application of rational decision-making criteria (e.g., V.A.N.).

The semi-quantitative estimation techniques provide for assigning a score (risk score) to the classes identified by the qualitative methods, whose functionality is linked to the classification and comparison of the identified risks.

To this end, the "probability/impact" technique can be "transformed" into a semi-quantitative estimation technique by assigning scores to the qualitative scales used to estimate probabilities and impacts.

Semi-quantitative techniques are certainly more helpful compared to qualitative methods, where you want to make a comparative assessment between different corporate risk profiles. However, they need to allow the limits already reported about qualitative techniques to be exceeded.

Quantitative techniques for estimating business risks make it possible to estimate the probability distribution of the random variables that are sources of risk.

The distribution of possible losses will be represented in pure corporate risks, while for speculative risks, the distribution of possible results will be described.

Once the distribution of the random variable has been estimated, it is possible to quantify the synthetic indicators capable of describing its characteristics, such as the expected value and standard deviation. The process of quantitative estimation of company risks is divided into three main phases:

- Definition of the model through which it is possible to determine possible realizations of the target random variable.
- Calculation of synthetic indicators of the random variables included in the model.
- It estimates the distribution of the random target variable and its synthetic indicators resolution of the model.

The Collection of Interviews with Managers, Experts, Consultants, Professionals, and Stakeholders

Collecting interviews with managers, experts, consultants, professionals, and stakeholders is essential for an integrated Risk Management system. These interviews must be carried out periodically to make the most of the elements collected, also in terms of statistical significance.

The collection activity can be conducted on an individual basis or with group techniques such as, for example, the organization of brainstorming and/or the Delphi technique.

The brainstorming technique consists of a process applicable about any level of the organization, aimed at encouraging creativity and the development of ideas by a group of people with adequate skills and experience in risk matters, as well as different professional backgrounds, helpful in identifying uncertainties, potential risks, and management strategies (Barber & Odean, 2001). The people involved in the process are guided and coordinated by an "expert facilitator," who ensures that all participants can express their opinions without limitation or influence. Therefore, the ideas/views generated by this process are intended to be collected for subsequent processing and evaluation.

This technique has as its strong point the simplicity and speed of configuration of the process, not requiring multiple input data and encouraging creativity. The weak point is the time this technique needs to organize the sessions since there must be no dominant positions within the group.

The Delphi technique can typically be used to collect the opinions of a group of experts about particularly complex problems characterized by considerable uncertainty.

In detail, the collection takes place through a series of sequential questionnaires compiled, anonymously and individually, by the group of experts, providing that they have access to the opinions of the other subjects involved during the process. This last aspect is substantiated in the review, by the topics involved, in a second questionnaire of the most shared opinions collected in the first questionnaire. In this way, at the end of the process, a set of views characterized by the consensus of all the participants in the process is collected.

This process is generally designed to solve problems at a strategic level, but it can be adapted and used to identify business risks and evaluate their probabilities and impacts.

The benefits of this technique include less hierarchical bias (anonymous questionnaires) and equal weight/value of all expert opinions. Conversely, the method is complex and requires time between completing the first and subsequent questionnaires; weeks/months can pass.

Identification of Risks and Risk Drivers

Numerous techniques are used in practice to achieve an adequate identification of risks. In addition to the more traditional methods based on the analysis of historical data, the analysis by scenarios, and on the classification of risks, two techniques assume importance as they provide for the breakdown of the problem in question—identification of potential risks—into "sub-problems," to make subsequent analysis and determination of the causes/drivers of the various risk factors easier: FMEA technique and SWIFT analysis.

The FMEA technique (failure modes and effect analysis) divides an object of analysis into sub-dimensions. For each sub-dimension, the different possible ways in which failure can be reached and the causes and effects of the loss are considered.

FMEA analysis was first used in the 1940s by the US military to predict and minimize adverse effects in the event of an operational failure. Once the Second World War was over, it was forgotten for about twenty years, only to be revived in the 1960s by the automotive industry. It was going through a highly competitive period and therefore needed systems to optimize production and "beat" the competition.

FMEA Analysis is used for systematic risk analysis in complex systems or processes. The purpose of the application is to recognize, understand, limit, and remedy potential weaknesses and risks and thus avoid errors. Failure Mode and Effects Analysis (FMEA) is a team-oriented analysis used to find potential sources of errors in products or processes early on, recognize their importance and evaluate them to derive adequate preventive measures to avoid them if necessary. In this way, the high costs of control and error can be avoided or significantly reduced.

This technique lends itself to the analysis of complex processes such as, for example, the company production process. Using this technique, it is possible to highlight each sub-dimension:

- Its function.
- Potential faults/errors.
- The causes that lead to such faults/mistakes.
- The impacts of such failures/errors.
- How to detect faults/mistakes.
- Provisions on how to act in the event of failures/errors.

In practice, there are two methods of FMEA analysis:

- Design FMEA analysis.
- Process FMEA analysis.

The Design FMEA methodology focuses on creating reliable products, while the Process FMEA methodology focuses on developing reliable processes.

While they can be used independently, they are often used together in a company's risk and failure analysis process. This is because both product design and business processes are at risk of failures and errors, and both contribute to the overall business quality.

The SWIFT technique (structured what-if technique) involves senior management. It consists of the use of the brainstorming technique, involving questions of the "what if" type, to bring the discussion together on issues such as, for example:

- Previously identified or already known risks.
- Sources and drivers of risk.
- Previous successes/failures.
- Regulatory requirements and constraints.

This is to achieve a complete review of the origins of corporate risk. This technique is suitable for capturing the impacts of inevitable organizational changes on the corporate risk profile. It leads to implementing a risk register, in which the risks are classified according to their potential impact, which can be used to establish treatment strategies.

The SWIFT technique has the advantage of applying to each dimension and/or organization's activity and is relatively rapid ("risk sources quickly become apparent within the workshop session"). The SWIFT technique requires that the group members participating in the analysis sessions have widespread skills and experience regarding the organization and the various activities involved. Otherwise, some risks may not be identified. Furthermore, this technique needs to correctly support subsequent control activities, requiring further subsequent analyses regarding the identified risk profiles.

Value at Risk (VaR)

VaR can be defined as an accurate risk indicator even if its use is widespread in the financial sphere. Following Risk.net Value at risk is a quantitative (statistical) "measure of the riskiness of financial entities or portfolios of assets. It may be defined as the maximum money amount expected to be lost over a given time horizon at a pre-defined confidence level. In the Anglo-Saxon literature, VaR is also considered capital at risk" (https://www.risk.net/definition/value-at-risk-var).

VaR was initially developed as a risk measure, especially for market risk, by the investment bank Morgan Stanley in 1994. In the last decades, VaR was developed for other risks with particular care to the default risk.

VaR can be calculated using different techniques. To calculate the VaR, it is necessary to know the distribution of the random variable in question; to this end, the same can be determined through simulations that consider various information as historical data and/or market information or through random simulations using Monte Carlo simulation.

Under the parametric method, also known as the variance–covariance method, VaR is calculated as a function of the mean and variance of the return's series, assuming a normal distribution. With the historical process, VAR is determined by taking the returns belonging to the lowest quintile of the series and observing the highest returns.

The VaR expresses the maximum loss an investment could suffer with a certain confidence level and in a particular time horizon. To fully understand the Value at Risk, it is, therefore, necessary to focus on two aspects:

- The time horizon is the period we need to calculate the loss.
- The level of statistical confidence is generally 95% or 99%, the probability that a loss more significant than that indicated by the VaR will occur.

To indicate the maximum loss, negative percentage numbers are usually used. But the use of absolute values is also widespread. In short, although it seems like a highly complex technique, VaR is quite simple since it uses only three variables:

- Amount of the loss.
- Its probability.
- Time.

Suppose a monthly VaR of –2% concerning an investment with a confidence level of 99%. This means there is a 99% chance that we will lose up to 2% in one month. Or that in the next month, it is possible, but very difficult, because the probability is only 1%, to record a loss greater than 2%.

Summary Considerations

The acceleration of economic dynamics and the interconnections created on a global scale in recent decades due to globalization and the development of technology have increased the complexity of business systems. Hence the growing search for tools suitable for preventing corporate crises and avoiding events that directly and/or indirectly can impact the company's survival and business continuity.

In practice, companies sometimes adopt behaviors aimed at pursuing risks, needing to understand that the approach to risk must be global and integrated for the company.

Global in the sense that risk management must increasingly become part of the managerial culture, determining behaviors including accounting consistent with the search for growing economic, financial, and equity sustainability; integrated since it must involve the entire company system and since risk management cannot be limited to certain functions or specific areas.

The dimensions of the risk in terms of exposure have increased. The speed with which risks manifest and change has increased.

Statistical tools can help companies and management, but they can do nothing if they lack an adequate culture and long-lasting planning based on progressive technology, processes, and skills investments.

References

Arena, M., Arnaboldi, M., & Azzone, G. (2011). Is enterprise risk management real? *Journal of Risk Research, 14*(7), 779–797.

Barber, B. M., & Odean, T. (2001). Boys will be boys: Gender, overconfidence, and common stock investment. *The Quarterly Journal of Economics, 116*(1), 261–292.

Baxter, R., Bedard, J. C., Hoitash, R., & Yezegel, A. (2013). Enterprise risk management program quality: Determinants, value relevance, and the financial crisis. *Contemporary Accounting Research, 30*(4), 1264–1295.

Farrell, M., & Gallagher, R. (2015). The valuation implications of enterprise risk management maturity. *Journal of Risk and Insurance, 82*(3), 625–657.

Gallati, R. R. (2022). *Risk management and capital adequacy*. McGraw-Hill.

Hopking, P., & Thompson, C. (2022). *Fundamentals of risk management* (6th edition). Kogan Page.

Paape, L., & Speklé, R. F. (2012). The adoption and design of enterprise risk management practices: An empirical study. *European Accounting Review, 21*(3), 533–564.

Power, M. (2009). The risk management of nothing. *Accounting, Organizations and Society, 34*(6–7), 849–855.

Tillema, S., Trapp, R., & van Veen-Dirks, P. (2022). Business partnering in risk management: A resilience perspective on management accountants' responses to a role change. *Contemporary Accounting Research, 39*(3), 1509–2233. https://doi.org/10.1111/1911-3846.12774

Wolke, T. (2017). *Risk management*. Walter de Gruyter.

Woods, M. (2007). Linking risk management to strategic controls: A case study of Tesco plc. *International Journal of Risk Assessment and Management, 7*(8), 1074–1088.

PART IV

Practical Experiences

CHAPTER 10

Case Studies: Pirelli–NatWest–Eni–Ocado–Ryanair

> *The benefits (and costs) of risk management vary by firm, a risk management strategy must be tailored to the individual company.* (Meulbroek, 2002: 55)

In this section, the cases of five companies are investigated to describe and discuss how firms implement risk management strategies and develop techniques to control operations. The five companies analyzed are:

- Pirelli
- NatWest
- Eni
- Ocado
- and Ryanair.

The selection is not random. The five companies operate in different sectors with different strategies and goals. Thus, the group proposed allows us to discuss multiple techniques and confront different approaches.

For each company, there is:

- A brief introduction discussing the history of the company and its main features.

A. Capocchi, *Vulnerability and the Corporate Immune System*, https://doi.org/10.1007/978-3-031-30254-1_10

- The risk management structure.
- The risk identification.
- And finally, a discussion of the risk management process.

The five case studies are exclusively based on information retrievable from companies' websites. The comments are based on the 2021 annual reports, the first 2022 quarterly reports if available, and all the information disclosed by the companies regarding the corporate governance structure, the risk management process, and future economic prospects. A brief list of questions to delve into the analysis is provided at the end of each case. This Chapter was conceived, elaborated, and written with the contribution of **Alessandro Paolo Rigamonti**, currently a Ph.D. student at the University of Pisa and collaborator at the University of Milan Bicocca.

Pirelli is an Italian manufacturer that produces tires focused on high-value products. Indeed, it is one of the largest world producers. Research and Development (R&D) is a crucial strategy to create value and competitive advantage. Employee turnover is vital because it protects or dissipates the know-how, and the Group tries to prevent the risk. Moreover, Pirelli allows us to understand how emerging risks that might seem unrelated to the business (such as the shortage of semiconductors) can profoundly impact business operations in an integrated and interconnected world.

NatWest is one of the four largest banks in the United Kingdom.[1] In this business case, the financial market plays a crucial role, and the analysis of the macroeconomic outlook does not provide only guidelines regarding growth prospects. Still, it is a vital part of the business strategy. The case is relevant because it allows the investigation of the reputational risk. NatWest was previously known as the Royal Bank of Scotland, but after a series of recent scandals, the Board decided to change the name of the bank and the way it is managed. Reputational risks do not involve specific monetary losses but impact the business's future financial sustainability. Moreover, after the 2008 financial crisis, governments issued new banking system regulations to reduce the probability of bankruptcy and systemic risk. By investigating the case of NatWest, it is possible to discuss

[1] Usually, to refer to the group of the four largest banks in the UK, the term "Big Four" is used.

the stress tests, the scenario analysis, and the sensitivity analysis using real examples.

ENI is an Italian company and one of the most prominent players in the energy sector, the most economically significant category of commodities. The main peculiarity is that the company cannot control the product's price outside the management's decision-making powers. Moreover, it operates in a highly volatile environment (regarding the economy, the political process, and the rule of law), which gained relevance during the pandemic and after the Ukraine war. In 2021 energy was one of the main drivers of inflation, and in 2022 the disruption of the value chain, shipments, and economic sanctions against Russia exacerbated the effect. To reduce the economic weight on the population, significantly the poorer and the working class, multiple governments increased the corporate tax rate on the excessive profits made with high energy prices. The example highlights the political sensitivity of the energy sector.

Ocado is a British technology company operating in the online grocery market. This example is fascinating. Doing business implies risks, especially in a fast-changing sector. Entrepreneurs are risk-takers and thrive in uncertainties by testing new ideas and innovating. Moreover, standard risk management practices differ because innovation requires significant capital to grow and display negative cash flows initially. Thus, investors select companies based on their ability to exploit new opportunities rather than the initial economic results. However, technological companies must implement risk management strategies for operational situations and uncertainties. For Ocado, relevant risks are keeping the talents and the capabilities inside the company, cybersecurity, managing the overall value chain, and intellectual property.

Ryanair is the leader in low-cost European airline travels. The annual report focuses mainly on the impact of the COVID-19 pandemic that disrupted the business operations of Ryanair. European governments-imposed lockdowns and restrictions on mobility by implementing new regulations (and standards) to travel across borders. The principal driver of the economic struggle is the 81% decline in airline traffic caused by the lockdowns, the restrictions, and new regulations (quarantine) that discouraged further travel. Furthermore, the pandemic does not only reduce the demand, but it has a significant impact on Ryanair's liquidity for two main reasons. First, it increases the related costs. Second, Ryanair refunded all the canceled flights.

Pirelli

Brief Description of the Company

Pirelli is one of the largest producers of tires and associated services globally. It has been listed on the Italian stock exchange since 1922. During 2015–2017, the Company was delisted following a period of reorganization and was listed again from the 7th of October 2017 as "Pirelli and C. SPA." The CEO is Marco Tronchetti Provera, appointed in 1991. In 2021 the total turnover was approximately 5.3€ billion, employing more than 30,000 people. The production of tires includes products for cars, motorcycles, and bicycles. The breakdown of revenues highlights the importance of the car sector, which generates around 92% of total turnover.

Furthermore, Pirelli strongly focuses on innovation and advanced products: 71% of the revenues are from selling high-value tires and 29% from standard tires. The company has 18 production plants operating in 12 countries, and the products are sold in more than 160 countries with a widespread distribution using more than 18,000 sales points. The total production capacity is seventy-three million tires. The headquarters and the research and Development (R&D) center have been in Milan since its foundation. Pirelli is involved in multiple competitions to sustain the image of cutting-edge technology and innovative brand. Since 2011, it has been the official and exclusive supplier of tires for the Formula 1 World Championship and World Rally Championship.

The Risk Management Structure

Pirelli implements the Enterprise Risk Management (ERM) model based on the framework "Enterprise Risk Management Integrating with Strategy and Performance," updated by the Committee of Sponsoring Organization of the Treadway Commission (COSO). Using such a framework, one can identify mitigation strategies to safeguard strategic objectives and create value for stakeholders. The company is an excellent example of COSO implementation. The risk management process of Pirelli is strictly integrated with the corporate governance structure. The Board of Directors plays a central role in adopting adequate internal control and risk management systems with the support of multiple teams such as Audit, Risk, Sustainability, and Corporate Governance Committees. The main goal is to design the risk management structure to contribute to the operation of a healthy and proper business, consistent with the company's objectives. The Board of Directors is responsible for identifying, managing, and monitoring the principal risks that could affect the company. The main feature of Pirelli's risk management approach stated multiple times in all the documents, is being proactive. Pirelli does not simply hedge against possible risks; it tries to grasp opportunities when not anticipated and turn risk and uncertainties to its favor. This should be the approach and the goal of an exemplary risk management implementation.

Risks Identification

The company assesses the risks by dividing three categories:

a. External Risks: whose occurrence is outside the influence of Pirelli.
b. Strategic Risks are characteristic of the relevant business and a potential source of competitive advantage.
c. Operational Risks: generated by the organization's processes and activities.

Another typology of risk, which fits into all the categories, is represented by the Corporate Social Responsibility, Environmental, and Business Ethics risks. These risks arise both in the supply chain and in the value chain. Pirelli does not disclose the plans and strategies to tackle the identified risks. The table below collects and summarizes the main risks described in the 2021 annual report divided into three related categories. If appropriate, the company adopts a local-for-local strategy, meaning that Pirelli must monitor, assess, and identify idiosyncratic risks in each of the 12 countries where it operates. Pirelli identifies Argentina, Brazil, Mexico, and Russia as the countries with higher instability regarding political, economic, financial, tax, and security uncertainties. Reallocating production capacity is a response to mitigate the under-utilization of total production capacity (Table 10.1).

The risks identified in Pirelli's 2021 Annual Report are divided—as represented in Table 10.1—into external, strategic, and operational.

Table 10.1 The risks identified in Pirelli's 2021 Annual Report

External	*Strategic*	*Operational*
Macroeconomic outlook	Exchange rate	Environmental issue
Country risk	Liquidity	Employee health and safety
Russia-Ukraine crisis		
Brexit	Interest rate	Defective product
Shortage of semiconductors	Price of financial assets	Litigation
Coronavirus	Credit	Personal data processing
Long-term demand	Human resources	Information system and Network infrastructure
Climate change		Business interruption
Price and availability of raw materials		Financial reporting process
Competition		

Discussion and Analysis

Most of the risks are standard across all companies. Thus, it is possible to focus on exciting risk factors specific to the company and the sector. Regarding the Russia-Ukraine crisis, the group established a special "Crisis Committee" team to constantly monitor the situation and develop mitigation measures and contingency plans to respond efficiently. Considering that few predicted the beginning of the war, the company implemented an effective risk management tool. The shortage of semiconductors arises because of the effect on supply and demand generated by the COVID-19 pandemic.

On the one hand, the lockdowns increased the demand for technologies heavily dependent on chips that require semiconductors. On the other hand, the lockdowns depressed supply because they reduced production. Furthermore, a 7.3 magnitude earthquake in Japan (involving the third largest automotive chipmaker) and a fire at the most significant world producer of chips exacerbated the situation. The automotive industry is vulnerable to these shocks and reduced car production, reducing tire demand. This example provides a good representation of the complexity of doing business. It also highlights the interconnections of the global value chain and the difficulties in anticipating emerging (or new) risks.

The evolution of long-term demand is one of the most critical risks for the future economic sustainability of the company. Long-term trends take work to predict and anticipate. However, cultural and generational changes suggest a reduction in mobility and the use of cars. In the Interim financial report (first quarter 2022), Pirelli displays an increase in all the critical financial (and performance) indicators. However, compared to the pre-pandemic volumes, there was a reduction of approximately 6% in the first quarter of 2019. The potential impact on the tire sector is difficult to forecast, but Pirelli should focus extensively on this issue, considering its peculiarity of serving only consumers.

Because of its focus on innovation, Pirelli identifies the loss of human resources as a relevant risk for the company. It is the only strategic risk it is possible to focus on. The loss is not monetary and is from two different perspectives. First, employees with strategic know-how are difficult to substitute. Second, when an employee changes companies, he/she can bring valuable knowledge to the competitors. In the operational risk category, personal data processing risks and the risks related to information systems and network infrastructure are interesting. These emerging risks are gaining relevance in the everyday activities of any company, and the potential consequences are catastrophic from both the financial and the reputational perspectives. Personal data processing risks involve full compliance with all data protection regulations in the countries where Pirelli operates. Information systems and network infrastructure risks are analyzed deeply in the annual report. Malfunctioning and unauthorized access are the worst scenarios, especially in remote working conditions. The company implemented multiple mitigation measures such as renewing infrastructure components to reduce technological obsolescence, increasing the staff in the Cyber Security Headquarters, period assessments, ad-hoc training sessions, and the setup of the Cyber Security Defense Center.

Questions

a. Considering the probability and the possible economic impact, create a rank of all the risks from the most relevant to the least appropriate.
b. Considering the probability and the possible economic impact, place all the risks in the table into the risk matrix.

c. Based on the type of company, the sector, and the strategy, select three risks from the table and provide a discussion.
d. Considering future trends, select possible risks that might become more relevant for the company.
e. When possible, confront the results with your colleagues and discuss the differences.

NatWest

Brief Description of the Company

NatWest Group plc is a financial service company providing a wide range of products and services to personal, commercial, large corporate, and institutional customers. It provides mobile and digital banking, finances startups and business, and offers financing, risk management, and trading solutions. The headquarter is in Edinburgh, Scotland. Formerly known as the Royal Bank of Scotland, in 2019, the chairman, Howard Davis, and the CEO, Alison Rose, declared the intention to change the group's name to NatWest Group plc (NWG). The rationale provided by the company to explain the name change is to align "the parent's name with the brand under which the substantial majority of services were delivered" (National Westminster Bank plc, 2021, NatWest Group plc, 2020 Annual Report and Accounts. Retrieved Online from NatWest Group—Reports archive 2020, p. 8). The change occurred on the 22nd of July 2020. However, it is considered a symbolic change trying to distance itself from past scandals.

For example, there have been multiple accusations, including money laundering, harmful practices such as selling garbage mortgages before the financial crisis, unnecessary expenses, and promoting itself as the "Oil & Gas Bank" because of the vast amount of loans to finance the operation of the oil and gas sector, and the most recent scandal for the exploitation of small businesses through its controversial global restructuring group. In 2008, the bank was bailout by the British government to avoid its collapse during the financial crisis. The government stake, held and managed through UK Government Investments, constantly dropped from 84 to 48%. The Group plans to sell all government participation by 2024. Following the bailout, the bank could not pay dividends until 2018. Since its bailout, the bank has constantly cut the number of employees yearly, attracting criticism from taxpayers and the British community. At the end of 2021, the permanent headcount is 59,915, equally distributed between males and females.

Total assets value amounted to 781.9£ billion makings, and market capitalization amounts to 27.1£ billion, making NatWest the fourth biggest bank in the UK considering both measures.[2] Given the dimension, the structure of NatWest Group is very complicated. The group uses many well-known brands: NatWest, Royal Bank of Scotland, Ulster Bank, Coutts, Adam & Company, Child & Co., Drummonds, Lombard, NatWest International, RBS International, Isle of Man Bank, and Holt's Military Banking. Operations are principally in the UK, Europe, Asia, and North America. Considering financial results, in 2021, RBS reported an operating profit before tax of £4032 million and delivered a dividend of 7.5 pence per share.

The group reduced operating expenses by £256 million (4%), increasing net retail and commercial business lending to £305.7 billion. The percentage of consumers using exclusively digital channels to interact with the company is constantly growing in retail and commercial segments. The result is relevant for the company's prospects because, in recent years, all the five largest banks in the UK have faced growing competition from the so-called "digital challengers" (Starling, Monzo Bank, or Revolut) that pushed for the transition to digital services. The analysis of the company is interesting because it highlights how reputational risk is relevant in our contemporary competitive economic environment. NatWest implements behaviors aiming at being perceived as a "good citizen" that contributes to society. Trust is one of the most important intangible assets in the banking sector that create sustained competitive advantage. And the Group needs to gain back its credibility.

The banking industry is highly regulated. The Basel Committee on Banking Supervision (BCBS) issues the Basel framework that sets international standards for banks. In November 2010, after the 2008 financial crisis pointed out the regulation's limitations, the committee issued Basel III, the new framework partially implemented starting from 2013 due to extensions. In 2017, the committee issued new standards with 1st January 2023 as the implementation date. However, the European Commission and the British government agreed to extend the beginning date to 2025.

[2] The ranking of the five largest British bank groups is HSBC Holdings, Lloyds Banking Group, Barclays, NatWest Group, and Standard Chartered.

Risk Management Structure

NatWest Group operates an enterprise-wide risk management framework. The framework's goal is to guarantee the appropriate control and management of principal risks by setting standards and defining the role of each division. The Group Chief Risk Officer is between the CEO of each subsidiary and the risk officer of the subsidiary and is a member of the executive committee. In addition to advising on NatWest Group's risk profile and the performance of its controls, the Chief Risk Officer plays a key role in advising the board.

NatWest has a Board risk committee that oversees and advises the Board of Directors regarding risk exposures, risk profile, and effectiveness of risk management framework. The committee 2021 focused on multiple vital matters such as:

a. Financial crime is a top risk for the Group.
b. Model risk is particularly relevant because it involves the bank's simulations.
c. The enhancement of the Enterprise-Wide Risk Management Framework.
d. The risk profile and reporting.
e. Capital, funding, and liquidity risk.
f. Financial and strategic risk.
g. Stress testing.
h. Recovery plans and the resolvability self-assessment.
i. Control environment. To check the effectiveness of the internal control system.
j. Non-financial risk.
k. Accountability and remuneration.

The Group establishes the risk appetite with qualitative measures by describing the actions that can be performed and their extent. NatWest sets limits to design the tolerance accepted in the day-to-day activities and communicates the operation guidelines to all the subsidiaries. Because financial markets are volatile, the Group must constantly review the risk profile and adjust accordingly.

Risk Identification

The risks identified in NatWest's 2021 Annual Report are divided into principal financial risks, principal non-financial risks, and emerging risks.

Table 10.2 reports the main risks discussed in the 2021 Annual report of the company. The emerging risks are divided into external and internal. For each risk, the annual report provides the definition, the sources of risk, the key developments in 2021, the governance (meaning, which is responsible for monitoring, assessing, and mitigating the risk), the risk appetite expressed in both qualitative and quantitative terms, monitoring and measurement, and finally mitigation.

The focus is mainly on credit risk, defined as "the risk that customers and counterparties fail to meet their contractual obligation to settle outstanding amounts" (National Westminster Bank plc, 2022. NatWest Group plc 2021 Annual Report and Accounts. Retrieved Online from NatWest Group—Annual Report 2021, p. 197). It originates from mainly the lending activity. Assessing the borrower's creditworthiness is the key, but methods vary depending on the borrower and the business it does (Fight, 2004). The assessment must consider the probability of default, which can occur internally or externally. External assessments are the credit ratings issued by the credit agencies such as Moody's, Standard & Poor, and Fitch. The rating influences the interest rate required. However, not all companies have publicly available data that credit agencies can analyze. Banks must have internal procedures to assess the probability

Table 10.2 The risks identified in NatWest's 2021 Annual Report

Principal financial risks	*Principal non-financial risks*	*Emerging risks*
Credit risk	Conduct risk	Climate-related risks
Traded market risk	Financial crime risk	Competitive environment
Non-traded market risk	Operational risk	COVID-19
Capital adequacy	Regulatory compliance	Cyber threats
Liquidity and funding	Model risk	Economic and political
Earnings stability	Climate risk	Regulatory, legal, and conduct
Pension risk	Reputational risk	Change risk
		Data management
		People risk
		Third-party suppliers

of default that consider the profitability, the solvency rate, and the cash flows. The Z-Score is a famous example[3]; it provides a score considering five financial ratios. If the score is lower than 1.81, the company has a high probability of default. However, its predicting power decreased because the companies influence the critical factors in the probability of receiving a loan. Thus, banks must constantly monitor and update their models if the predicting power decreases. NatWest implements mitigation activities such as avoiding credit concentrations to an individual customer or a group of borrowers or using derivatives like Credit Default Swaps (CDS). The non-market risk is defined as "non-traded market risk, the risk to the value of assets or liabilities outside the trading book, or the income risk, that arises from changes in market prices such as interest rates, foreign exchange rates, and equity prices, or from changes in managed rates" (Annual Report, 2021, p. 266). The definition of market risk provided is "the risk arising from changes in fair value on positions, assets, liabilities or commitments in trading portfolios as a result of fluctuations in market prices" (Annual Report, 2021, p. 275).

Discussion and Analysis

NatWest's risk management process must be highly dynamic and flexible. The definition of clear limits for operations and implementing control systems are crucial to the business's success. NatWest Group's financial strength is assessed using a stress test that quantifies and evaluates the impact of specific changes in risk factors. Scenario testing includes scenario analysis which examines how a hypothetical future state would affect risk factors by analyzing the future state's impact by assessing the future state's influence, and sensitivity analysis, where one or more incremental changes to a risk factor are examined. The process is divided into four steps:

a. Define scenarios: Understand and reach a consensus over possible events that could take place in the future. The events must be relevant to the operations and have direct and measurable consequences

[3] The Z-Score (Altman, 1968) considers the working capital, retained earnings, EBIT, market capitalization, and sales in period t. All scaled by total assets in period t. The financial ratios assess profitability, leverage, liquidity, solvency, and activity. Different coefficients are used to multiply each percentage. There are different versions of the Z-Score for private companies, firms in emerging markets, non-manufacturers firms, and others.

on the Group. Usually, a company provides at least one optimistic scenario, one negative, one in line with strategic plans, and, for each scenario, a probability.

b. Assess impact: Identify the key drivers of the events to assess the effect on financial measures and cash flows. This step is critical to understanding the drivers that must be monitored and providing estimates for the limits based on the risk appetite.
c. Calculate results and implications: aggregate all the results to get the total impact on the company. The company needs to assess the consequences for the business.
d. Develop and agree on management options: the results are analyzed to develop response actions and mitigation plans. The Board reviews the results and the plans to approve or suggest improvements.

Calculating the minimum liquidity level is the primary purpose of stress testing by understanding the net liquidity outflows under multiple severe but plausible scenarios. The test evaluates three scenarios: the idiosyncratic risk, where only NatWest suffers an extreme stress event, and the market perceives an increased credit risk; market-wide risk, where all the participants suffer with equivalent exposure to market risk, credit risk, and possible contagion; a combined scenario where both idiosyncratic and market-wide risk occurs. Liquidity is monitored daily. The bank must constantly ensure that the hypothesis underlying the simulations is valid. Especially during unexpected large shocks, when previous conditions vary, reviewing and asses if the stress test is reliable becomes necessary.

Questions

a. Considering the probability and the possible economic impact, create a rank of all the risks from the most relevant to the least appropriate.
b. Considering the probability and the possible economic impact, place all the risks in the table into the risk matrix.
c. Based on the type of company, the sector, and the strategy, select three risks from the table and provide a discussion.
d. Considering future trends, select possible risks that might become more relevant for the company.
e. When possible, confront the results with your colleagues and discuss the differences.

ENI Group

Brief Description of the Company

Eni is one of the most significant oil and gas players and the most prominent Italian listed company considering its market capitalization (78.22 billion $[4]). In the period 2003–2013, it was the Italian company reporting the most significant turnover. The Italian government owns more than 30% of the share and still has control. The Group "engages in oil and natural gas exploration, field development and production, as well as in the supply, trading, and shipping of natural gas, LNG, electricity, and fuels. Eni processes crude oil and other oil-based feedstock through refineries and chemical plants to produce fuels, lubricants, and chemical products supplied to wholesalers or through retail networks or distributors" (Eni S.p.A., 2022. Eni Annual Report 2021. Retrieved Online from Downloads—Eni Annual Report 2021). Thus, it operates along the value chain, starting from the exploration and ending with product commercialization. In 1992 it became a listed company; Eni is now listed on the New York Stock Exchange and the FTS-Mib index of the Italian stock exchange. The foundation occurred in 1953 as a state-owned enterprise with Enrico Mattei as president and CEO. The CEO is Claudio De Scalzi (appointed in May 2014), and Lucia Calvosa is the Chair of the Board of Directors (established in May 2020). The employees are more than 32,000 in 69 countries in the world.

Analyzing the company is interesting for several reasons. First, the business model of the oil and gas sector is peculiar because it is highly capital-intensive. It requires cash in advance to explore reserves of natural resources and to construct the extraction sites. Thus, it shows a negative cash flow in the beginning years of a project and high fixed costs. When a company decides whether to invest in a project, it projects the future price of the oil, which is the critical driver of profitability. However, the company has no control over the cost of the product (oil), and it is exposed to price volatility. Second, it is possible to investigate the importance of political connections and relations. Eni operates in 69 countries with different legal systems and social practices. Not all of them are democracies. The oil and gas industry is famous for its lobby activity,

[4] As of January 2022.

and a large proportion of the population needs a better perception of the business and the integrity of the corporations.

In 2017, Eni and its chief executives were accused (together with Royal Dutch Shell) of international corruption in the deal involving the most extensive African oil reserves estimated to contain more than 9 billion crude oil barrels (Financial Times, 2020). In 2011, Eni and Shell acquired the OPL 245 offshore oilfield for $1.3 billion, but prosecutors had alleged that most of the money was used to bribe Nigerian politicians and officials (Financial Times, 2012, 2014). In March 2021, after three years of trial, the Italian court acquitted all the defendants. The example highlights the complexity of such business and the possible repercussions on reputation and external perceptions. Third, the United Nations set the goal of carbon neutrality in 2050. As a major oil producer, Eni needs to change its business model. Therefore, it mainly invests in sustainable resources to reduce its carbon footprint.

Risk Management Structure

"The IRM Model is characterized by a structured approach, based on international best practices, and considering the guidelines of the Internal Control and Risk Management System (see page 42), that is structured on three control levels. Risk Governance attributes a central role to the Board of Directors, which defines the nature and level of risk in line with strategic targets, including in the evaluation process all the elements that can be relevant given the Company's sustainable success." The Board outlines the guidelines for risk management with the support of the Control Committee and the Risk Committee. The goal is to identify, assess, manage, and monitor the principal risks by considering the strategic target and compatibility with the company's overall strategy.

ENI's risk management process is divided into four steps: risk governance, methodologies, and tools; risk strategy; integrated risk management; risk knowledge, training, and communication.

Risk Identification

The risks identified in ENI's 2021 Annual Report (Eni S.p.A., 2022. Eni Annual Report 2021. Retrieved Online from Downloads—Eni Annual Report 2021) are divided into external, strategic, and operational (Table 10.3).

Table 10.3 The risks identified in ENI's 2021 Annual Report

External risk	*Strategic risk*	*Operational risk*
Biological	Price volatility	Accidents
Geopolitical	Climate change	Cyber security
Country risk	Exposure to long-term contracts	Investigations and proceedings
Energy sector regulation	Decreasing demand	Safe, security, and environmental
Relationship with stakeholder	Competitive environment	Unsuccessful drilling
Permitting	Ukrainian war	Development of projects
Weather conditions	Replacement of reserves	
Income taxes and royalties	Interest rate	
Sanctions	Foreign exchange rate	
	Liquidity risk	

"The Group performance is exposed to the volatility of crude oil and natural gas prices and changing margins of refined and chemical products" (Eni S.p.A., 2022. Eni Annual Report 2021. Retrieved Online from Downloads—Eni Annual Report 2021, p. 122). The price volatility can impact operating expenses and revenues, influencing the marginality. The price relates to supply, demand, inventory levels, and spare capacity. Oil production is not flexible, and in the short run, oil producers cannot respond promptly to significant variations in needs. Unpredictable events like wars, pandemics, economic crises, extreme weather, and others can influence supply and the market. Thus, the sector is pervaded by uncertainty, and the critical driver of profitability is outside management's control. Eni mitigates the risk by improving resilience, efficiency (regarding capital discipline and synergies with the renewable division), and business flexibility. Furthermore, the Group uses derivatives to hedge against price volatility and commercial exposures.

Political risk does not have a single definition; following Fitzpatrick (1983), it is possible to identify three categories: the first focuses on the consequences of explicit or implicit government interferences with business operations, the second regards constraints imposed on the firms or the industry, or political events that can be relevant for the firm or the industry, the third concerns discontinuity in the environment surrounding the firm because of political changes. Such risks apply to international businesses like Eni. In the aftermath of the Ukraine war, the Group intends to divest its interests from a joint operation with Gazprom (the Blue Stream, a pipeline to move natural gas from Russia to Turkey), the Russian company. Eni decided not to sign any new contracts involving the supply of Russian oil, which represents 18% of the total volume. The Group implements geographical diversification to reduce political risk, creates strong relations with local authorities, and requests guarantee letters to protect its credit position.

The long-term demand is exciting. Two forces negatively impact the long-term market. First, the main feature of a commodity is low product differentiation, implying intense consumer loyalty. Increasing competition can reduce sales and volumes, impacting profitability. Second, governments are shifting toward renewable sources to reduce the use of fossil fuels. Both mechanisms affect future demand and the economic sustainability of the operations. To mitigate the negative impact of a competing environment, the Group focuses on the efficiency of operational costs. It provides valuable services to buyers as a differentiation strategy to create value. A key component is the ability to access and exploit future investment opportunities. To mitigate the second dynamic, Eni is investing in the renewable sector to diversify its portfolio, it creates a scenario with low carbon consumption to assess the resilience of the business, and it is increased flexibility regarding strategy and investment. The Group expects oil consumption to peak in 2035. Thus, it is fundamental to manage the green transition appropriately.

Discussion and Analysis

"In the four years, Eni's management foresees an investment plan of €28 billion (on average about €7 billion/year). Eni plans investments in renewable sources, efficient energy, circular economy, and flaring reduction of over €7 billion. The plan is characterized by high flexibility with more than 55% of investments in the 2024–25 period not yet contracted" (Eni S.p.A., 2022. Eni Annual Report 2021. Retrieved Online from Downloads—Eni Annual Report 2021). Thus, properly implementing a risk management strategy is fundamental to guarantee the success of the investment plan. The vast amount of money invested points out the strategic importance of the project.

Oil and gas extraction is highly capital-intensive and requires large cash outflows in the starting phases (Gray et al., 2019); therefore, firms reduce investments during periods of considerable unpredictability. After the COVID-19 pandemic hit, oil producers reduced their investments in production because financial discipline was fundamental to survival. During economic hibernation, firms use the minimum amount of cash to cope with the crisis (Didier et al., 2021). Tight supply in the following years is the primary consequence influencing oil prices. The mechanism explains what happened in 2021 and 2022 and why energy commodities are responsible for the inflation in Europe when lockdowns and restrictions were lifted. The volatility and the price dynamics are determinants for the sustainability of investment plans. It is possible to highlight the intersection between the abovementioned risks. An extended period of sustained turbulence will have consequences for Eni.

Questions

a. Considering the probability and the possible economic impact, create a rank of all the risks from the most relevant to the least appropriate.
b. Considering the probability and the possible economic impact, place all the risks in the table into the risk matrix.
c. Based on the type of company, the sector, and the strategy, select three risks from the table and provide a discussion.
d. Considering future trends, select possible risks that might become more relevant for the company.
e. When possible, confront the results with your colleagues and discuss the differences.

Ocado[5]

Brief Description of the Company

Ocado Group is a British technology company specializing in online grocery solutions. The Company provides home delivery of a wide range of products and services to the world's largest grocery retailers, such

[5] Ocado's annual report discusses the 52 weeks from 1 December 2020 to 28 November 2021.

as Kroger, Coles Group, and Auchan. Thus, it sells the logistic platform and organizes the deliveries of strong global brands. It has a joint venture which operates like an online supermarket (Ocado.com) with Marks and Spencer. The company was founded in the UK in 2000 by former Goldman Sachs bankers. The company rapidly grew, and in 2006 it delivered 50,000 orders per week. In 2010 was listed on the London Stock Exchange. Ocado also focused on improving technology, adopting systems for automating logistics processes and robots for warehouse management over the years to keep pace with an ever-increasing amount of work. Software based on machine learning and artificial intelligence is also fundamental. Its focus on cutting-edge technology implies a significant cash burn and reports constant loss despite increased revenues and EBITDA.

The case is interesting for multiple reasons. First, the focus on technological development implies challenges. On the one hand, Ocado must retain talent and critical workers. The internal know-how must be protected and preserved. On the other hand, it must protect intellectual capital. In December 2020, Ocado acted against the Norwegian company Auto Store specializes in storage systems. The legal actions focus on patent infringement and breaches of competition law. They are in several jurisdictions: the US International Trade Commission, the US District Court, the UK High Court, and the German district courts of Mannheim and Munich. Ocado states that it was the inventor and rightful owner of certain patents, and the complaints focus on two products, the Blackline robot and the software Router. In December 2021, Ocado won the trial, but Auto Store declared the intention to challenge the decision, and the result is still an open question (Financial Times, 2021).

The example highlights the difficulties of protecting knowledge to sustain a competitive advantage in a growing market. Second, Ocado is a company that thrived during the lockdowns and has now adapted the business to a post-Covid era. During the pandemic, restrictions forced the population to online shopping and online groceries. Stock value floated at more than 2000£ per share from May 2020, recording peaks of more than 2800£. As of July 2022, the value plummeted to 770£ because of negative prospects. In the first quarter of 2022, the average basket value had fallen 15% compared to the previous year, to £124, as the ease of restrictions changed the daily lifestyle again. The company assumed that the increase in online grocery consumption was permanent. But the proportion of online shopping dropped from 20% to 14% (still up compared to the pre-Covid levels), and higher fuel prices decreased the margins. Ocado invested capital in innovation and competed in a market with reduced demand and margins. The 2021 annual report completely overlooks this obstacle. Finally, because Ocado is proliferating and is searching for opportunities, it needs external financing to support the existing plans. 2021 results report total revenues 2499£ million, 61£ million EBITDA and a loss of 220£ million. Total employees are 20,132 (+17.59% from 2020) across 13 countries.

Risk Management Structure

Ocado follows the UK Corporate Governance Code 2018 ("the Code"). Ocado implements a bottom-up approach with five central bodies in its risk management structure. Starting from the bottom, an ad-hoc risk committee for a specific topic supports the second-line team. The risk committee reviews the relevant risks and emerging risks. It is supported by the Group Enterprise Risk Management team, which controls the framework's appropriate implementation. The Board oversights all the structure. It is responsible for setting a strategy and monitoring its implementation while approving all the key and emerging risks identified by the divisions. The Board delegates the Audit committee responsible for reviewing the effectiveness of risk management processes and internal control systems and monitoring the quality of financial statements. To ensure internal control across all the Internal Audit Team structures. One of the critical features of the design is the clear segregation of duties. This should reduce confusion over who is responsible for the risks.

The risk management process involves four critical steps with loop feedback.

1. Strategy setting: the Board sets the strategy and the purpose. The strategy is the starting point to develop and communicate goals across the company.
2. Risk evaluation: the most significant risks are evaluated by the Executive Directors. Furthermore, each department prepares a report highlighting and communicating the division's significant risks.

3. Implement mitigation: each division prepares a report describing how each relevant risk will be managed, mitigated, or accepted. The Group summarizes each action into the company mitigation plan.
4. Review risks: assess the reliability and efficacy of the process. Risk evaluation and mitigation (steps 2 and 3) are reviewed.

Risk Identification

Ocado identifies 12 principal risks. For each risk, the company provides the following:

I. A brief description of the issue.
II. How they plan to manage it. This differs from a plan where the company describes the plan to respond if the risk occurs. Ocado provides a list of actions it implemented to reduce the risk.
III. Risk level: If the risk has increased, decreased, or remained constant compared to the previous year.
IV. The target tolerance: in the 2021 annual report, Ocado uses "minimal, cautious, flexible, and open" to describe the level of risk appetite it has in each category. Minimal means that the company is highly conservative and accepts options with a low probability of failure. Cautions signal a limited tolerance and get the options only if the evidence of a cost–benefit analysis strongly favors the option. Flexible means that Ocado will accept some risks to exploit possible opportunities. Open signals the willingness to take justified risks to maintain the position and deliver a higher return.
V. The emerging threats: risks are not static, and the initiating event change over the years. Moreover, the increased complexity varies the consequences of the issue. Here are two examples. First, the pandemic is a new source of risk for the safety and well-being of workers inside the company. Second, Ocado's exponential growth increased the supply chain and network complexity.
VI. The owner of the risk: Ocado identifies the manager responsible.
VII. The reference to the ESG materiality reference: if the risk relates to Environmental, Social, or Governance.

VIII. What component of the strategy is impacted by the risk identified? The strategic pillars identified are revenue growth, optimization of OSP economics, delivery of transformational technology, delivery of client commitments, and development of global scale-up skills (Table 10.4).

The risks identified in Ocado's 2021 Annual Report are divided on the variation of risks in increased risk, no variation, and decreased risk.

It is possible to focus on business interruptions because they threaten the company's reputation. The company is investing heavily in technologies and supports large brands. Business interruptions cause delays and reduce consumer satisfaction which poses a risk to the long-term profitability of the Group. Ocado describes the risk as "major service disruption, customer confidence, and increased costs arising from a failure at key location" (Ocado Group plc., 2022. Ocado Group plc Annual Report and Accounts for the 52 weeks ended 28 November 2021. Retrieved Online from Annual Report | Ocado Group, p. 89). The causes are physical events (i.e., the fire mentioned in the introduction), technical events, and mechanical failure caused by accidental components. The company mitigates the risk by having a dedicated engineering team supporting the operations and conducting maintenance daily. It also updates the continuity plans and structures the IT system to operate in such situations.

Table 10.4 The risks identified in Ocado's 2021 Annual Report

Increased risk	*No variation*	*Decreased risk*
Cybersecurity and data	Business interruptions and catastrophic events	Product (OSP) proposition and commercial viability
Supply chain	Safety and wellbeing	
Climate change—transition	Legal and Regulatory Noncompliance	
	Talent and capabilities	
	Product (OSP) delivery and service	
	Product (OSP) innovation and safety	
	Intellectual property	
	Geopolitical and Economic uncertainty	

Discussion and Analysis

By identifying each risk, the owner has reduced uncertainty inside the organization. Choosing to highlight in the annual report the person and his position within the company responsible for risk compliance is crucial in the segregation of duties and reduces doubts within the organization. The immediate consequences are clear guidelines, clear roles, and precise tasks.

Questions

a. Considering the probability and the possible economic impact, create a rank of all the risks from the most relevant to the least appropriate.
b. Considering the probability and the possible economic impact, place all the risks in the table into the risk matrix.
c. Based on the type of company, the sector, and the strategy, select three risks from the table and provide a discussion.
d. Considering future trends, select possible risks that might become more relevant for the company.
e. When possible, confront the results with your colleagues and discuss the differences.

Ryanair Group plc[6]

Brief Description of the Company

Ryanair is an Irish low-cost airline founded in 1984 and headquartered in Dublin. In origin, it offered flights to connect Waterford to London Gatwick, which nowadays is the largest carrier in Europe. The company is strictly linked to the person of Michal O'Leary appointed Chief Financial Officer in 1988 and CEO in 1994. When O'Leary was appointed, Ryanair was experiencing negative results and did a restructuring process which gave success to the company. In 1997 it went public and is now listed on the Irish Stock Exchange (Euronext Dublin), has the American

[6] Ryanair issues the annual report that covers the period 1 April–31 of March. Thus, the 2021 annual report provides information about 2020–2021, including the pandemic. So, the analysis has some differences compared to the other companies.

Depositary Shares listed on the NASDAQ, and has a standard listing on the London Stock Exchange.

Before the pandemic, Ryanair reported 149 million passengers annually, more than 2000 flights daily, and operates in 37 countries. Ryanair follows a cost leadership strategy, and the business model focuses on efficiency (both technical and economic). During the '70s, Southwest Airlines, an American carrier, was the first to introduce a low-cost strategy. Ryanair was one of Europe's first to adopt such an approach in 1992.[7] The focus must be on cost reduction and capacity utilization to implement the low-cost strategy. To reduce costs, Ryanair's flights are often defined as "no frills" because the company eliminated services and comfort once guaranteed. In the short term, much of the costs are fixed, and a relevant component of the strategy is maximized revenues to reduce the incidence of fixed costs. Sustain such a process is challenging because the target consumers are price sensitive, not loyal to the brand, and their willingness to pay is low.

Furthermore, low margins represent a high risk for the company because it increases the probability of having noncompetitive pricing and, consequently, the risk of going out of the market. The low-cost strategy takes time to implement. The reduction in Europe of entry barriers in the airline industry increased the competition. Several examples of carriers that went bankrupt such as Debonair (2000) and Buzz (acquired by Ryanair in 2002 and closed in 2004). To sustain the high flight turnover, the company needs high efficiency in avoiding mistakes.

Consequently, Ryanair suffered relevant strikes which compromised operations. Business interruption is a pertinent risk because, on one side, it reduces consumer satisfaction. On the other side, it increases refund requests with an impact on cash flow and profitability.

Risk Management Structure

Ryanair follows the U.K. corporate governance code. The Board comprises one Executive and nine Non-Executive Directors, with a gender proportion of 40% female and 60% male. There is a detailed description of the system that manages risks in Ryanair. First, because it is impossible to avoid risks, the system focuses on managing the risks rather

[7] The main European competitor, EasyJet, was founded in 1995 and implemented that strategy.

than eliminating them.[8] It is possible to extrapolate some quotes from the Annual Report to summarize the process: "The Board is ultimately responsible for the Company's system of risk management and internal controls and for monitoring its effectiveness. (...) Executive management review and monitor the controls in place, both financial and non-financial, to manage the risks facing the business. (...) A clearly defined organizational structure along functional lines and a clear division of responsibility and authority in the Company, including appointing a Chief Risk Officer. (...) Providing key performance indicators and financial results for each major function within the Company. (...) A detailed budgetary process which includes identifying risks and opportunities and which is ultimately approved at Board level" (Ryanair Group plc., 2021. Ryanair Group annual report 2021. Retrieved Online from: Ryanair | Results Centre).

The Board establishes multiple committees with different aims. It is possible to extrapolate from the annual report the names and the description of their tasks:

a. Audit committee: it has several responsibilities, including reviewing the effectiveness of the Group's internal financial controls and risk management systems. The tasks are performed by checking the management's reports and by conducting an annual assessment of the operation of the Group's internal control system.
b. Executive committee: which performs the Board's tasks when there is not enough time to organize a meeting with all the Directors.
c. Nomination committee: It supports the Board in nominating the components by assessing the skill, knowledge, and experience; establishing the process to identify suitable candidates; by overseeing the succession plan. Finally, it guarantees a balanced composition.
d. Remuneration committee: It determines the reward of the Company's Senior Executives in salary and shares.
e. The safety and security committee reviews and discusses air safety and security-related issues.

[8] "The Directors acknowledge their responsibility for the system of risk management and internal control which is designed to manage rather than eliminate the risk of failure to achieve business objectives and can provide only reasonable and not absolute assurance against material misstatement or loss" (Annual Report, 2021).

Risk Identification

The risks identified in Ryanair's 2021 Annual Report are divided into company risks, industry risks, and ownership risks (Table 10.5).

Fuel costs constitute a large share of Ryanair's operating expenses. Respectively, around 22% and 37% of the 2021 and 2020 expenses are represented by such costs. In the case of a company that implements a low-cost strategy, controlling the costs is a source of competitive advantage because it means protecting the marginality required to survive. The Company hedge against this risk using derivatives,[9] generally through forwards contract, which cover up to 18 months of the anticipated fuel

Table 10.5 The risks identified in Ryanair's 2021 Annual Report

Company risks	*Industry risks*	*Ownership risks*
Decline in demand	Airborne diseases	Restriction of ownership
Cyber security	Passenger compensation	Right to vote
Data protection	Economic conditions	Conversion of the shares
Fuel costs	Environmental/ government taxes	Fluctuation of operations
Pricing	Policy uncertainty	Dividends payment
Liquidity	Environmental regulation	CSD
Legal challenges	Extreme weather	Repurchasement
Grounded aircraft	Perception of low-fare airlines	
Debt financing	Loss and liabilities	
Currency rate	Uncertainty	
Brexit	Safety-related undertakings	
Supplier delay	State aid	
Risk related to expansion		
Labor relation		
Dependency on external contractors		
GDSs		
Tax rates and audits		
Restructuring		

[9] Ryanair also disclosed that derivatives are used for "changes in the fair value of aircraft purchase commitments, through foreign currency contracts to hedge against fluctuations in the Euro/U.S. dollar exchange rates on jet fuel and aircraft deliveries for the term of the contract with the aircraft manufacturer, i.e., through 2024" (Annual Report, 2021).

need. The jet fuel price involves different risk factors that the derivatives hedge. With the fluctuation of commodity prices and the related foreign exchange rate risk, jet fuel prices are usually denominated in US dollars, and Ryanair uses the Euro.[10] The Company acknowledges it is a short-term strategy because it cannot hedge against permanent or future increases. Moreover, Ryanair relies on forward contracts to cover "approximately 60% of its estimated requirements for the fiscal year 2022 and approximately 35% of its estimated requirements for the fiscal year 2023"[11] (Ryanair Group plc., 2021. Ryanair Group annual report 2021. Retrieved Online from: Ryanair | Results Centre).

Another relevant risk is represented by debt sustainability. 66 new Boing 737 aircraft of the fleet (15.6% of the 422 airplanes) were purchased relying on external financing in the form of loans supported by a guarantee from Ex-Im Bank. Furthermore, "the Company has raised unsecured debt via capital market bond issuances and syndicated bank loans. The Company had outstanding cumulative borrowings under the above facilities of €5,243.7 m with a weighted average interest rate of 1.30% on March 31, 2021" (Ryanair Group plc., 2021. Ryanair Group annual report 2021. Retrieved Online from: Ryanair | Results Centre).

Finally, it is essential to note that 11% of the average ticket cost is environmental taxes. Considering the future trends, it represents one of the significant risk sources for Ryanair.

Discussion and Analysis

The discussion is based on the sensitivity analysis of such factors. Using data from 2021, the Company predicts that "a change of US$1.00 in the average annual price per metric ton of jet fuel would have caused a change of approximately €0.8 m in Ryanair's fuel costs" (Ryanair Group plc., 2021. Ryanair Group annual report 2021. Retrieved Online from:

[10] "Ryanair's revenues have been denominated primarily in two currencies, the euro, and the U.K. pound sterling. The euro and the U.K. pound sterling accounted for approximately 67% and 27% of Ryanair's total revenues in fiscal year 2021".

[11] The use of derivatives is indeed extensive. To give a perspective, "the Company entered into a series of forward contracts, principally euro/U.S. dollar forward contracts to hedge against variability in cash flows arising from market fluctuations in foreign exchange rates associated with its forecast fuel, maintenance, and insurance costs" (Annual Report, 2021).

Ryanair | Results Centre). It might seem small, but oil prices have fluctuated dramatically recently. Starting from an average of around 68$ per barrel at the end of 2019, during the pandemic, the price fell to 19$ per barrel in April 2020 and rose to 133$ per barrel in the aftermath of the Russian invasion of Ukraine. The difference between the dip and the peak means a possible economic effect of approximately 91 million €. Moreover, the sensitivity analysis on the foreign currency exchange rate assumes a variation of 10%. If the exchange rate decreases, the estimated economic effect is "a positive impact of €40 m on the income statement (net of tax) (2020: €246 m; 2019: nil)" and a "negative €372 m impact (net of tax) on equity." If the exchange rate increases, the estimated economic effects are "a negative impact of €33 m on the income statement (net of tax) (2020: €235 m; 2019: nil) and a "positive €304 m impact (net of tax)" on equity. Finally, "based on the levels of and composition of year-end interest-bearing assets and liabilities, including derivatives, at March 31, 2021, a plus one-percentage-point movement in interest rates would result in a respective increase of €6.4 m (net of tax) in net interest income and expense in the income statement and a minus one percentage-point movement in interest rates would result in a respective increase of €47.8 m (net of tax) in net interest income and expense in the income statement (2020: €10 m; 2019: €10 m)" (Annual Report, 2021).

The pandemic hit the technical efficiency of Ryanair particularly. In 2021 the booked passenger load factor was 71% compared to an average of 95% in the four previous years, with consequences on profitability and marginality. The main result is the average cost per passenger increase because fewer consumers share overhead costs.

Questions

a. Considering the probability and the possible economic impact, create a rank of all the risks from the most relevant to the least appropriate.
b. Considering the probability and the possible economic impact, place all the risks in the table into the risk matrix.
c. Based on the type of company, the sector, and the strategy, select three risks from the table and provide a discussion.
d. Considering future trends, select possible risks that might become more relevant for the company.

e. When possible, confront the results with your colleagues and discuss the differences.

References

Altman, E. I. (1968). Financial ratios, discriminant analysis, and the prediction of corporate bankruptcy. *The Journal of Finance, 23*(4), 589–609.

Didier, T., Huneeus, F., Larrain, M., & Schmukler, S. L. (2021). Financing firms in hibernation during the COVID-19 pandemic. *Journal of Financial Stability, 53*, 100837. https://doi.org/10.1016/j.jfs.2020.100837

Eni S.p.A. (2022). *Eni annual report 2021.* Retrieved Online from Downloads—Eni Annual Report 2021 (https://report.eni.com/annual-report-2021/en/servicepages/downloads.html)

Fight, A. (2004). Credit risk management (Ser. Essential capital markets). Elsevier.

Financial Times. (2012, July 20). Nigeria oil deal puts focus on energy sector.

Financial Times. (2014, September 11). Eni chief executive under investigation over $1bn Nigerian oil deal.

Financial Times. (2020, March 05). Eni and Shell's Nigerian bribery trial delayed.

Financial Times. (2021, June 27). Ocado's largest warehouse shut after robot collision causes fire.

Fitzpatrick, M. (1983). The definition and assessment of political risk in international business: A review of the literature. *Academy of Management Review, 8*(2), 249–254.

Gray, S. J., Hellman, N., & Ivanova, M. N. (2019). Extractive industries reporting: A review of accounting challenges and the research literature. *Abacus, 55*(1), 42–91.

Meulbroek, L. (2002). The promise and challenge of integrated risk management. *Risk Management and Insurance Review, 5*(1), 55.

National Westminster Bank plc. (2021). NatWest Group plc 2020 Annual Report and Accounts. Retrieved Online from NatWest Group—Reports archive 2020 (https://investors.natwestgroup.com/reports-archive/2020)

National Westminster Bank plc. (2022). NatWest Group plc 2021 Annual Report and Accounts. Retrieved Online from NatWest Group—Annual Report 2021 (https://investors.natwestgroup.com/annual-report.aspx)

Ocado Group plc. (2022). Ocado Group plc Annual Report and Accounts for the 52 weeks ended 28 November 2021. Retrieved Online from Annual Report | Ocado Group (https://www.ocadogroup.com/investors/annual-report)

Pirelli & C. S.p.A. (2022). A beautiful place, the art of manufacturing. Annual report 2021. Retrieved Online from: Annual Report 2021 | Download (https://corporate.pirelli.com/corporate/en-ww/investors/annual-report-download-2021)

Ryanair Group plc. (2021). Ryanair Group annual report 2021. Retrieved Online from: Ryanair | Results Centre (https://investor.ryanair.com/results-centre/)

The Economist. (2020, May 24). Ocado, the tech start-up you thought was a supermarket.

PART V

Conclusion

CHAPTER 11

"Rational Globalization" and the Search for an Alternative Way Out

When I look around and observe how companies and, more generally, all economic players behave, I wonder about the meaning and role of management today.

The question is not trivial and is not only for experts. Management is indeed a science that, over the years, has helped companies grow, develop, and enhance elements and assets that today we would define as soft or intangibles, such as creativity, intelligence, and the individuals who work within the company and the organization up to involving decision-making processes.

In Italian literature, the role and centrality of management have been well described by Giovanni Ferrero (Ferrero, 1987) by analyzing the relationship between needs and economic activity and the role of the company as an "instrument" to produce goods and services aimed at the market and satisfaction of human needs.

Ferrero observes how creative activity is essential for the satisfaction of human needs and for making goods and services available in the processes of consumption (Ferrero, 1987: 3). Giovanni Ferrero defines management as an "administrative activity." He identifies two closely related dimensions: management in the objective aspect and management in the subjective element (Ferrero, 1987: 54).

In the objective aspect, management highlights the content of the activity and the unitary set of operations through which corporate

A. Capocchi, *Vulnerability and the Corporate Immune System*,
https://doi.org/10.1007/978-3-031-30254-1_11

management is expressed. In the subjective element, management refers to the relationships established within the company between the bodies and functions of the administrative activity, generating the corporate organization from which the structure and the dimension of the human element with which planning is based derive (Ferrero, 1987: 54).

The integration between the objective and subjective aspects has generated essential effects on corporate decision-making processes, to which more and more attempts have been made to give rationality. The rationality of decision-making processes must consider the objectivity of the data that management produces on the one hand and requires on the other. Over time, the search for greater rationality has favored the integration between accounting data and non-accounting data: the former is produced internally by the company, while the latter comes from the company and partly from the system external to the company itself.

The integration between accounting and non-accounting dimensions has marked the evolution of corporate information systems. From information systems of an exclusively accounting nature, we moved on to increasingly integrated information systems, first with monitoring company processes and then with customer relationship management systems.

The evolution of corporate information systems is at the basis of the development of mathematical-statistical models with which algorithms and software have been designed to govern decision-making processes by making them faster and reducing the margins of error. Mathematical-statistical models use historical trends and measure complex variables, generating forecasts on market trends and economic-financial variables.

The evolution of corporate information systems has also changed managerial tools and the role humans assume in decision-making processes. In this regard, the growing space occupied by mathematical-statistical models and the reduction of subjectivity in decision-making processes is evident. More and more humans must adapt to technology with a consequent imbalance between the objective and subjective aspects.

Today everything is changing, or instead, everything has changed. From the factory and the product, we first moved toward the individual, not as a person capable of thinking, evaluating, and deciding, but as a customer with his purchasing or spending capacity—the willingness to pay: factories are no longer necessary; they can be moved, closed, and reopened; the tangible or intangible product has become a mere tool for hooking up or creating a need and indirectly or directly the customer's spending power; and the customer has become a set of byte inside a server kept in a cloud in which information, numbers, and data are recorded which then complex algorithms created by man process and translate into predictions.

Predictions are already the real lever with which the market tries in every way to “manipulate” the behavior of Consumer Customers, pushing them to exhaust all their spending capacity. It is interesting to think that the algorithms created by man are the binding man himself to a minimal set of bytes, while the market (generally) and companies (more in detail) today chase the spending power of bytes as they did in cartoons of Tom and Jerry: behavior that in economics is well described by the expression cash-cow.

This scheme needs an important actor capable (once) of regulating the game between the market and the customer: the State. Unfortunately, today even the State sees its role changed, and the State must fight not only with the market but also with the web. Hence the total ineffectiveness of traditional tools with which the State cannot think today, of introducing even simple rules such as the opening hours of shops. Rules that cannot be implemented on the web and which would paradoxically end up benefiting the same actors who have generated the profound changes that we try to face in a “traditional” way.

And what happened to management? Management has become the science of rationality, which, with numbers, algorithms, and bytes, wants to predict the future and decide for everyone by directing and manipulating decision-making processes. Rationality with algorithms and mathematical models on one side and the web on the other.

Fortunately, even in the era of “rational globalization,” there is always at least one alternative: the alternative of doing business differently, the alternative of not bowing to the law of mathematics and statistics, and the alternative of being accessible without doing demagogy. As? Simply by placing the individual at the system’s center, not the bytes, to restore dignity to the product and, through the product, go back to the factories where goods are not created, but well-being is created. Well-being already. Not only economic but, above all, social and cultural well-being.

Many years ago, a great Italian entrepreneur understood all these things and would still be a forerunner of management theories today. He is a great entrepreneur who has given us a tangible testimony of his work and vision. Adriano Olivetti is an example that I hope the new generation, not only in Italy, can rediscover today more than ever.

Reference

Ferrero, G. (1987). *Impresa e Management*. Giuffré.

Index

A. Capocchi, *Vulnerability and the Corporate Immune System*,
https://doi.org/10.1007/978-3-031-30254-1

C

D

www.ingramcontent.com/pod-product-compliance
Ingram Content Group UK Ltd.
Pitfield, Milton Keynes, MK11 3LW, UK
UKHW020835290926
15470UKWH00004B/1361
9783031302534